T0360568

Conversations about Calling

"The ability to answer the question "to what am I called?" is foundational to the search for meaning at the interface between person and work. However we might understand vocation or calling, we are unlikely to have plumbed the construct's rich history across spiritual, psychological, sociological, and organizational perspectives. Here in one readable volume we are given access to this broader intellectual landscape. We are led by a wise guide who has assembled interdisciplinary wisdom providing entrée to a full understanding of a lodestone construct critical to personal fulfillment."—Andre L. Delbecq, Santa Clara University, USA

"*Conversations About Calling* is the definitive and comprehensive treatise on the field of calling. This book offers an in-depth review of the historical trends of both secular and spiritual approaches to callings, multi-faith perspectives on calling, inspiring and provocative conversations on calling from the practitioner point of view and much more. Reading this, one would think the author had dedicated a lifetime to the study of theology, another lifetime as an academic, and a third lifetime as a practitioner. Myers weaves these strands into a beautiful tapestry that will enrich any reader's understanding of calling in a way that makes this field fresh and alive."—Judi Neal, Ph.D., Chairman, Edgewalkers International

"Valerie Myers' provocative *Conversations about Calling* builds on emerging interest among management scholars about a special type of very deeply meaningful work. Myers calls for bringing the sacred and transcendent back into management conversations about callings, arguing for an older, more focused conceptualization of callings. Surprisingly, she argues for such narrowing in order to make our understanding broader and richer; and looks to past scholarship in order to chart out new avenues for research. Myers' book should be on the reading list of anyone seriously interested in the role of callings at work!"—Michael Pratt, Boston College, USA

"Dr. Myers has done an excellent job of integrating and synthesizing disparate approaches to work as a calling across management and theological disciplines that do not usually interrelate. The book thus fills a unique niche in providing approaches to and examples of work as a calling across a variety of perspectives."—Jerry Biberman, University of Scranton, USA

Conversations about Calling explores management perspectives related to the calling construct. Using Max Weber's seminal work, *Protestant Ethic and the Spirit of Capitalism*, as a starting point, Myers seeks to enrich management perspectives of calling by integrating the contributions of other disciplines to the literature.

While the word 'calling' is casually used as shorthand for 'my ideal job', the calling concept has provoked deeper and varied interest among the secular and spiritual circles of both scholars and practitioners. Structured around the idea of four conversations, the book aims to promote a holistic examination of calling. Each conversation has a different focus, elucidating important dimensions of calling, and together they provide a truly comprehensive view. Part I of the book examines existing conversations in management, while part II explores calling across disciplines and eras, from the 1500s to the present. Finally, part III unifies all conversations into a comprehensive theory, then discusses its application and implications for practitioners and organizations.

With a strong theoretical grounding, the book also incorporates practical applications supported by case studies. Anyone interested in ethics or management and spirituality will benefit from reading this book.

Valerie L. Myers is a faculty member at the University of Michigan's Ross School of Business in Ann Arbor, USA, and is the president of Myers Management Consulting, LLC.

Conversations about Calling

Advancing Management Perspectives

Valerie L. Myers

 Routledge
Taylor & Francis Group

NEW YORK AND LONDON

First published 2014
by Routledge
605 Third Avenue, New York, NY 10017
4 Park Square, Milton Park, Abingdon, Oxon OX14 4RN

*Routledge is an imprint of the Taylor & Francis Group,
an informa business*

Library of Congress Cataloging-in-Publication Data

Myers, Valerie L.
Conversations about calling : advancing management
    perspectives / Valerie L. Myers.—1 Edition.
        pages cm
    Includes bibliographical references and index.
    1. Vocational guidance.   2. Vocation.   3. Occupations.   I. Title.
    HF5381.M89 2013
    331.702—dc23
    2012050990

ISBN: 978-0-415-50745-5   (hbk)
ISBN: 978-0-415-50746-2
ISBN: 978-0-203-12633-2

Typeset in Garamond
by Apex CoVantage, LLC

This book is dedicated to my parents, Frederick and Teresa, and their parents, all of whom modeled ways to live a calling against the odds.

Contents

Preface

I searched for a theory of calling; this book is what I found. Nearly 20 years ago, I became intrigued by the idea of calling while working in management for a multinational corporation and volunteering at my church. During that time, I was captivated by the biblical story of Joseph—a story that continually provides me with new insights. My interest in Joseph coincided with two important academic trends—the spirituality at work movement in management and faith-based intervention research in the social sciences more broadly. The synthesis of management, service, and curiosity about these social science trends led me to pursue graduate studies at the University of Michigan, where my quest to find a theory began in earnest.

Inspiration

Joseph's story is common to Judaism, Christianity, and Islam. Joseph was the favorite son among 12 Hebrew brothers (and 1 sister) whose father gave him the beautiful multicolored coat. His brothers sold him into slavery in Egypt. After working as a servant, house steward, and prison supervisor, Joseph became Egypt's second-highest-ranked political leader. Being a leader fulfilled a youthful dream. In that role, Joseph devised revolutionary economic and social policies that sustained the nation through crisis and left a lasting legacy. Firmly believing that narratives about Joseph's work ethic clearly illustrated how a calling is lived throughout the life course, I used the details of his work history—his job, career, volunteer service, and duty to family and community—to develop educational materials to promote calling, career development and employee engagement.[1] I used these materials to conduct workshops with young adults in the United States and South Africa in the late 1990s. Although Joseph's story gave me a largely theological view of calling, it was a portal to search for relevant social science theories.

Joseph's story, while not explicitly theoretical, ignited my intuitions about the mechanism of calling and the elements of theory that I might discover in graduate school. I discovered that some theories are "ready-made" by other people; others are not. There was no coherent theory of calling; if I wanted one, it would be a do-it-yourself project. I took a course called Theory Construction, taught by Professor David Tucker, who introduced us to the very tedious process of making meaningful contributions to academic progress.[2] As a result, I gleaned theoretical insights from Joseph's story about leadership, developing talent, the vicissitudes of work in a calling, the practical value of diversity and how it is (mis)managed, and the role of faith at work. I have since written a series of business case studies about Joseph,[3] to which I refer throughout this book. That was my first step into theory construction; the next was to understand the important questions and theoretical propositions embedded in all major works about calling. That was when I "met" Max Weber.

Investigation

While reviewing management literature about calling, I realized that all scholars working in this domain cited Weber's *The Protestant Ethic and the Spirit of Capitalism*. The citations were quite similar; they were typically brief and did not explain Weber's perspective of calling. I needed to know more. So, I read *The Protestant Ethic and the Spirit of Capitalism*. Then, I read it again and again and again, dissecting it until I fully understood Weber's core assertions about calling. To say that this was an exercise in persistence is an understatement, particularly given the language of his day. But it was well worth it. I discovered that his perspective about calling was not fully or accurately represented in the literature, even to critique it. Yet Weber's theology has been widely critiqued by theologians. For example, Lee Hardy refused to "spill any ink" on Weber's ideas, and Dorothy Sayers professed that the ethic about which Weber wrote was nothing more than enlightened self-interest. Nevertheless, Weber's sociological assumptions about calling have not been extracted to create a theory.

Once I discovered that Weber warned against the secularization of calling, and that the secular trajectory was exactly what management scholars were pursuing, I felt compelled to dig deeper. I wanted to understand what Weber thought religion added to calling and if, indeed, there might be something considered a "secular calling." I also wanted to know whether or not management scholars were asking the right questions. Were they using appropriate measures? Was the work relevant to people's philosophical and phenomenological experiences of work? Moreover, how might emerging social science research about religion inform calling scholarship? Here, I do not focus solely on Weber's assertions but instead scan the field of knowledge on calling to test the validity of his claims. Little did I know that the exercise of dissecting Weber was a primer and prerequisite for a deeper dive into more convoluted writings about calling dating back to the 1500s.

These steps were essential in my process of disciplined theory construction,[4] which culminated in the publication of a paper that I presented at the Critical Management Studies Conference in Manchester, England, in July 2007, "An Ontology of Calling: Examining Mechanisms and the Transcendent Possibilities of Work Orientation Theory."[5] Two years later, in 2009, a more exhaustive version of my paper, "What Did Weber Say? A Comprehensive Materialization of His Implicit Theory of Calling,"[6] was accepted by the Academy of Management's Management Spirituality and Religion group, which I presented in Chicago, Illinois.

Before departing for Chicago, my own calling as the eldest daughter of an ailing father came to the forefront; upon returning home, his illness appropriately brought my work to a halt and radically reoriented my priorities. Managing his care and affairs during his final months was the most important work of my life. Months later, I resumed my work on calling. A series of events and the persistent lack of a theory led me to submit the proposal for this book to Sharon Golan, acquisitions editor of business, management, and accounting books at Routledge Press. It was a step forward in my professional calling.

Some might ask, "Why bother?" If Weber's assertion is true—that calling influenced the growth of capitalism in any way—then calling has important implications for both established and emerging economies. More specifically, instability, decline, and ethical lapses in the established economies of the United States and Europe, in particular, may find that work as a calling can ameliorate related problems and correct the future course. In emerging economies, particularly across BRICS—Brazil, Russia, India, China, and South Africa—we know that faith matters. But we know little about ideologies that are comparable to calling, how calling might influence the spread of capitalism, and how emerging economies might avoid some of the missteps in the capitalistic experiment that Weber warned against. As a management scholar, I hope that we export positive evidence-based practices, not missteps. To be clear, however, I am not interested in or advocating for calling merely to improve business outcomes, although that might be a by-product. I, like many scholars, am interested in calling because of its transcendent value for individuals and its potential to "make the world a better place."

My approach in this book is interdisciplinary, proceeds from a Positive Organizational Scholarship (POS) perspective, and is informed by my Christian faith. I believe that it is important for me to clarify what this means at the outset. First, the idea of calling and the audience for this book reach across disciplinary boundaries. Therefore, multiple perspectives are needed to understand it—history, economics, sociology, anthropology, theology, and political science, to name a few. I also draw on practitioner and folk wisdom, based on the belief that knowledge knows no ZIP code or pedigree. Therefore, the examples I use may resonate with an array of leaders and readers. Although my emphasis is clearly on management and organizational psychology, my analysis of calling touches all of the aforementioned disciplines—in which I am admittedly not an expert. Nevertheless, my expertise as an organizational scholar enables me to focus on multiple levels of analysis simultaneously and resist the drift toward only a microlevel focus on individuals that threatens to diminish calling and make research less meaningful.

Second, although calling is frequently discussed in the context of POS, I have intentionally avoided a quixotic approach that ignores the paradoxical nature of work and shadow aspects of calling or religious involvement. I proceed from the standpoint that these challenging aspects of calling should not be ignored or casually dismissed with saccharine platitudes and prescriptions. Instead, I seek to understand how people can use their existing cosmologies to manage those tensions and elevate themselves to higher ground—even when that sometimes means holding steady.

Third, I am a Christian. This is not, however, a "Christian book," and I do not proselytize. It is a management book about a historically Christian idea—the Protestant Reformation's sacred calling to secular work. Still, I refer frequently to the teachings of Christianity and Judaism because (1) Christianity was the basis for the Protestant ethic that pervades Western thought and life; (2) most social science research about faith-based interventions has been conducted with Christian populations; (3) even authors who write about calling from a secular perspective cite stories from Christianity and Judaism to illustrate salient theoretical points about calling; and (4) I am a Christian whose fundamental understanding of calling is rooted in my faith and examined through the lens of organizational scholarship. Through my research, I have discovered that the theoretical foundations of calling have implications for understanding how this idea relates to other faiths, philosophies, and worldviews.

My three goals for this project are to understand the state of management scholarship about calling, identify theoretical elements of calling, and assemble those elements into a coherent theory that can advance research and practice across disciplines. Toward these ends, I have organized the book in three parts that follow the overview in Chapter 1. Part I, "Management Conversations about Calling 1980–2012," reviews three different management perspectives about calling and critically analyzes the evolution of management scholarship, which gained momentum about 20 years ago.

Part II, "Other Conversations about Calling 1520–2012," explores diverse perspectives about calling beyond management. My sources include popular literature, academic literature, historical references, as well as personal and collective narratives. I also use the tools of social science to identify theoretical assumptions that are embedded in a literature that the majority of management scholars avoid—theology. My goal is to analyze these sources to make implicit assumptions about calling explicit, consider them in light of multiple sources of evidence, and suggest steps toward a coherent theory of calling that can be explained in psychological, sociological, and ideological terms. Through this process, I seek to advance the conversation about calling across disciplines and denominations and propose an integrative theory that can be tested and expanded by a broad array of scholars and practitioners.

In Part III, "Connecting Conversations in Theory and Practice," I integrate insights from the preceding chapters to present a comprehensive theory of calling. The theory draws on diverse perspectives and is relevant across cultures, disciplines, and philosophical traditions. Because conversations about calling include diverse perspectives, I also discuss the possibility of atheists having a calling. It is up to subsequent research to tease out how sacred, spiritual, and nontheistic callings are manifest and how the theory applies to different cultures and ideologies. I also provide examples of how to apply the theory and suggest ways to cultivate callings through institutional partnerships.

A book of this breadth has required some difficult choices about how much to cover, in how much detail, who to cite, with how much scholarship, and at what level of complexity. The calling literature is voluminous; I focus on the past 500 years. Hence, I have not reviewed every published study and article, which may disappoint some scholars whose work I did not cite. This book is not a meticulous literature review; it is a book about a grand, enduring, revolutionary idea that is being discussed in many different conversations that may be more fruitful if they were unified. With the hope of bridging these conversations, I deliberated about the topics that would be most relevant to advancing interdisciplinary dialogue and research. I am indebted to the University of Michigan for creating a climate in which interdisciplinary research is normative and thrives. For topics such as calling, interdisciplinary understanding is essential.

My approach to the topic is somewhat unique, given that I integrate management research, theology, and popular literature. It is important, therefore, that I clarify what this book is and is not.

What This Book Is Not

- It is not an undergraduate text. The case studies referenced in Chapter 11, which are published by GlobaLens.com, however, can be used in undergraduate, graduate, and executive education, as well as community and professional settings.
- It is not a self-help book that offers five keys, seven steps, or nine principles. Nor is it filled with various assessments to guide you on the path of your calling. There is no shortage of such books on the market (and one day I may add to their number.). If you gain insights into your calling by reading the different perspectives in this book, I will be gratified.
- It does not pay homage to Max Weber, although for historical and scholarly reasons, I use his work as a frame of reference because he is prominently cited by many management scholars in their publications about calling. Like Weber, my perspective is somewhat sociological, however, recognizing that how we think about calling is influenced by the political, economic, institutional, and cultural forces of our time.
- It is not a reductionist perspective that views calling as "it"—your dream job for life. Instead, it explores the complexities of calling as it has evolved over centuries.

What This Book Is

- This book is an effort to refine theory by reviewing different literatures to identify the essential variables that can be tested empirically and to understand how to enhance the professional practices of clergy, psychologists, and managers, among many others.
- It challenges management scholars to at least *allow* for a postpositivist approach to their work on calling and to devise appropriate measures to examine beliefs—sacred or secular—in constructing and enacting calling.
- It is a challenge to include variables in research that have been excluded yet are relevant to the general population of workers and practitioners who encourage them (e.g., managers, career counselors, parents, clergy, psychologists, consultants).
- It is an effort to advance the discourse among social scientists and practitioners so that our collective body of work is more socially

relevant and impactful. It is an invitation to join a richer conversation; indeed, it is not a conclusion.

NOTES

1. Leoneda Inge-Barry, "Career Lessons from the Biblical Joseph," *Michigan Today* 32, no. 2 (2000).
2. L. Laudan, *Progress and Its Problems: Toward a Theory of Scientific Growth* (Berkeley: University of California Press, 1977).
3. Valerie L. Myers, "Calling and Talent Development: Not Your Average Working Joe Case #1-429-200," GlobalLens.com (2011).
4. See the special issue of the *Academy of Management Review* 14, no. 4 (1989).
5. Valerie L. Myers, "An Ontology of Calling: Examining Mechanisms and the Transcendent Possibilities of Work Orientation Theory," in *Critical Management Studies Conference Proceedings,* convened by Scott Taylor, Emma Bell, and Roy Jacques (Manchester, UK: Manchester Business School, 2007).
6. Valerie L. Myers, "What Did Weber Say? A Comprehensive Materialization of His Implicit Theory of Calling," in *Academy of Management Annual Conference—Management, Spirituality and Religion Division,* organized by Debu Mukerji (Chicago, IL: Academy of Management, 2009).

Acknowledgments

Like Joseph, I did not anticipate the long, circuitous route between points *A* and *B*—the people that I would meet or the path that my idea would take. I am especially grateful to professors from my graduate program at the University of Michigan. Jerry Davis and Kris Siefert, thank you for introducing me to macro theories and intervention design research, respectively. The intervention course enabled me to understand how elements of Joseph's story could reinforce desirable organizational behaviors, and institutional theory helped me locate developments in the field in a broader sociological context. I am also grateful to David Tucker, who at my insistence, taught a small seminar in Theory Construction. John Wallace and Robert Taylor, I appreciate your mentoring and examples of scholarship about religion, showing me that it was not only possible but also worthwhile and achievable. I appreciate the late Chris Peterson's instruction, serving on my dissertation committee and for his groundbreaking work in Positive Psychology. Our last exchange in 2012 was a conversation about character and calling. Richard Saavedra, thank you for encouraging me to explore this line of inquiry in graduate school, before it was a popular topic. It is gratifying to know that a growing body of literature now affirms my calling to undertake this work years ago.

To my academic colleagues: Scott Taylor of the University of Birmingham—the Critical Management Studies Conference that you organized in Manchester, England, was the catalyst for me to finally crystallize my thoughts about calling in an academic publication. I still remember the day I received the acceptance notice—thank you! Jane Dutton, Kim Cameron, and Laura Morgan Roberts—thank you for reading and providing feedback on the manuscript that I submitted to the Academy of Management; it was the foundation for this book. Thanks also to Jane and the POS community for opportunities to refine this work through different POS activities. To anonymous reviewers of various manuscripts, I appreciate your feedback, critiques, and especially recommended readings that helped me to advance this project. Lynn Wooten, thank you for connecting me with Routledge Press. Tom Sy and Scott Greer, thanks for your encouragement and sense of humor along the way. Scott, I really appreciate your feedback on selected chapters of the book and for recognizing that *Millhands and Preachers* was the story that I referenced—I didn't know about the book.

A team of people was responsible for this book, and parts of it, being published. GlobaLens.com, at the University of Michigan's William Davidson Institute, it's been a pleasure working with the team on the "Not Your Average Working Joe" business cases. I am indebted to anonymous reviewers of my book proposal; without your positive feedback, this project would not have materialized. Sharon Golan, thank you for believing in this project and shepherding it through the review process, as well as your patience in bringing it to print. I have really enjoyed working with you and getting to know you. To editors Leslie Wilhelm-Hatch, with whom I worked locally, and to Denise File and her team at Apex CoVantage, thank you for contributing your skill and insights to help bring this book to print. Stephanie Gehani, thank you for the graphic design work.

Finally, I appreciate the encouragement, support, and love of friends and family over the years. In your own way, you've each reminded me why this project was important, to keep going, and also to take a break. Thank you for listening, laughing with me, inspiring me, and being there.

Cover Art

The cover design reflects how I've come to think of calling. The text and illustration convey ideas throughout the book and the metaphor that I have used to describe calling theoretically. The cover is the product of my conversations with Sharon Golan, the acquisitions editor at Routledge Press.

Calling is a grand idea that looms large over the illustration, as it does over lives, but it is sometimes elusive. Some people "know" early on what they are called to do; for others it's not so obvious. Similarly, some people are quite clear about the meaning of calling, for others the meaning is murky and emerging. It takes many conversations, literally and figuratively, to understand calling.

Many metaphors have been used to describe calling, but I like the architectural metaphor of spiral stairs best. The stairs illustrate that, at a most basic level, calling is a continuous summons in a forward and ascending direction. It is an enduring challenge to transcend and rise up to meet our circumstances as a light illuminates the path. The spiral stairs are analogous to a whole-life journey and its inherent shifts; calling is not simply an occupational destiny, nor does it unfold in a linear manner. It is an ongoing process of transcending from youth that winds and turns through retirement and the end of life. *What* or *who* is calling you higher is mystical and personally subjective. *How* you interpret the calling and the influence that the different meaning systems have on behavior is a topic for study. Similarly, where calling ultimately ends is a personal philosophical question. The light above, however, connotes pursuing the positive and transcendent through our work and throughout life.

Steps in the foreground are an invitation to you to join a journey through centuries of scholarship and perhaps climb higher in your own calling. How do we begin? Gradually and incrementally. Calling is fulfilled, just as theory is constructed—step-by-step in day-to-day mundane work and less so in large heroic leaps. Thus, there are no wasted experiences—they all serve to cultivate essential competencies for the path ahead. I am explicit both about the steps that I've taken to construct a theory and about steps that various people have taken to live their callings. Often, it is only in retrospect that can we make sense of the many elements that constituted our calling.

This path, of course, is idealized. Rarely does a calling unfold so elegantly and rhythmically. I do not suggest that calling is always about passion, perfect alignment, and enjoyment. Sometimes, calling is striving to transcend less-than-ideal circumstances. Even the most gifted, self-assured people have challenges to overcome—or they will at some point in their lives. Even people with a clear vision and meticulous plan in youth may find that their idea of calling morphs as they respond to life's rhythms. Certainty can shift with age and circumstances. Furthermore, the path is sometimes obscure. The way becomes more apparent, however, with each courageous step we take toward becoming our highest selves.

The construction of the stairs, in all their complexity, also illustrates that context matters. But context is often ignored in management research about calling. First, the railing reminds us that we need a guide and supports along the path. In fact, mobility and progress are contingent on the infrastructure of one's ascent. Family, community, leaders, organizations, and society can foster or frustrate calling with supportive structures or burdensome barriers that must be overcome. The context of calling cannot and must not be ignored. Second, calling is paradoxical. The juxtaposition of light and shadow, sharp edges and sinewy curves is analogous to positive and negative influences on one's calling from society and within. Shadowy individual aspects of calling include resistance, reluctance, habits, and fear that stall our progress. Further, just as it is possible to ascend, it is also possible to descend, stall, or fall. Third, the winding intersection of horizontal and vertical planes parallel the converging intellectual planes of theology and management theory, of calling research and practice, and they show how centuries of philosophy and, more recently, research can become a coherent whole.

Finally, spiral stairs have personal meaning for me. They are a tribute to my father's architectural designs and his encouragement to persevere and climb higher.

1

Conversations about Calling

"How does it make you feel?" "Does it have a positive impact on others?" "Does it turn up the volume and increase the vibration of your life?"[1] Media mogul Oprah Winfrey posed those questions to help her readers gain insights about their "callings." Contributing authors to the "Find Your True Calling"[2] issue of *O Magazine* echoed the core themes embedded in her questions—personal alignment, intense emotions, prosocial intent, and something transcendent (e.g., vibration). Interestingly, these same themes dominate contemporary management scholarship—not surprising given that management scholars' renewed interest in calling coincided with Winfrey's ascent as an "arbiter of truth"[3] during the 1990s.

Modern management scholars generally agree that a calling entails engaging in work that is intrinsically rewarding because it is aligned with one's passion, core interests, abilities, and perceived destiny. Consequently, work in a calling is energizing, elicits commitment, and sometimes benefits society. Similar themes are evident in definitions of calling that guide management scholarship.[4] More specifically, the *Encyclopedia of Career Development* states:

> The idea of viewing one's work as a calling came into common usage with Max Weber's concept of the Protestant work ethic. While a calling originally had religious connotations and meant doing work that God had "called" one to do, a calling in the modern sense has lost this religious connotation and is defined here as consisting of enjoyable work that is seen as making the world a better place in some way. Thus, the concept of a calling has taken on a new form in the modern era and is one of several kinds of meanings that people attach to their work.[5]

This definition suggests that modern management has made considerable progress beyond historic theological notions of calling—but not all management scholars agree.[6] Although encyclopedic definitions have the cache of authority and dominate the discourse, some management scholars contend that calling is still a transcendent or religious concept, but they are in the minority. The source of discord among management scholars can be traced to fault lines that frame conversations about calling. In this chapter, I explain the contours of those fault lines, resulting conversations about calling, and overall implications for calling scholarship and practice.

Fault Lines That Define Conversations about Calling

Calling is an old idea that found new life in management scholarship at the end of the 20th century. *The* conversation about calling is centuries old and has spawned multiple conversations as religious adherents, philosophers, social scientists, and cultural trends have influenced its meaning. New actors and epochs have spawned revolutionary changes in the meaning of calling and evolutionary changes[7] that reflect incremental shifts in our understanding and its application.

Three historical epochs carved fault lines that now define calling scholarship: (1) the Protestant Reformation of the 1500s, which defined calling as a sacred approach to ordinary work; (2) the simultaneous birth of management studies and the introduction of calling into it in the early 1900s; and (3) renewed interest in calling in the 1980s. These epochs are illustrated in Figure 1.1. Revolutionary changes in the meaning of calling are illustrated by large, dramatic flashes, while more incremental evolutionary changes are represented by minor flashes along a continuum from before the Christian era (B.C.E.) to the present.

Revolutionary conversations about calling originated with being *called* to the Christian faith after the ministry of Jesus Christ. Shortly thereafter, an evolutionary shift in meaning denoted calling as a summons to religious occupations and service.[8] Sacred meanings of calling as religious service persisted for more than 1,500 years.

In the mid-1500s, a revolutionary shift occurred when Protestant Reformers Martin Luther and John Calvin appropriated the term *calling* and declared that all ordinary work was sacred, not just work in a monastery. For the remainder of the millennium to the present, theologians have continued to theorize, sermonize, and write about the sacred calling in secular life.[9] (Theological perspectives of calling will be examined in Chapter 9.) As Figure 1.1 shows, there has been no widely accepted revolutionary shift in the meaning of calling since the 1500s; truly revolutionary changes are both rare and disruptive.

The next notable evolutionary shift in meaning occurred nearly 500 years later, when calling was catapulted into management studies at the dawn of the 20th century. The issue that interests us here is whether modern management's perspective of calling in the 21st century is best described as revolutionary, evolutionary, or something else.

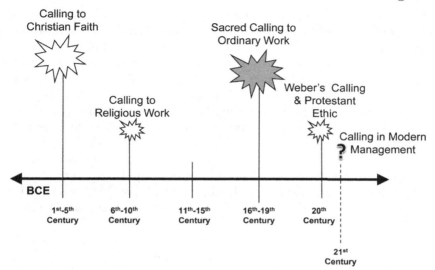

Figure 1.1 Twenty centuries of revolutionary and evolutionary shifts in the meaning of calling.

Origins of Calling in Management Studies

Renowned sociologist Max Weber introduced the idea of calling to the nascent discipline of organization studies in the early 1900s with his book *The Protestant Ethic and the Spirit of Capitalism*[10] (hereafter *Weber*). His ideas about calling were evolutionary in the larger context, but injecting calling into the new field of management studies was indeed revolutionary for management. *Weber* referred to the theological writings of Protestant reformers Martin Luther and John Calvin to describe calling as a "peculiar ethic" that infused ordinary work with religious or sacred meaning. He hypothesized that a sacred calling resulted in highly motivated employees who approached work in ways that "enormously increase performance," thereby contributing to remarkable economic growth. Intrigued by these ideas, industrialists and clergy experimented with integrating spirituality and work during this era, which I examine in Chapter 9. Yet, Weber was concerned that the robust religious construct might become a ghost of its former self in the new economic system—with good cause.

Weber considered religion an important dimension of modern life in the industrial age, as did his contemporaries, psychologist William James and sociologist Emile Durkheim. Yet Weber's perspective was eclipsed by two academic trends—Scientific Management and positivism. Frederick Taylor's book *The Principles of Scientific Management*,[11] was the cornerstone of management studies and was published shortly after

Weber's book. Scientific management sought to enhance employee performance with exhaustive measurement—not meaning and motivation. Taylor used time and motion studies to measure and improve observable work practices, which resonated with industrialists and managers. Moreover, Taylor's techniques were validated by the second academic trend—positivism in scientific research.

Positivists, and logical positivists, measure what is distinctly observable. The goals of positivist approaches to research are to identify and predict cause-and-effect relationships in order to control those causes and outcomes. This research tradition seeks to verify or falsify claims or deem them meaningless. However, since metaphysical, spiritual, and religious constructs are not easily observable, knowable, or verifiable, they were not considered "serious" topics for social science research in that era.[12]

Positivism prevailed from the 1920s to the 1950s, coinciding with management's Human Relations movement of the 1920s–1940s, when psychologists redirected their attention from time studies toward human need; indeed, careerism and fitting a person with his or her environment (i.e., Person-Environment [P-E] fit) followed.[13] As these ideas prevailed, Weber's calling receded in importance and lay dormant for decades.[14] Calling was a dead topic in management during most of the 20th century.

It stands to reason that in 1968, when calling reemerged in management scholarship—having been filtered through Taylorism and positivism—that the definition was quite different from Max Weber's original idea. Richard Hall resurrected calling with a study of professions and bureaucracy during the ascent of careerism. Hall's definition reflected the prevailing academic zeitgeist: "A sense of calling to the field—this reflects the dedication of the professional to his work and the feeling that he would probably want to do the work even if fewer extrinsic rewards were available."[15] Hall's assertion is notable because he decoupled calling from religion, God, and sacred notions of work. Further, he tightly coupled calling and career by associating it with professions (e.g., law, medicine, and accounting).

Nearly 20 years later, in 1987, Phillip Schorr published an article about public service as a calling,[16] in which he defined calling as "joyous service" to a profession. Having traced the origins of calling from ancient Greece to the Bible to Weber, Schorr believed that the utility of calling could be increased by disconnecting it from religion and making it *broadly applicable* to *non-religious endeavors* such as public service and administration. He asked, "Can we promote the contemporary equivalent of the calling by creating commitment and passion for the public service by means of an administrative theology?"[17] Apparently, Schorr was unaware that reformers' revolutionary idea of calling applied to *non-religious endeavors* and was *broadly applicable* to all work. For Schorr, an "administrative theology" had more practical utility than an actual theology of work, as Weber suggested. (I discuss the risks of an administrative theology in Chapters 8 and 9.)

The 1980s publication that had the greatest influence on management thought about calling was *Habits of the Heart*,[18] by Robert N. Bellah, Richard Madsen, William M. Sullivan, Ann Swidler, and Steven M. Tipton (hereafter *Habits*). *Habits* emphasized the importance of institutions in strengthening community and society as a means of moderating the rise of expressive individualism, which is characterized by strong feelings, rich sensual and intellectual experiences, self-expression, and luxuriating in one's interior world.[19] In *Habits*, the authors did not dismiss religious notions of calling as Schorr did; instead, they suggested that it had been weakened and displaced, which is precisely what Weber feared. Thereafter, calling became an intriguing topic in management, and publications proliferated.

Given the trajectory of calling scholarship in management, it is "logical" that the dominant conversation asserts that calling is a secular orientation toward occupational work. If this is true, however, the notion would represent the first revolutionary shift in meaning in 500 years! While some might think it's about time, and it may be, not reflecting on the context, causes, and consequences of such a momentous change is intellectually reckless. So, I consider them here.

The Revival of Calling in Historical Context

Each epochal shift in the definition of calling to date—from the call to religious belief and behaviors, to a call to religious service, to the sacred call to ordinary work—has added layers and texture to its meaning, making calling more robust and relevant for daily life. Through the lens of institutional theory,[20] layered and increasingly complex meaning can be expected over time, as new voices enter a conversation. Notably, as new voices entered the discourse about calling, they did not negate prior meanings; multiple meanings of calling have coexisted for centuries. However, the dominant management perspective about calling is a conversation stopper; nearly 20 years of scholarship has insinuated itself into a 20-centuries-old conversation, disrupting and dismissing sage voices without fully listening to them or understanding the implications of silencing them. Conversationally speaking, that's just rude.

As sociologist Stephen Kalberg noted, "Cognizance of ideas teaches that the present is closely connected to the past: if forces as fragile as ideas can remain viable over centuries, despite their inherent dependence upon social carriers, then the past must be acknowledged in general as powerfully influencing the present."[21] Since management scholars are neither the authors nor social carriers of the idea of calling, it is imprudent to uncritically accept the dominant secular perspective as definitive—it is not the only management definition of calling.

Competing conversations about calling began during the 1980s and 1990s, similarly reflecting themes of alignment, passion, and prosocial intent that Winfrey espoused. However, these conversations were differentially influenced by economic, social, technological, and ideological trends. The confluence of economic recovery, information technology, creeping individualism, post-positivism, and religious revival formed the zeitgeist that led some scholars to persist in their belief that calling is transcendent or sacred. Such scholars were influenced not only by historic fault lines but also by new ones carved in response to contemporary cultural and academic trends. In the sections that follow, I briefly describe these trends and representative characters[22] of the era (in addition to Winfrey) who depicted personality traits, tastes, and behaviors that were considered good, legitimate, and culturally appropriate going into the 21st century. I discuss these trends, icons, and implications for calling scholarship in management.

Capitalism, Individualism, and Technology

In 1981 Ronald Reagan became president of the United States during an economic recession in which 11% of Americans were unemployed. The national mood became more hopeful as economic recovery ensued, buoyed by a technology revolution, although tinged with increasing individualism. The images of fictional and actual success icons dominated the media, representing the competing cultural ideals of civic-minded and communitarian ethics versus triumphant individualism in modern capitalism.[23] Those icons and images influenced business practices, career aspirations, and consumer tastes.

For more than a decade, fictional television characters from *Dallas* and *Dynasty*[24] gave weekly lessons about how triumphant individuals amass, enjoy, and display the fruits of capitalism on a grand scale. Gordon Gekko, a ruthless stockbroker in the movie *Wall Street* (1987), embodied the period's unrestrained utilitarian individualism with his "greed is good" mantra that heralded a hypercompetitive and amoral spirit of capitalism. These characters influenced national culture and represent some risks of the secular individualistic calling that I describe in Chapter 2. At the same time, real management gurus multiplied, as Tom Peters sent us *In Search of Excellence* and W. Edwards Deming encouraged *Total Quality Management*[25] to gain competitive advantages in global commerce. These fictional and actual icons defined business and individual "success" for a generation—the baby boom generation.

Baby boomers (i.e., those born between 1946 and 1964) came of age in industrialized countries and yuppies—young upwardly mobile professionals—became icons for individualism, conspicuous consumption, and how to scale the corporate ranks. Iconic entrepreneurs Oprah Winfrey and Martha Stewart catered to and cultivated the tastes of baby boomers and aspiring yuppies with their unique brands of expressive individualism;[26] they offered lessons in introspection, emotional expressiveness, and sensual domestic experiences (albeit, on a more modest scale than fictional television icons).

The parallel yet divergent trajectories of Stewart and Winfrey highlight tensions of that era of capitalism. Stewart used her platform of evangelical domesticity[27] for purely utilitarian purposes—to cultivate consumers' tastes for household products (many her own brand). She promoted her products through corporate partnerships that comprised her vertically integrated empire. Eventually, Stewart went to prison for insider trading and was confronted with the challenge of preserving her tarnished brand. In contrast, Winfrey used her media platform toward communitarian, individual, and economic ends. As a communitarian, Winfrey launched new talent and promoted literacy, social advocacy, health awareness, global education, and activism. She promoted triumphant individualism with self-improvement programming; economically, her legendary product endorsements were an entrepreneur's dream and a retailer's delight. During this era, the cultural call seemed to summon people to *be* their best, *buy* the best, and *build* a bigger, better enterprise—sometimes winning at any cost. *Habits'* authors sought to counter negative aspects of that call by encouraging civic engagement and greater reliance on traditional institutions to prevent the societal trend toward creeping individualism.

One individual stands out as *the* business icon of the era, Microsoft cofounder Bill Gates. Gates, a college dropout whose technology empire made him one of the world's richest people. He embodied the inventive, entrepreneurial, and competitive spirit of modern capitalism. Gates also demonstrated a communitarian conscience through the work of the Gates Foundation.

Developments in information and manufacturing technologies during the 1980s and 1990s made anything seem possible; these advances also influenced new thinking about science more broadly. In an interview with *Business Week*, Laura Nash, then a professor at the Harvard Business School, described how technology broke the positivist frame.

The New Economy is causing a deep seated curiosity about the nature of knowledge and life, providing a fertile environment for this new swirl of non-materialist ideas. In this kind of analytical framework, suddenly it's O.K. to think about forces larger than yourself, to tap into that as an intuitive source of creative, analytical power. Furthermore, the Internet's power to blast through old paradigms and create previously impossible connections is inspiring fervent feelings that border on the spiritual. This new sense of spontaneity has caused even the most literal-minded to say, "Wow, there's this other force out there."[28] Suddenly, studying religion, spirituality and the metaphysical were no longer considered taboo in mainstream social science.[29]

In 2001 management scholars Charles Fornaciari and Cathy Lund Dean pondered the possibilities of using post-positivist scientific methods such as quantum physics and chaos theory to advance research about spirituality and management.[30] Later, Deborah Bloch and Lee Richmond applied complexity theory directly to calling and career development.[31] They argued against quantitative studies that measured small differences (positivism) and for the use of narrative methods to explore the dynamic, self-regenerative nature of calling and the nonlinear way that it develops (post-positivism).

Post-positivism, Faith and Professional Practice

Post-positivism was the most important philosophical shift in scientific thought in the 20th century.[32] Instead of the positivist approach that accepts only observable measures as ultimate truth, a post-positivist approach is interested in layers of deep structures that underlie what we observe. Post-positivists understand that observable reality is socially constructed and fluid, and is therefore fallible, prone to researcher bias, and reflects *a* truth, but not *the* truth. Consequently, post-positivist scholars seek multiple perspectives to gain insight into truth.[33] During this era, one post-positivist perspective included faith.

A popular religious revival occurred near the end of the 20th century, due in part to the felt need for deeper meaning in life and work that transcended the hypercompetitive, consumption-oriented, rapidly changing world.[34] People were searching for something more. To aid their search, an explosion of Christian book sales ushered in the "purpose-driven"[35] end of one millennium and the beginning of a new one. Religious practices, alternative practices, and philosophies became more mainstream and more pervasive in the social sciences.

Although the scientific study of religion in the social sciences had been underway for decades, research escalated during the 1980s and 1990s with support from entities such as the Fetzer Institute, the Templeton Foundation, and the Lily Endowment. Furthermore, professional associations created religion and spirituality subgroups as forums for practitioners to share knowledge about how to use faith to achieve secular goals in practice. Professionals' shift to acknowledge and include clients' beliefs was less about professionals' own beliefs, but rather the need to offer more culturally relevant, client-centered, and holistic practices.[36] Medicine, psychology, social work, and public health were among the professions that created faith subgroups in their professional associations; management was one of the last professions to embrace the trend when, in 1999, the Management Spirituality and Religion interest group was formalized as part of the Academy of Management (AOM). This lag by AOM is notable given that the Faith at Work movement started 14 years earlier.[37]

Even though there was a long history of combining faith with work in practice (which I examine in Chapters 7, 8, and 9), social, economic, and political trends of the 1980s inspired business leaders to combine faith and work in new ways. While some sought to address macro issues of social, economic, and environmental justice, others sought more integration of their beliefs and work lives. According to David Miller,[38] former business leader turned theologian, integration occurred in one of several ways, by (1) infusing religious *ethics* into work; (2) engaging in *evangelism* explicitly or implicitly by viewing work as part of one's vocation; (3) *experiencing* work in spiritual terms (e.g., calling) rather than merely instrumental terms; and/or (4) seeking personal *enrichment* and transformation through contemplative practices (e.g., prayer, meditation, and study). The Faith at Work movement spawned new partnerships between clergy and corporations, workplace ministries, and the role of corporate chaplains.[39] Notably, the movement was not led by religious institutions.[40]

Related business publications followed. Best-selling business books of the 1980s such as *The Road Less Traveled* and *The 7 Habits of Highly Effective People* were published as antidotes to the amoral and hypercompetitive approach to capitalism. Although the authors of both books had religious backgrounds, they muted religious beliefs in their writings. Instead, they promoted expressive individualism through hope and pursuing one's passions, and, to varying degrees, they espoused the importance of character development. In contrast, best-selling business books of the 1990s boldly combined management and spirituality, but neither Deepak Chopra's *The Seven Spiritual Laws of Success*[41] nor Laurie Beth Jones's *Jesus CEO*[42] were scholarly books. Finally, in 2003, two scholarly publications brought legitimacy and rigor to synthesizing faith and management: *The Handbook of Workplace Spirituality and Organizational Performance* and *Business, Religion, and Spirituality.*[43] Only this latter work mentioned calling or vocation.

Despite the scientific shift toward post-positivism, increased interest in spirituality across professions, and the well-documented Faith at

Work movement, the majority of management scholars were reluctant to or timid about engaging religion or spirituality.[44] Therefore, it is not surprising that, today, a secular perspective of calling dominates management scholarship, while a faith perspective of calling is relegated to being a faint minority voice.

In sum, epochal shifts from the Protestant Reformation of the 1500s, to the ascent and subsequent decline in calling's popularity in management during the early 1900s, to major cultural, scientific, and technological shifts in the 1980s have profoundly shaped ideas about calling. Those shifts, along with other factors, have resulted in three distinct conversations about calling in management.

Three Conversations about Calling in Management

Although *Habits* was first published in 1985, and the pace of academic publications has accelerated during the past decade, scholars have yet to agree on a single definition, robust measure, or theory of calling.[45] Instead, three research enclaves have formed due to scholars' different ontological, phenomenological, and epistemological foci.

Epistemologically, management scholars are united by their references to *The Protestant Ethic and the Spirit of Capitalism* and *Habits of the Heart* as the basis of their truth claims about calling. They differ, however, in degree to which they (1) have preserved Weber's and *Habits'* ideas, (2) implicitly extend different vocational guidance theories, and (3) are based on explicit psychological theories. Phenomenologically, scholars differ in their focus on the individual, the work itself, work organizations, and society at large—but those differences are relatively minor. The main point of contention is ontological—that is, whether calling is secular, transcendent, or sacred and how calling relates to work and life.[46] These ontological differences have resulted in three conversations about calling in management: (1) secular individualistic; (2) transcendent, meaning it is a spiritual yet secular concept; and (3) sacred. Management scholars widely acknowledge the fact that these differences have not been reconciled and impede progress.[47] The question is why?

Why, after 28 years, is there still no consensus about the definition, measure, or theory of calling? What are the unexamined assumptions that cause this fragmentation to persist? What are the consequences of this fragmentation in practical terms? What insights and evidence can help us overcome this conceptual quagmire? And, how do we transform the cacophony of voices into a harmonious chorus that promotes progress in research and practice? I offer insights and answers to these questions throughout this book.

Advancing the Discourse

Indeed, conversations about calling have been socially constructed and the meaning has changed over centuries as philosophers from Aristotle to Oprah entered the discourse. Historic and contemporary social, economic, scientific, and cultural shifts shaped the context in which management scholarship about calling began in earnest, as well as the dominant and emerging ways that we think about it. At present, a vocal and dominant group of management scholars contend that calling is secular, negating its essential core. This is both radical and risky.

Radical ideas are important because they have the potential to promote progress. Conversely, radical ideas can be reckless if pursued uncritically. With regard to calling, perhaps after 2,000 years it is time to think about it in secular terms as well. However, this thinking is risky if we unquestioningly accept assertions that calling is *only* secular without fully considering individual and social reasons for dismissing the sacred, the attendant implications for organizations and society, or how the wisdom of other voices could inform our scholarship in nontheological ways. I explore various radical, risky, and rational ideas about calling throughout this book.

Although *the* conversation about calling has been underway for hundreds, indeed thousands, of years, the management conversation is just beginning. After 20 years, there is no consensus about the definition of calling or how it should be measured, nor is there an overarching theory that can guide research and practice. This is a perfect time, therefore, for management scholars and others interested in the topic to consider how to thoughtfully advance the conversation about calling in the 21st century. That is my goal throughout this book. As ensuing chapters will show, each conversation describes elements of a theory, advances our understanding of key features and core dimensions of calling (e.g., personal alignment, intense emotions, prosocial intent, and something transcendent), and illuminates unexamined dimensions.

In Part I of this book, I explore aforementioned conversations about calling in management. In each conversation, I present illustrative research, intellectual contributions, theoretical foundations, and implicit or explicit assumptions. I then highlight the strengths, limitations, and implications of each conversation. (I trust that my reasons for not "vacuum cleaning"[48] the literature by citing every published study will be apparent to readers by the end of each chapter.) I conclude Part I with Chapter 5, "Calling in the Iron Cage," in which I explain why the dominant perspective gained academic legitimacy, implications for privileging it over marginal perspectives, and describe steps to progress toward a coherent theory of calling (which I present in Chapter 10). Although Part I is aimed at researchers, nonacademic readers may find it interesting to peek behind the curtain to gain insights into the process of knowledge construction.

In Part II, I explore conversations about calling outside of management scholarship; they yield major insights that can make management theorizing more relevant and robust. More specifically, Chapters 6 and 8 examine practitioner perspectives of calling, including psychologists, journalists, consultants, and religious authors. Chapter 7 illustrates how people have navigated the vicissitudes of pursuing a calling. In Chapter 9, I explore and directly quote theologians to reveal elements of theory scattered across the 16th through 20th centuries. Because Part II examines popular books, personal stories, familiar narratives, and history, it is less research oriented and more accessible. It will be of interest to readers who are deeply interested in the topic of calling, either to motivate themselves or others, as well scholars and practitioners (e.g., counselors, consultants, and clergy).

In Part III, I connect all of the conversations in a theory of calling and use a case study to illustrate how it can be applied in practice. Finally, drawing on innovations in post-positivist social science research, I conclude by suggesting ways to cultivate the callings of youth and adults, with hopes of restoring the calling's former vigor in modern life.

Persistent divisions and discordant conversations about calling matter. On one hand, different voices expand notions of what it means to have a calling. On the other, they impede advances within management scholarship and management's ability to work across disciplines. Setting aside ideologies and preferences, the question for us to consider going forward is not "Which conversation is right or wrong?" Instead, we must discern what is gained or lost by amplifying or silencing the many different voices.

NOTES

1. O. Winfrey, "The Oprah Challenge: Three Questions That Will Help You Find Your True Calling," *O Magazine,* 2011. http://www.oprah.com/spirit/How-to-Find-Your-True-Calling-What-Am-I-Meant-to-Do.
2. Ibid.
3. Tirdad Derakhshani, "Oh, Woe! No O; Why Did the Prospect of Oprah's Presence—Now Dashed—Create Such a Frisson in Philadelphia? She Is That Very Rare Celebrity Who Inspires Trust," *Philadelphia Enquirer,* March 25, 2010, http://www.lexisnexis.com.proxy.lib.umich.edu/hottopics/lnacademic/?verb=sr&csi=247189.
4. A. Wrzesniewski, K. Dekas, and B. Rosso, "Calling," in *The Encyclopedia of Positive Psychology,* ed. S. J. Lopez and A. Beauchamp, 115–18 (Chichester, UK: Blackwell Publishing, 2009).

5. Amy Wrzesniewski and Jennifer Tosti, eds., "Career as a Calling," Reference Online Web ed., *Encyclopedia of Career Development* (Thousand Oaks, CA: Sage, 2006).

6. B. D. Rosso, K. H. Dekas, and A. Wrzesniewski, "On the Meaning of Work: A Theoretical Integration and Review," *Research in Organizational Behavior* 30 (2010); J. W. Weiss, M. F. Skelley, J. C. Haughey, and D. T. Hall, "Callings, New Careers and Spirituality: A Reflective Perspective for Organizational Leaders and Professionals," *Research in Ethical Issues in Organizations* 5 (2004): 175–201.

7. Philip Anderson and Michael L. Tushman, "Technological Discontinuities and Dominant Designs: A Cyclical Model of Technological Change," *Administrative Science Quarterly* 35, no. 4 (1990): 604–33.

8. See William C. Placher, *Callings: Twenty Centuries of Christian Wisdom on Vocation* (Grand Rapids, MI: Eerdsman, 2005).

9. Ibid.

10. Max Weber, *The Protestant Ethic and the Spirit of Capitalism* (London: Routledge, 1904/1992).

11. Frederick Winslow Taylor, *The Principles of Scientific Management* (New York: Harper & Brothers, 1911).

12. Robert J. Furey, *Called by Name: Discovering Your Unique Purpose in Life* (New York: Crossroad, 1996).

13. J. L. Holland, *Making Vocational Choices: A Theory of Careers* (Englewood Cliffs, NJ: Prentice-Hall, 1973).

14. Weber's work remained relevant and of interest to sociologists and other disciplines; it was not a focus in organizational behavior.

15. Richard H. Hall, "Professionalization and Bureaucratization," *American Sociological Review* 33, no. 1 (1968): 93.

16. Philip Schorr, "Public Service as a Calling: An Exploration of a Concept," *International Journal of Public Administration* 10, no. 5 (1987): 465–93; Philip Schorr, "Public Service as a Calling: An Exploration of a Concept. Part II," *International Journal of Public Administration* 13, no. 5 (1990): 649–88.

17. Schorr, "Public Service as a Calling"; Schorr, "Public Service as a Calling. Part II," 658.

18. Robert N. Bellah, Richard Madsen, William M. Sullivan, Ann Swidler, and Steven M. Tipton, *Habits of the Heart: Individualism and Commitment in American Life: Updated Edition with a New Introduction* (Berkeley: University of California Press, 1996).

19. Ibid.

20. W. Richard Scott, *Institutions and Organizations,* Foundations for Organizational Science (Thousand Oaks, CA: Sage, 1995).

21. S. Kalberg, "Should the 'Dynamic Autonomy' of Ideas Matter to Sociologists?: Max Weber on the Origin of Other-Worldly Salvation Religions and the Constitution of Groups in American Society Today," *Journal of Classic Sociology* 1 no. 3 (2001): 294.

22. Bellah et al., *Habits of the Heart.*

23. Ibid.

24. The original *Dallas* series was broadcast from 1978 to 1991, and the original *Dynasty* series was broadcast from 1981 to 1989.

25. W. Edwards Deming, *Quality Productivity and Competitive Position* (Cambridge, MA: Massachusetts Institute of Technology Press, 1982).

26. Bellah et al., *Habits of the Heart.*

27. Mary Ann Glynn, "Evangelical Domesticity and Martha Stewart Living Magazine, 1990–2002," in *Interdisciplinary Committee on Organization Studies,* ed. University of Michigan (Ann Arbor: University of Michigan Press, 2003).

28. Michelle Conlin, "Religion in the Workplace: The Growing Presence of Spirituality in Corporate America," *Business Week,* November 1, 1999, 6.

29. The *Journal for the Scientific Study of Religion* was founded in 1961, so religion research was not new. However, such topics were taken more seriously and deemed legitimate across professional disciplines (e.g., anthropology, economics, health sciences, religious studies, psychology, and political science).

30. Charles J. Fornaciari and Kathy Lund Dean, "Making the Quantum Leap: Lessons from Physics on Studying Spirituality and Religion in Organizations," *Journal of Organizational Change Management* 14, no. 4 (2001): 335–51.

31. Deborah P. Bloch and Lee J. Richmond, "Complexity, Chaos, and Nonlinear Dynamics: A New Perspective on Career Development Theory," *The Career Development Quarterly* 53, no. 3 (2005): 194–207.

32. See http://www.socialresearchmethods.net/kb/positvsm.php. Mats Alvesson and Kaj Skoldberg, "(Post-)Positivism, Social Constructionism, Critical Realism: Three Reference Points in the Philosophy of Science," in *Reflexive Methodology: New Vistas for Qualitative Research,* 2nd ed. (Thousand Oaks, CA: Sage, 2009).

33. See Alvesson and Skoldberg, "(Post-)Positivism," for a more detailed explanation of philosophies of science.

34. John Naisbitt and Patricia Aburdene, *Megatrends 2000: Ten New Directions for the 1990s* (New York: Avon Books, 1990).

35. The bestseller *The Purpose Driven Life,* by pastor Rick Warren, was a symbol of religious revival and individuals' search for meaning.

36. Valerie L. Myers, *An Interdisciplinary Analysis of Faith-Based Human Services: Analyzing Latent Organizational, Social and Psychological Processes* (PhD diss., University of Michigan, 2003).

37. David W. Miller, "The Faith at Work Movement," *Theology Today* 60, no. 3 (2003): 301; David W. Miller, *God at Work: The History and Promise of the Faith at Work Movement* (New York: Oxford University Press, 2007).

38. Miller, *God at Work.*

39. Conlin, "Religion in the Workplace"; Miller, *God at Work.*

40. Miller, *God at Work.*

41. Deepak Chopra, *The Seven Spiritual Laws of Success: A Practical Guide to the Fulfillment of Your Dreams* (San Rafael, CA: New World Library / Amber-Allen Publishing, 1994).

42. Laurie Beth Jones, *Jesus, CEO: Using Ancient Wisdom for Visionary Leadership* (New York: Hyperion, 1996).

43. Robert A. Giacalone and Carole L. Jurkiewicz, eds., *The Handbook of Workplace Spirituality and Organizational Performance* (New York: M.E. Sharpe, 2003); Oliver F. Williams, ed., *Business, Religion and Spirituality: A New Synthesis* (Notre Dame, IN: University of Notre Dame Press, 2003), 94–110.

44. Weiss et al., "Callings, New Careers and Spirituality" James E. King, "(Dis) Missing the Obvious: Will Mainstream Management Research Ever Take Religion Seriously?" *Journal of Management Inquiry* 17 (2008): 214.
45. Rosso, Dekas, and Wrzesniewski, "On the Meaning of Work"; Valerie L. Myers, "What Did Weber Say?: A Comprehensive Materialization of His Implicit Theory of Calling," in *Academy of Management Annual Conference— Management, Spirituality and Religion Division* (Chicago, IL: 2009).
46. Valerie L. Myers, "An Ontology of Calling: Examining Mechanisms and the Transcendent Possibilities of Work Orientation Theory," in *Critical Management Studies Conference Proceedings,* ed. Scott Taylor, Emma Bell, and Roy Jacques (Manchester, UK: Manchester Business School, 2007).
47. Ibid.; Myers, "What Did Weber Say?"; Rosso, Dekas, and Wrzesniewski, "On the Meaning of Work"; Tamara Hagmaier and Andrea E. Abele, "The Multidimensionality of Calling: Conceptualization, Measurement and a Bicultural Perspective," *Journal of Vocational Behavior* 81, no. 1 (2012): 39–51.
48. Mats Alvesson and Jörgen Sandberg, "Has Management Studies Lost Its Way? Ideas for More Imaginative and Innovative Research," *Journal of Management Studies* (2012). doi: 10.1111/j.1467-6486.2012.01070.x.

Part I

Management Conversations about Calling 1980–2012

2

Secular Individualistic Callings

The secular individualistic calling is the dominant management perspective. Conversations about this type of calling typically ensue using a job-career-calling framework that was derived from *Habits of the Heart*.[1] On one hand, *Habits* asserts that calling was replaced by job and career due to cultural shifts, yet contends that "something of the notion of calling lingers on, not necessarily opposed to, but in addition to job and career."[2] This is one of many conundrums about calling in management scholarship. In this chapter, I explore this conceptualization of calling, related research, and assumptions that guide it. In addition, I discuss practical and theoretical implications of accepting the secular individualistic calling as the authoritative voice in the management discourse.

Revolutionary Ideas about Calling: Secularism and Individualism

At the dawn of the 21st century, many management scholars dismissed or marginalized the religious aspect of calling as irrelevant, despite its long history, and asserted that calling is now a secular construct.[3] According to Novak, even an atheist can have a calling.[4] Douglas Hall and Dawn Chandler claimed that "although some people may pursue a calling out of religious beliefs, such a set of beliefs is neither a necessary nor a sufficient condition for having a calling."[5] Organizational research provides some support for this view; indeed, studies have shown that religiosity does not predict a sense of calling,[6] no longer "constrains" calling,[7] and is in fact only loosely associated with it. (I will describe contradictory studies in Chapter 4.)

Management scholarship about secular callings examines the meaning that people derive *from* their work in paid employment[8] with some studies focusing on specific occupational groups such as administrative assistants,[9] zookeepers,[10] health care workers,[11] or business leaders.[12] Calling is described as a feeling that one has toward a particular career domain.[13] The overarching idea is that people with a calling engage in work because the work itself is enjoyable, fulfilling, meaningful, and socially useful—not for the monetary rewards of a job or the occupational status and power of a career.[14]

In addition to secularism, this conversation indicates that calling is now considered far more individualistic than in past eras. Not only is the experience of calling highly individualized, but so is its meaning. In fact, the meaning of calling has been compared to a Rorschach test;[15] much like interpretations of Rorschach ink blots, a person's definition of calling projects their own individual psychology—or so says this line of scholarship.

Amy Wrzesniewski, along with her colleagues, noted that secularism, individualism, and prosocial intent now define conversations about calling in modern management. They offered the following definition of calling, which has dominated the field:

> The concept of calling has continued to transform over time, largely losing its religious cast in the modern era. Most definitions of calling are now focused in general on the individual experience of work as deeply meaningful and engaging, intrinsically motivating, and having a positive impact on the wider world. Thus, the concept of calling has taken on stronger individualistic tones . . . Perhaps the two most salient dimensions of a calling in modern research revolve around the calling as a source of intrinsic enjoyment and as a means to serving a greater good.[16]

Research Developments

Research commenced two decades ago and has been guided by assumptions embedded in the preceding definition. Studies largely have examined the presence or absence of a calling among modern workers, as compared to a job or career orientation, and have shown that between 15% and 62% of people report having a sense of calling, depending on the population examined.[17] The prevalence of calling among respondents suggests that it remains a socially relevant topic and a fruitful line of inquiry for modern management.

Several research findings are particularly interesting. First, people across occupational classes and at different levels within occupational hierarchies may experience their work as a calling.[18] It has also been argued that calling is a class-based luxury that can be constrained by myriad social barriers, including race, gender, and social status;[19] as such, people might need help to live their callings in nonwork settings.[20]

Theoretically, scholars have shed light on the antecedents of calling, how it operates in daily life, and its expected outcomes. More specifically, a calling can be acquired by active search, inner insight, and serendipity or nurtured and increased by being exposed to related activities in one's youth or affiliating with peers who have similar aspirations.[21] Shosana Dobrow[22] states that this type of calling originates within the individual, whereas Wrzesniewski and her colleagues assert that it is derived from the work itself and the work context.[23] Research has also shown that although calling is characterized by passion, passion can fade with time and as a result of negative work experiences.[24] Further, studies that examine emotional aspects of calling indicate that it is a malleable and fluid state, not a fixed trait—and can therefore be influenced by time and context.[25] Attention to the work context and waning passions offer interesting new directions for calling research.

Finally, findings have shown a positive relationship between calling and desirable individual outcomes (e.g., psychological well-being, personality development, and job satisfaction) and organizational outcomes (e.g., employee commitment and engagement).[26] These positive outcomes reinforce the notion that scholarship about calling, in this case a secular individualistic calling, is practically useful.

This body of theoretical and empirical scholarship about secular individualistic callings has made important contributions to the grand conversation about calling. Foremost, these scholars helped revive a dead but potentially vibrant topic in management studies. Further, by injecting calling into social science research, calling is no longer the sole purview of theological conversations that are typically devoid of empirical evidence.

Conversely, dominance of the secular individualistic perspective is curious, given the history of the word, Weber's concern about secularization, and *Habits*' concern about creeping individualism. Before uncritically accepting and advancing the secular individualistic perspective, it is imperative that we examine *Weber* and *Habits*' core claims, and make implicit assumptions explicit. More specifically, is it true that calling is no longer religious or sacred? Is the concept improved by being more individualistic? And is the secular individualistic calling a truly unique theoretical construct in management research?

Assumptions and Analysis

Calling: Is It No Longer Religious?

The only evidence that calling is no longer religious is derived from the aforementioned management studies and truth claims in academic publications. Beyond that, there is compelling evidence to the contrary. During the 1990s and 2000s, when calling scholarship gained momentum, religious and philosophical publications on the topic flourished.[27]

As evidence, I've provided a list of books (Table 2.1) that were written by practitioners (e.g., theologians, counselors, psychologists, and consultants). From 1996 to the present, the chain of religious, quasi-spiritual, and philosophical publications is unbroken, and this list is by no means exhaustive.

Table 2.1 A Sample of Religious and Philosophical Books about Calling, 1990–2012

	A Sample of Religious and Philosophical Books About Calling, 1990–2012
1990	*Fabric of This World: Inquiries into Calling, Career Choice, and the Design of Human Work* by Lee Hardy
1996	*The Fabric of Faithfulness: Weaving Together Belief and Behavior* by Steven Garber (2nd ed., 2007)
1996	*Called by Name: Discovering Your Unique Purpose in Life* by Robert J. Furey
1996	*Lifekeys: Discover Who You Are* by Jane A. G. Kise, David Stark, and Sandra Krebs Hirsh
1996	*Business as a Calling: Work and the Examined Life* by Michael Novak
1997	*Callings: Finding and Following an Authentic Life* by Gregg Michael Levoy
1998	*The Call: Finding and Fulfilling the Central Purpose of Your Life* by Os Guinness
1998	*Find Your Calling, Love Your Life: Paths to Your Truest Self in Life and Work* by Martha I. Finney and Deborah Dasch
1999	*Let Your Life Speak: Listening for the Voice of Vocation* by Parker J. Palmer
1999	*Courage and Calling: Embracing Your God-Given Potential* by Gordon T. Smith (2nd ed., 2011)
1999	*The Purpose of Your Life: Finding Your Place in the World Using Synchronicity, Intuition, and Uncommon Sense* by Carol Adrienne and James Redfield
2000	*The Other Six Days: Vocation, Work, and Ministry in Biblical Perspective* by R. Paul Stevens
2001	*Career and Calling: A Guide for Counselors, Youth, and Young Adults* by Ginny Ward Holderness and Forrest C. Palmer Jr.
2002	*The Purpose Driven Life* by Rick Warren (Anniversary ed., 2012)
2003	*Vocation: Discerning Our Callings in Life* by Douglas James Schuurman
2004	*Revisiting the Idea of Vocation: Theological Explorations* by John C., S. J. Haughey
2004	*Working with Purpose: Finding a Corporate Calling for You and Your Business* by Jane A. G. Kise and David Stark
2005	*Callings: Twenty Centuries of Christian Wisdom on Vocation* by William C. Placher (ed.)
2005	*Live Your Calling: A Practical Guide to Finding and Fulfilling Your Mission in Life* by Kevin Brennfleck and Kay Marie Brennfleck

(Continued)

Table 2.1 (Continued)

	A Sample of Religious and Philosophical Books About Calling, 1990–2012
2005	*Sustaining the Spirit: Callings, Commitments, & Vocation Challenges* by Catherine Cronin Carotta and Michael Carotta
2005	*Living Your Heart's Desire: Gods Call and Your Vocation* by Gregory S. Clapper
2006	*A Sacred Voice Is Calling: Personal Vocation and Social Conscience* by John Neafsey
2007	*Directionally Challenged: How to Find and Follow God's Course for Your Life* by Travis Collins
2007	*The Other Calling: Theology, Intellectual Vocation and Truth* by Andrew Shanks
2008	*Culture Making: Recovering Our Creative Calling* by Andy Crouch
2008	*Crossroads: Navigating Your Calling and Career* by Colin Creel and Joe White
2009	*Leader's Life Purpose Handbook: Calling and Destiny Discovery Tools for Christian Life Coaching* by Tony Stoltzfus
2010	*The Calling: Live a Life of Significance* by Kurt Martin Senske
2011	*Kingdom Calling: Vocational Stewardship for the Common Good* by Amy L. Sherman, Steven Garber, and Reggie McNeal
2012	*The Great Work of Your Life: A Guide for the Journey to Your True Calling* by Stephen Cope

Most notably, Rick Warren's *The Purpose Driven Life* was published in 2002 to help people find "it." Book sales indicate that people are searching for their purpose or calling and that search ensues globally. By 2007, 30 million copies of *The Purpose Driven Life* were sold, and the book has been published in different languages to reach a global audience (e.g., Chinese, German, Urdu [Pakistani], Korean, Arabic, Thai, Spanish, Mongolian, Rumanian, Hungarian, Polish, and Portuguese).

This continuous thread of religious books about calling, and the economic incentives to publish them, unequivocally refutes the notion that calling is no longer thought of in religious terms—it is. Assertions made by a majority of management scholars contradict both historic and contemporary reality. In fact, many management scholars even cite these books as they espouse the secular individualistic perspective. So how do we reconcile research data that show an apparent disconnect between calling and religion, compared with a stable and growing market for religious books on the topic? In the spirit of positivism, let's begin with the data—or lack of data about book readers, institutional influences, and sampling methods.

Books and the Individual Quest for Calling

People who read religious books about calling are engaged in a form of self-directed search. Little is known, however, about how widespread the search is or the efficacy of this approach.

When vocational psychologist John Holland developed the *Self-Directed Search* assessment to help people in their quest to align their personality and work, he rigorously tested the instrument. However, no commensurate research has been conducted to assess the efficacy of reading religious books in a self-directed search for one's calling, even though advances in social science research provide the insights and tools to do so.[28] Thus, contradictory research results may simply reveal that (1) existing books are inadequate to facilitate one's individual quest to link faith and calling; or (2) that the self-directed search for one's calling is a suboptimal way to explore or understand the concept. Holland might lean toward the latter.

Holland developed the *Self-Directed Search* to help individuals "simulate . . . what counselors, parents, psychologists, and personnel workers do in more intuitive and less precise ways."[29] He realized that discovering one's fitting work was ideally a product of social construction; the paper tool was a complement to human interactions and influences. Weber agreed, noting that calling is "the product of a long and arduous process of education"[30] and that education occurs in "the religious atmosphere of the home community and the parental home"[31]—not just from books. To date, studies have not measured the efficacy of reading books about calling or the degree to which education about calling has been provided by or absorbed from the institutions that Weber mentioned.

Institutional Influences on Calling

The meaning of calling was once communitarian; organizations and communities held similar ideas about what calling meant. Although there were denominational variations regarding particulars, Protestant faith communities generally agreed that all work had dignity and should be performed in ways that glorified God.[32] The fact that the meaning of calling has recently been compared to interpretations of Rorschach tests[33] suggests that institutions, for whatever reason, no longer espouse or reinforce shared meaning about calling. Empirical data lend support for this assertion.

Lori Fox reviewed published studies from 1960 to 2000 to analyze trends in church-based vocational development programs. She found a steady decline in professional publications about church-based vocational programs during the same time that popular book sales on the topic increased; programs at the local level were sporadic, at best.[34] Despite years of scholarly recommendations to improve faith-based vocational development programming[35] (e.g., large-scale systematic interventions and training laypeople), clergy and administrators have not heeded those recommendations—or at least have not published their activities.

Furthermore, although workplace ministries forged by clergy and management scholars commenced during this era, the effectiveness of those programs has not been examined empirically. Management scholarship lags behind medicine and other disciplines in systematically integrating and analyzing faith and the profession.[36]

In sum, apparent evidence of the secularization of calling may actually reveal respondents' lack of education, ineffective education from self-directed search, exclusion of book readers from research studies, or institutional indifference about calling. Without effective education by institutions, we cannot expect much of a religious connection to calling. On the other hand, the lack of religious connection may be due to respondents' lack of religiosity.

Sampling Bias

It is possible that either people who hold religious beliefs were excluded from the pool of study participants or that religiosity is declining. However, mid-2009 statistics about religion showed that more than 80% of people on six of seven continents adhere to some religious faith.[37] Furthermore, all major world religions and philosophical traditions espouse positions about the meaning of work and work ethics.[38] In the United States, even though the *American Religious Identification Survey* showed that fastest growing group is nonreligious,[39] their numbers pale in comparison to 77% of the population that self-identifies as Christians, Muslims, Jews, Buddhists, and Hindus.[40] Therefore, it is unlikely that the majority of study participants were agnostic or atheist. In fact, most studies don't inquire about religiosity.

These revelations about calling and religious faith are a reminder of Mats Alvesson and Kaj Skoldberg's caution that "the observed reality is not all there is—and the researcher can reach behind it and reveal more fundamental layers."[41] In this case, we need to understand the fundamental layers that comprise the antecedents or preconditions of calling.

Research about secular individualistic callings commenced with an underlying assumption that the preconditions for calling naturally exist. But Weber stated that calling "is by no means a product of nature."[42] Yet few if any studies have measured the degree to which participants have actively cultivated their callings individually, at work, or in religious or other institutions. Therefore, research indicating that calling is secular may actually reveal more about the efficacy of reading books about calling, institutional influences on calling, and sampling and research methods. Hence, before measuring the presence or absence of calling, management scholars need to answer several questions. How do, and in fact do, traditional institutions (e.g., family and religious organizations) educate members about calling in the modern era? If not, why not? If so, which methods are effective? Given the plethora of religious books about calling, have they been influential? And, if it's true that many people have come to think about calling as secular and individualistic, what are the broad implications of these shifts?

Implications of Secularization and Individualism

Weber commented on the trend toward the secularization of calling as it commenced 100 years ago: "In the field of its highest development, in the United States, the pursuit of wealth, stripped of its religious and ethical meaning, tends to become associated with purely mundane passions, which often actually give it the character of sport."[43] He predicted that as capitalism gained momentum, its corrosive effects would dilute the sacred calling and deplete the spirit that acted as its catalyst. He feared that as calling devolved, it would become a utilitarian ethic driven by hypercompetitiveness, a passion for "quantitative bigness," and "winning," a term infamously popularized by Hollywood bad boy, Charlie Sheen (admittedly an extreme example).

Both *Weber* and *Habits* cautioned against the trend toward expressive individualism because of its implications for calling, individuals, and society more broadly.[44] Both contended that because the secular individualistic calling focused on aligning individual interests and emotion, one who pursued that type of calling did so untethered from any collectively held standards—moral or religious. A calling guided by purely self-referent or subjective criteria[45] opens the door to all kinds of organizational mischief. One may approach work and life with anticipation, energy, and excitement[46] but without anything to moderate individualistic impulses toward hedonistic, reckless, careless, greedy, or nefarious ends. The idea, therefore, that a secular individualistic calling somehow "transcends" historic notions of calling is naive. Weber warned that "for of this last stage of this cultural development, it might well be truly said: Specialists without spirit, sensualists without heart; this nullity imagines that it has attained a level of civilization never before achieved."[47] Weber used the phrase "specialists without spirit" to describe the potential fate of workers in the United States as the culture drifted from a sacred ethical calling toward a secularized, individualistic, utilitarian calling.

Specialists without Spirit

Kenneth Lay, former CEO of Enron, exemplifies a specialist without spirit whose secular, individualistic calling ran amuck.[48] Lay, the son of a Baptist minister, professed a calling to business. Business was aligned with his interests and proved to be enjoyable; presumably, Lay had good intentions toward society. Lay's strong impulse to amass wealth, however, led him to perpetrate a fraud so catastrophic that shareholders lost $11 billion and he was convicted on 11 criminal counts.[49]

Not all specialists without spirit are so notorious. We encounter ordinary specialists without spirit every day: careless contractors, rude receptionists, greedy investment bankers who game the system for personal benefit, manufacturers who knowingly distribute contaminated food or faulty products to make quarterly sales projections, physicians who are repeatedly let off the hook for mindless practices and medical errors, clergy and coaches who abuse children and the administrators who transfer rather than punish them, managers who ignore employees' safety concerns to "get 'er done" and collect their bonuses, professors who plagiarize students' and colleagues' work, hourly workers who pad their time cards, lobbyist-enriched government employees who fast-track drugs without adequate testing, lawyers who underprepare and overbill, athletes who use performance enhancing drugs to pursue their passion and win, and clerks whose phone calls and sidebar conversations are more important than the customers standing before them. Must I continue? Recent economic jolts, corporate catastrophes, employee malaise, and quality failures suggest that Weber's predictions were prescient.

In the 1980s, manufacturing errors in the United States sparked the Total Quality Movement[50] and establishment of the Malcolm Baldrige National Quality Award;[51] the goals of both were to improve performance across industries. Later, insidious effects of corporate malfeasance and the 2008 economic collapse that rippled around the globe increased the urgency to strengthen the ethical infrastructure of commerce—globally and domestically. Numerous business schools rose to the challenge to establish learning goals related to ethical practices and corporate social responsibility. But *every* profession needs specialists *with* spirit—people who ethically and effectively practice their craft. It is curious then that the majority of management scholars have unquestioningly adopted and advanced the secular individualistic calling, devoid of spirit and specialization in the tradition sense.

Specialists with Spirit

Specialists are devoted to an occupation or branch of learning.[52] As a specialist, you are devoted to centering your attention wholly and purposefully, not necessarily because it is your *ideal* work, but because it is *your* work. As Richard Sennet, author of *The Craftsman*,[53] suggests, a specialist values doing a job well for its own sake—it is a moral obligation to the craft and community, an ethic that *Weber* described. That type of specialization, however, is not included or measured in research pertaining to the secular individualistic calling, even though *ethic* was part of the title of Weber's book. Furthermore, in our current era of increasingly fragmented attention, in which multitasking is considered a virtue, we do not specialize or focus on a single task very well.

Adopting the traditional meaning of "specialist" as part of calling offers an opportunity to expand how we think about calling, moving from meaning and "fit" to behaviors—purposive, skillful, and collegial work. Matthew Crawford, author of *Shop Class as Soulcraft*, agrees: "One has to have certain personal qualities, more than a well-defined set of competencies tied to the fulfillment of specific organizational ends."[54] Spirit is a personal quality that differentiates calling from other ways of working; it is the animating force or vital principle that gives life.[55]

A *spirit* is a disposition or attitude that can be sacred, virtuous, apathetic, wounded, or malevolent. Hence, the abusive coach, careless contractor, mindless physician, shifty lawyer, or any other person on the theoretically infinite list of previously described workers, is not actually without spirit. More accurately, their spirits are malevolent, narcissistically unethical, or merely apathetic—in a word, uncultivated. They do not reflect the spirit of a calling.

The authors of *Habits* imply that specialists *with* spirit are an antidote to individualism and a prescription for greater social cohesion. To illustrate their point, they applied the concept to social science and management education in the following two quotes:

> And if we remember that "calling or vocation," with the implication of public responsibility, is the older meaning of "profession," then we would see that a really "professional social scientist" could never be only a specialist. He would also see social science as, in part, public philosophy. That is, he would do his work in the spirit of community, at minimum, and ideally in a spirit of ethics and integrity.[56]

> Management would become a profession in the older sense of the word, involving not merely standards of technical competence but standards of public obligation that could at moments of conflict override obligations to the corporate employer. Such a conception of the professional manager would require a deep change in the ethos of schools of business administration, where "business ethics" would have to become central in the process of professional formation.[57]

Habits describes the spirit of community and the spirit of integrity as central to calling, such that transcendence is not framed in religious terms but as a social obligation that transcends corporate interests and altruistic intentions. These ideas cannot be found in secular individualistic calling research. In fact, *Habits* reveals the practical limits and deficits of a secular individualistic calling—it lacks a positive spirit that animates the work; it is devoid of traditional specialization that is a product of social influences that result in careful methods; and we are left with a calling that is merely specialization in a desired and fitting occupation.

Is a Secular Individualistic Calling a Distinct Concept?

At the turn of the century, Frank Parsons founded the vocational guidance movement, with the goal of "helping people find jobs they do well and that are fulfilling."[58] In 1927, Stanford University psychologist Edward K. Strong developed a scale to measure occupational and leisure interests with the goal of helping military veterans find appropriate jobs when they reentered civilian life after the war. Over the years, several psychologists revised and refined Strong's Interest Inventory, among them John Holland.

In his book *Making Vocational Choices*,[59] Holland espoused his theory of Person-Environment fit (P-E fit), which aligned personality type (person) with the desired characteristics of a work context (environment). The six types of personalities and environments are realistic, investigative, artistic, social, enterprising, and creative. Holland's central thesis was that "people search for environments that will let them exercise their *skills* and *abilities,* express their *attitudes* and *values,* and take on agreeable problems and *roles.*"[60] Furthermore, "[v]ocational satisfaction, stability, and achievement depend on the congruence between one's personality and the environment in which one works."[61] For example, a fitting environment allows a person to use skills that they prefer or to engage in work that is congruent with their values, world outlook or personality."[62] Holland's validated theory of P-E fit is still used today.

In Table 2.2, I highlight similarities between P-E fit and secular individualistic calling. Although the comparison is imperfect linguistically, conceptually the terms are only differentiated by prosocial intent—and even then, a parallel could be drawn. Under both conceptual umbrellas, people pursue pleasurable and intrinsically rewarding activities, seek work that is aligned with important personal values, preferred roles, and have a particular worldview. Do we really need a term as lofty as *calling* to link altruism to P-E fit? No.

Parallels between P-E fit and calling are important for several reasons. First, the P-E fit measure of calling is frequently used in published,

Table 2.2 Comparing Constructs: Person-Environment Fit and Calling

Person—Environment Fit	*Secular Individualistic Calling*
People seek work environments in which they can exercise their skills and abilities, perform activities they prefer, use special competencies, and deal with agreeable problems.	People seek work for its intrinsic enjoyment. They feel good about the work because they love it.
They seek work environments in which they can express their attitudes and values and that reinforce their personal disposition and personality traits.	Their work is a vital part of who they are; it is one of the first things they tell other people about themselves.
They seek preferred roles.	They are pleased that they are in this line of work.
They seek work environments that are in agreement with their special outlook on the world.	Their work makes the world a better place.
	Their work serves a greater good.

mainstream studies. Thus, a great deal of published research actually measures P-E fit and not calling; at best, it measures a dimension of calling and not the most important dimension, as we will see in Chapters 3 and 4.

Second, since the secular individualistic calling is analogous to P-E fit, then the job-career-calling typology really describes a continuum of emotions related to P-E fit. More specifically, at the negative end of the continuum, a job or career may be a very "bad fit" for any number of reasons (e.g., physical burden or misalignment of interests with responsibilities). At the middle of the continuum, the job may be a good fit that is aligned with personal interests and aptitudes but is fraught with the normal burdens of work. It's important to remember that not everyone despises his or her "job," and not everyone wants a "career"; people can be very satisfied with well-fitting jobs. More positive still is a desired and fitting career with growth potential. The most positive extreme of all, then, would be a calling—a blissfully perfect fit! Therefore, measures that use the job-career-calling framework actually assesses positive emotion and expressive individualism related to P-E fit or P-E fit plus altruism—but not a calling. (The fact that positive emotions are not inherent in a calling is explored in greater detail in subsequent chapters.) Since a secular individualistic calling is virtually indistinguishable from P-E fit and lacks the specialization and spirit that are germane to calling, our quest to build a theory must continue.

Advancing the Discourse

The majority of management scholars espouse a secular and individual-istic view of calling, that reflects the cultural zeitgeist of the 1980s and beyond, when the conversation about calling began in management. Generally speaking, the majority of management scholars agree with Oprah Winfrey about the meaning of calling as work that aligns with one's occupational *destiny*: the individual feels a strong inner urge or external pull toward the occupation, it involves intensely positive emotions, and calling demonstrates a concern for others and society. Unlike Winfrey, they dismiss transcendence. Although scholars' conceptualization has some basis in history, framing the concepts of alignment, emotions, and prosocial intent as calling, while simultaneously eliminating tran-scendence, ignores 2,000 years of theological philosophy, other social science trends, popular culture, demographic data, and psychological insights about elements that differentiate calling from other types of motivation.

Management scholars' emphasis on individuals and individualism has eclipsed the important role of institutions and community in the for-mation and reinforcement of calling. Consequently, the negative effects of a highly individualistic calling have been grossly underexamined and underestimated, despite *Weber* and *Habits'* admonishments. Moreover, if every individual holds a different meaning of calling, then the con-cept is utterly meaningless. The socially shared meaning of calling was a source of its power, which I will describe in Chapter 7. Management scholars' focus on individual versus institutional aspects of calling has had important implications for the questions that were posed, answers that were unquestioningly accepted, the trajectory of our scholarship, and its cultural credibility and organizational relevance.

Regarding secularism, there is no evidence that calling is no longer religious. However, scholars in this conversation have argued that a case might be made for secular and nontheistic types of callings. That idea seems counterintuitive since calling is an inherently religious construct. Therefore, we need to understand, theoretically, what might unite such divergent worldviews and link them to the calling ideal. Otherwise, claims about atheism and calling will be just as specious as those that contend calling is now only secular. Insights from *Weber* and *Habits* indicate that morals and ethics may be the missing link.

Morals and ethics are omitted from extant measures of calling; both concepts can potentially connect atheists and believers to the idea, which I explore in Chapter 3. More importantly, a case can be made for secular callings without dismissing transcendent, spiritual, and sacred callings that have endured for centuries. A minority group of manage-ment scholars has done just that. Their emerging conversations reveal an interest in the spirit that animates calling, which I discuss in Chapters 3 and 4. We can use the tools of post-positivist social science to better understand that spirit in action.

Finally, what are the implications of insisting that calling is secular and individualized? Based on demographic and publication trends, this group of management scholars will theorize themselves into irrelevance for a majority of the working population worldwide. Elevating the individual while ignoring institutions and the *spirit* of calling, whether that means a religious, moral, or ethical spirit, is the most vapid version of calling there is—in fact, it is not a calling. Emerging conversations in the following chapters offer insights into what is.

NOTES

1. Robert N. Bellah, Richard Madsen, William M. Sullivan, Ann Swidler, and Steven M. Tipton, *Habits of the Heart: Individualism and Commitment in American Life: Updated Edition with a New Introduction* (Berkeley: University of California Press, 1996).
2. Ibid., 66.
3. Richard H. Hall, "Professionalization and Bureaucratization," *American Sociological Review* 33, no. 1 (1968); Bellah et al., *Habits of the Heart*; Amy Wrzesniewski, Clark McCauley, Paul Rozin, and Barry Schwartz, "Jobs, Careers, and Callings: People's Relations to Their Work," *Journal of Research in Personality* 31, no. 1 (1997): 21–33; S. Dobrow, "Extreme Subjective Career Success: A New Integrated View of Having a Calling," paper presentation at the Academy of Management Annual Conference, August 2004; Michael Novak, *Business as a Calling: Work and the Examined Life* (New York: Free Press, 1996).
4. Novak, *Business as a Calling*.
5. Douglas T. Hall and Dawn E. Chandler, "Psychological Success: When the Career Is a Calling," *Journal of Organizational Behavior* 26, no. 2 (2005): 161.
6. S. R. Dobrow and J. Tosti-Kharas, "Calling: The Development of a Scale Measure," *Personnel Psychology* 64, no. 4 (2011): 1001–49; R. D. Duffy, "Spirituality, Religion and Work Values," *Journal of Psychology and Theology* 38, no. 1 (2010): 52–61; Andreas Hirschi, "Callings in Career: A Typological Approach to Essential and Optional Components," *Journal of Vocational Behavior* 79, no. 1 (2011): 60–73.
7. Michael F. Steger, N. K. Pickering, B. J. Dik, and J. Y. Shin, "Calling in Work," *Journal of Career Assessment* 18, no. 1 (2010): 82–96.
8. Wrzesniewski et al., "Jobs, Careers, and Callings": Amy Wrzesniewski and Jennifer Tosti1, eds., "Career as a Calling," Reference Online Web ed., *Encyclopedia of Career Development* (Thousand Oaks, CA: Sage, 2006).
9. Wrzesniewski et al., "Jobs, Careers, and Callings."
10. J. Stuart Bunderson and Jeffrey A. Thompson, "The Call of the Wild: Zookeepers, Callings, and the Dual Edges of Deeply Meaningful Work," *Administrative Science Quarterly* 54, no. 32 (2009): 32–57.

11. M. Teresa Cardador, Erik Dane, and Michael G. Pratt, "Linking Calling Orientations to Organizational Attachment via Organizational Instrumentality," *Journal of Vocational Behavior* 79, no. 2 (2011): 367–78.
12. Novak, *Business as a Calling.*
13. Hall and Chandler, "Psychological Success"; Dobrow and Tosti-Kharas, "Calling."
14. Wrzesniewski and Tosti, "Career as a Calling"; Hall, "Professionalization and Bureaucratization"; Bellah et al., *Habits of the Heart*; Wrzesniewski et al., "Jobs, Careers, and Callings."
15. Bryan J. Dik and Ryan D. Duffy, *Make Your Job a Calling: How the Psychology of Vocation Can Change Your Life at Work* (West Conshohocken, PA: Templeton Press, 2012).
16. A. Wrzesniewski, K. Dekas, and B. Rosso, "Calling," in *The Encyclopedia of Positive Psychology*, ed. S. J. Lopez and A. Beauchamp (Blackwell Publishing, 2009), 116, 117.
17. J. D. Davidson and D. P. Caddell, "Religion and the Meaning of Work," *Journal of Scientific Study of Religion* 33, no. 2 (1994): 135–47; Wrzesniewski et al., "Jobs, Careers, and Callings"; Dik and Duffy, *Make Your Job a Calling.*
18. Wrzesniewski et al., "Jobs, Careers, and Callings"; Amy Wrzesniewski and Jane E. Dutton, "Crafting a Job: Revisioning Employees as Active Crafters of Their Work," *The Academy of Management Review* 26, no. 2 (2001): 179–201; B. A. Allan and E. M. Bott, "Calling and Life Satisfaction Among Undergraduate Students: Investigating Mediators and Moderators," *Journal of Happiness Studies* 13, no. 3 (2012): 469–47.
19. B. J. Dik and R. D. Duffy, "Calling and Vocation at Work: Definitions and Prospects for Research and Practice," *The Counseling Psychologist* 37, no. 3 (2009): 424–50.
20. Justin M. Berg, Adam M. Grant, and Victoria Johnson, "When Callings Are Calling: Crafting Work and Leisure in Pursuit of Unanswered Occupational Callings," *Organization Science* 21, no. 5 (2010): 973–94.
21. Dobrow, "Extreme Subjective Career Success."
22. Ibid.
23. Wrzesniewski et al., "Calling"; S. Dobrow, "Dynamics of Calling: A Longitudinal Study of Musicians," *Journal of Organizational Behavior* (2012). doi: 10.1002/job.1808.
24. Judith MacIntosh, Judith Wuest, Marilyn Merritt Gray, and Marcella Cronkhite, "Workplace Bullying in Health Care Affects the Meaning of Work," *Qualitative Health Research* 20, no. 8 (2010): 1128–41.
25. Valerie L. Myers, "An Ontology of Calling: Examining Mechanisms and the Transcendent Possibilities of Work Orientation Theory," in *Critical Management Studies Conference Proceedings*, ed. Scott Taylor, Emma Bell, and Roy Jacques (Manchester, UK: Manchester Business School, 2007); Dobrow, "Dynamics of Calling."
26. See B. D. Rosso, K. H. Dekas, and A. Wrzesniewski, "On the Meaning of Work: A Theoretical Integration and Review," in *Research in Organizational Behavior* (2010).
27. Michelle Conlin, "Religion in the Workplace: The Growing Presence of Spirituality in Corporate America," *Business Week*, November 1, 1999.

28. V. L. Myers, "Planning and Evaluating Faith-Based Interventions: Closing the Theory-Practice Divide," in *Independent Sector Conference Spring Research Forum: The Role of Faith-based Organizations in the Social Welfare System*, competition hosted by the Rockefeller Institute, Washington, D.C., February 2003.
29. J. L. Holland, *Making Vocational Choices: A Theory of Careers* (Englewood Cliffs, NJ: Prentice-Hall, 1973), 87.
30. Max Weber, *The Protestant Ethic and the Spirit of Capitalism* (London: Routledge, 1904/1992), 62.
31. Ibid., 39.
32. William C. Placher, ed., *Callings: Twenty Centuries of Christian Wisdom on Vocation* (Grand Rapids, MI: Eerdsman, 2005).
33. Dik and Duffy, *Make Your Job a Calling*.
34. Lori A. Fox, "The Role of the Church in Career Guidance and Development: A Review of the Literature 1960–Early 2000s," *Journal of Career Development* 29, no. 3 (2003): 167–82.
35. Ibid.
36. Valerie L. Myers, *An Interdisciplinary Analysis of Faith-Based Human Services: Analyzing Latent Organizational, Social and Psychological Processes* (PhD diss., University of Michigan, 2003).
37. See www.adherents.com and http://www.thearda.com/internationalData/regions/.
38. Quist Albertson, *The Gods of Business: The Intersection of Faith in the Marketplace* (Los Angeles, CA: Trinity University Alumni Press, 2007).
39. Barry A. Kosmin and Ariela Keysar (with Ryan Cragun and Juhem Navarro-Rivera), "American Nones: The Profile the No Religion Population 2008," report published from the American Religious Identification Survey 2008 (2009), http://commons.trincoll.edu/aris/publications/american-nones-the-profile-of-the-no-religion-population/.
40. Barry A. Kosmin, Egon Mayer, and Ariela Keysar, "American Religious Identification Survey" (2001), http://commons.trincoll.edu/aris/surveys/aris-2001/.
41. Mats Alvesson and Kaj Skoldberg, "(Post-)Positivism, Social Constructionism, Critical Realism: Three Reference Points in the Philosophy of Science," in *Reflexive Methodology: New Vistas for Qualitative Research* (Thousand Oaks, CA: Sage, 2009), 18.
42. Weber, *The Protestant Ethic*, 62.
43. Ibid., 182.
44. Bellah et al., *Habits of the Heart*.
45. Hall and Chandler, "Psychological Success."
46. Christopher Peterson, Nansook Park, Nicholas Hall, and Martin E. Seligman, "Zest and Work," *Journal of Organizational Behavior* 30, no. 2 (2009): 161–72.
47. Weber, *The Protestant Ethic*, 182.
48. Novak, *Business as a Calling*.
49. Krysten Crawford, "Lay Surrenders to Authorities: Ex-Enron Ceo Turns Himself in after Indictment, Pleads Not Guilty in Massive Accounting Fraud," *CNN/Money*, July 12, 2004, http://money.cnn.com/2004/07/08/news/newsmakers/lay/; Claire Suddath, "Top 10 Ceo Scandals: Kenneth Lay, Enron," *Time Magazine*, August 10, 2010.

50. W. Edwards Deming, *Quality Productivity and Competitive Position* (Cambridge, MA: Massachusetts Institute of Technology Press, 1982).
51. See http://www.nist.gov/baldrige/.
52. *Merriam-Webster's Collegiate Dictionary*, 11th ed., s.v. "specialist."
53. Richard Sennett, *The Craftsman* (New Haven, CT: Yale University Press, 2008).
54. Matthew B. Crawford, *Shop Class as Soulcraft: An Inquiry into the Value of Work* (New York: Penguin Press, 2009), 149ff.
55. Ibid.
56. Bellah et al., *Habits of the Heart*, 300.
57. Ibid., 290.
58. Holland, *Making Vocational Choices*, 85; F. Parsons, *Choosing a Vocation* (Boston: Houghton Mifflin, 1909).
59. Holland, *Making Vocational Choices*.
60. Ibid., 4.
61. Ibid., 9.
62. Ibid., 10, emphasis added.

3

Transcendent Callings

Several psychologists, unconvinced that the definition of calling based on person-environment (P-E) fit was adequate, have explored the possibility of a transcendent calling. That is the focus of this chapter. Social psychologists Tamara Hagmaier and Andrea Abele developed the *Multidimensional Calling Measure*[1] and used it to analyze the degree to which five dimensions represented a sense of calling. They found that "transcendent guiding force" was the strongest predictor of a sense of calling (31%), followed by "identification with one's work" (22%), "person-environment fit" (20%), and "value driven behavior" (18%). Sense and meaning (9%) were least predictive of a sense of calling. Notably, the "transcendent guiding force" dimension has religious, nontheistic spiritual and individualistic measures, including the following:

- The one who is calling to do something is God.
- An inner force gives me the power and certainty that the job I do is what I should do.
- A person who is called has a feeling of determination. The person knows what he or she has to do.[2]

Similarly, counseling psychologists Bryan Dik and Ryan Duffy[3] also discovered that a transcendent guiding force was central to calling among college students, over and above P-E fit and using one's gifts. While some psychologists contend that the calling is from within—an inner voice, spirit, or an indescribable leading,[4]—Dik and Duffy contend that the calling is external and may originate from the needs of society, fate, family legacy, and possibly God (but not necessarily),[5] as well as circumstances, chance human encounters, and serendipitous opportunities.[6] Although these scholars disagree about the origins of the summons, they agree that discerning the call entails a variety of strategies such as listening, reflecting, seeking advice, and conducting assessments. How individuals identify the calling and interpret it as transcendent likely depends on their guiding cosmology. Most important, a growing literature now shows that a transcendent or spiritual calling remains relevant in the modern era; transcendence is its most salient feature.

Developments regarding the centrality of transcendence to the essence of a calling raise questions about the validity of previous studies that have excluded it, focusing instead on P-E fit. In this chapter, I examine the work of scholars who study calling as spiritual or self-transcendent, but without being explicitly religious. I call this the *transcendent calling*—it is secular yet also spiritual. As such, scholars in this conversation are concerned with the *spirit* of specialists and seek to make some implicit factors explicit, which is essential for theory construction.

This emerging conversation about transcendent callings challenges the dominant management perspective that callings are secular and individualistic—at minimum, calling is spiritual and has a social dimension. In the sections that follow, I summarize scholarly insights about how a transcendent calling is lived and influenced by social forces, as well as potential new trajectories for research. (I explore religious-based callings in the next chapter.)

Dik and Duffy have published exhaustively on this topic and offered an alternative to the secular individualistic definition of calling: "A calling is a transcendent summons, experienced as originating beyond the self, to approach a particular life role in a manner oriented toward demonstrating or deriving a sense of purpose or meaningfulness and that holds other-oriented values and goals as primary sources of motivation."[7] The addition of transcendence to calling research expands the field's narcissistic gaze to include the collective and beyond—collective goals, values, and norms, as well as a higher force. After reviewing the literature, I have identified three core elements of the transcendent calling: (1) one is *called by* transcendent forces (previously described), (2) one is *called to* specific transcendent purposes (not just making the world better), and (3) one is *called to behave or be accountable* to a collective.

Research Developments

Called to . . .

A literature review reveals different "calls to" that can be described as *individualistic altruism* or *purposeful communitarian*. (I use these terms only to make distinctions, not to suggest the need for new labels or definitions.) Both have an altruistic dimension that differentiates them from mere P-E fit and a secular individualist calling, but they differ in the degree to which they are transcendent. Both "calls to" also lead us toward other theories, beyond P-E fit, which elucidate the mechanisms of calling.

Individualistic Altruism

The call to individualistic altruism entails finding a fit that aligns with one's interests and activities across multiple roles, always with the goal of serving others. Dik and Duffy described it this way: "discerning a calling is, after all, fundamentally about finding and establishing a fit."[8] But they acknowledge that "PE−fit can only get you so far," and that additional tools are needed to consider different life circumstances. So, they have drawn on Donald Super's life-span, life-space[9] career theory to enhance their idea of calling. In so doing, they, like others,[10] indicate that calling is not limited to a career but can apply to any life role, such as parenting, hobbies, and service, throughout one's life. The life-span view is consistent with Weber's and the reformers' original ideas about calling.[11] Consequently, finding "it" or a "fit" may occur multiple times throughout one's life and even into retirement.

Dik and Duffy wrote: "Imagine feeling like your job aligns with what you think is most important in life and allows you to live out a sense of purpose. Imagine feeling like your gifts and talents are being used well, that other people are benefitting from your effort, that your 9 to 5 is actually making the world a better place. Imagine having a job you'd want to do for free, one that makes you cringe at the thought of retirement."[12] They blend P-E fit and the life-span model to create what *Habits* described as expressive individualism or luxuriating in one's inner experience of enjoyment, but with an altruistic slant. So the call to be an individualistic altruist is an incremental step above the secular individualistic calling, in that one feels summoned to fit into multiple roles throughout one's life. The next step up, however, is the purposeful communitarian.

Purposeful Communitarian

The purposeful communitarian is called to purposeful action[13] and has three defining features, beyond the summons and multiple fitting life roles. First, while it can be argued that all work is purposeful, studies have shown that some people feel *called to* advance specific transcendent purposes such as caring for people,[14] the environment,[15] or animals[16] (as opposed to finding a fitting and enjoyable occupation). Fulfilling this kind of calling uses ones gifts and may be enjoyable, but it is not inherently enjoyable; it may involve suffering and sacrifice. Second, the transcendent purposes are specific (e.g., caring for people) and have been socially defined as valuable (as opposed to generically making the world a better place). Third, research has shown that the call to purposeful action was linked to desirable work behaviors. The following examples illustrate these defining features.

A study of the transcendent call to environmentalism[17] revealed how a calling can inspire people to embrace the paradoxical nature of their work—the simultaneity of fulfillment with frustration,[18] delight with drudgery, and managing difficult emotions while sustaining commitment. This last item is important because the passion of a calling wanes.[19] Similarly, psychologist and consultant Richard Treadgold found that transcendent vocations were associated with more problem-focused coping.[20] Environmentalists who felt a transcendent call reframed work challenges as minor compared to the significance of their work and viewed difficulties and uncertainties as "transformative learning opportunities";[21] surmounting these challenges provided a sense of renewal. The cycle of challenge, learning, and renewal is similar to the feedback loop associated with calling as a type of psychological success.[22]

Although research has not yet examined the reasons why a calling might be associated with endurance, coping, learning, and renewal, Tim Hall and Dawn Chandler hypothesized that people with a calling have "career meta-competencies" (identity and adaptability) that help them navigate work challenges and transitions. Dik and Duffy agreed: "They have strategies for fitting their work into the broader context of their lives in satisfying ways."[23] While we don't know the origins of their metacompetencies and inner resources, Jessica Kovan and John Dirkx offer some insights.

In their study of environmentalists, Kovan and Dirkx found a connection between environmentalists' calling and their sense of connection to others; a sense of meaning, purpose, and hope; an awareness of a larger reality with some coherence; and a sense of connection to God or a larger force—all elements of spiritual well-being.[24] (Note, however, that they didn't use the term *spiritual well-being*.) Spiritual well-being, therefore, may be an unexamined antecedent of calling that promotes psychological success. Research is needed to understand how these concepts relate.

In sum, while the individualistic altruist is slightly different from a secular individualistic calling, the purposeful communitarian calling is theoretically distinct from both in important ways. First, the call to transcendent purposes can be described as the pursuit of ultimate ends[25] and the highest form of job design.[26] Rokeach described "ultimate ends" as good in and of themselves,[27] and job design recognizes that people are motivated when they consider the task significant,[28] not just because it "fits." Therefore, the call to be a purposeful communitarian is distinct because (1) alignment is not merely between important personal values and work, but between transcendent or ultimate ends and work; (2) the action or role has socially defined significance, not just individually defined significance; (3) spiritual well-being is a transcendent resource that may precede and/or energize a calling; and (4) the confluence of ultimate meaning, social significance, and spiritual well-being may be the causal mechanisms underlying positive individual outcomes that accrue from calling (e.g., satisfaction, enjoyment, and commitment), but that relationship has not been examined empirically.

Second, although a link presumably exists between calling and coping (and presumably metacompetencies), no research has explained this connection or the source of unique coping skills or metacompetencies. While scholars imply that workers with a calling have some guiding framework that helps them cope, navigate, and situate their work in a larger context, we don't know what that guiding framework is. Based on research, spiritual well-being or spiritual cosmologies might be the guiding framework that (1) provides psychological resources that help people cope with challenging aspects of their calling, (2) helps them navigate uncertainty and transitions, and (3) produces generative qualities (e.g., learning and renewal).

Therefore, the call to be a purposeful communitarian is distinguished from a secular individualistic calling, an individualistic altruist, and simply mundane work[29] because of the pursuit of socially defined ultimate ends; having inner resources to learn, adapt, and cope; and generativity that yields personal benefits. How these factors interrelate is a topic for research, as well as how they relate to behavior.

Called to Behave . . .

Studies have shown that some people expressed a *call to behave* in ways that are consistent with collectively held standards. This call to behave goes beyond prosocial values or other-oriented goals to include adhering to other-defined, collectively constructed standards, in this case occupational standards. Stuart Bunderson and Jeffrey Thompson found an example of this in their study of zookeepers,[30] whose sense of calling included feelings of moral obligation and sacred responsibility to uphold professional behaviors. In Thomas Conklin's[31] study of environmental workers, he too discovered that workers had a sense of duty to uphold professional values and norms. This sense of duty sometimes involves personal sacrifice, discomfort, and difficulty. Bunderson and Thompson have labeled this a "neoclassical" calling and assert that it is more expansive and inclusive than the "traditional calling" because it is not religious and can be applied across cultures. Dik and Duffy also acknowledged that morals might be a dimension of calling (but they didn't consider morals a psychological phenomenon[32]).

The transcendent call to behave is an important addition to management scholarship because it highlights the mechanism by which prosocial intentions might actually result in prosocial outcomes. Zookeepers' and environmentalists' sense of obligation to their profession highlights a different social dimension of calling; in addition to defining task significance, the social group influences one's calling and defines behavioral norms. For example, Conklin[33] found that human encounters and social networks influenced the formation of one's calling, give meaning to, and sustain one's calling during difficulties. The social influences on one's calling are not always positive, however. Some social influences unfairly delay or deny people the ability to fulfill their callings.

Delayed or Denied Callings

Scholars in the transcendent conversation described, as did Weber, how contextual and social factors can inhibit enacting and realizing one's calling. These factors include the larger economy, family background, socioeconomic status, and opportunity structures, or lack thereof.[34] Curiously, although scholars described the evidence and outcomes of social injustices abstractly (e.g., discrimination at work), they have ignored its origins, that is, how managers and organizational cultures are instrumental in its production.

Social barriers can result in denied callings, delayed callings, and the inability to engage in "fitting" or enjoyable work, which can do violence to one's soul.[35] Alternatively, people may find that they are occupied in the right work, but over time, discover that it no longer fits, which puts them on the precipice of a transition toward a new calling. Either way, a person may confront existential challenges that prevent them from switching jobs or careers. In the interim, they need strategies to manage denied and delayed callings. "If it is low confidence, where can you find encouragement and boldness?" asked Dik and Duffy. Indeed, where?

As a remedy for delayed and denied callings, Dik and Duffy recommend job crafting, which entails changing how one thinks about the work, rearranging work tasks, and reconfiguring relationships to make the work more personally satisfying.[36] They suggest that through job crafting, people can turn their jobs into callings. I think, however, that in such circumstances, people need transcendent resources as well.

Assumptions and Analysis

Insights and advances related to transcendence, morals, ethics, and the socially constructed nature of calling highlight interesting new possibilities for research that are distinct from the dominant conversation about secular individualistic callings. Paradoxically, the emerging conversation about transcendent callings also crystalizes significant shortcomings in management scholarship that can be overcome quite easily. Before I conduct in-depth analysis, however, it's important to highlight several implicit and explicit assumptions that merit attention at the outset.

Putative Discoveries about Calling

Foremost, the "discovery" that calling is duty *and* destiny reveals more about social science research than it does about the calling concept. It is not a discovery; two different disciplines have been studying calling for decades but refer to it using two different labels—Protestant work ethic (PWE) and calling. Bifurcation between disciplines suggests that neither fully understood the premise of Weber's book, the original meaning of calling, or the *"ethic of calling."*[37]

About 20 years before the idea was en vogue in management, psychologists began exhaustively studying the PWE, which encompasses the moral or duty dimension of calling.[38] There is a high degree of consensus about the meaning of PWE; measures are well developed and empirically validated. In contrast, management scholars have primarily studied calling as P-E fit and have failed to reach consensus about its meaning. To date, management scholars' inordinate focus on calling as enjoyment, alignment, occupational *destiny*, and making the world better has obscured the *duty* dimension of calling. We can make a giant leap forward, however, by integrating these literatures and measures.

Second, relanguaging[39] calling and assigning new labels does not advance the discourse. For example, the revolutionary idea behind a neoclassical calling is, in fact, not new. The term *neoclassical* has been used to differentiate a traditional religious calling to secular work from a calling that is defined by a sense of moral duty that is not inherently religious. Presumably, the term *neoclassical* makes calling more inclusive and expansive,[40] but a literature review shows that it doesn't. Moral duty was always a part of calling from the reformers through Max Weber; it became peripheral as the culture shifted toward individualism, which Weber feared.[41] Furthermore, morals, and ethics are not just part of calling; indeed, they constitute it. *Weber* and *Habits* agreed on this point.

The "duty" dimension of calling, not destiny or P-E fit, was the focus of Weber's book *The Protestant Ethic and the Spirit of Capitalism*; he was interested in the *ethic* that animated work:

> Truly what is here preached is not simply a means of making one's way in the world, but a peculiar ethic. The infraction of its rules is treated not as foolishness but as forgetfulness of duty. That is the essence of the matter. It is not mere business astuteness, that sort of thing is common enough, it is an ethos. This is the quality which interests us.[42]

Similarly, the authors of *Habits* stated: "The absence of a calling means an absence of a sense of moral meaning.[43] . . . In the strongest sense of a 'calling,' work constitutes a practical ideal of activity and character that makes a person's work morally inseparable from his or her life."[44] The preceding quote from *Habits* has often been misinterpreted in the secular individualistic conversation to suggest that work as a calling is inseparable from life. This errantly makes work central to one's life rather than making morals central to one's life. Moral duty is the common thread that is woven across life domains. Morals, ethics, and a sense of duty differentiate calling from a P-E fit, resulting in a qualitatively different *way* of working that has yet to be defined in the secular individualistic conversation. (Re)introducing morals to the conversation about calling is important because, through them, the prosocial intent of calling can actually be realized in organizations and society.

Third, when Weber introduced calling to the field of management, he was interested in the influence of religious *and* cultural norms on economic systems, not only in the United States but also globally. Weber acknowledged that similar work ethics were common across faith traditions worldwide, and contemporary scholars agree.[45] (Weber focused on Protestantism because of its relationship to capitalism in Europe and the United States.) To demonstrate that calling was not only religious, at least in the context of management, he warned against disconnecting calling from "the highest cultural values";[46] thus, one need not be religious to have the calling ethic. Therefore, calling was and is inherently inclusive—culturally and ideologically. It is incumbent on management scholars to identify other underlying mechanisms by which this is possible; indeed, this is my goal throughout the book. So, the neoclassical label is a distinction without a difference that threatens to muddy keyword searches. Reconstituting calling with its original features of moral obligation to community and profession is neither a revolutionary nor evolutionary idea. It simply maintains the integrity of the original idea.

On a fourth, related note, much of the language that we need to define and measure calling already exists in other disciplines. One example is spiritual well-being, another is transcendence. These terms are not germane to management, but they are well established in the social sciences. Applying existing, validated measures in management research can greatly accelerate the pace of progress; those measures don't have to be reinvented.

Finally, the real contribution of the transcendent conversation is that it redirects us to the sociological and theological roots of calling with empirical support. Further, it reminds us that the combination of transcendence, duty, and destiny resulted in a powerfully different way of working—and those features weren't the only source of its power. In the sections that follow, I highlight others, as well barriers to calling.

Having dispelled notions of "discoveries" related to calling, I now examine implicit and explicit assumptions about job crafting, the defining features of calling, the moral dimension, and supporting cosmologies of transcendent callings.

Delayed and Denied Callings: Job Crafting versus Soul Crafting

In response to the challenges of work life in the form of delayed and denied callings, Dik and Duffy suggested job crafting as a temporary solution that can make ill-fitting work more tolerable—and even turn a job into a calling. Similarly, Howard Gardner and his colleagues recommended that workers "expand [their] domain" by rearranging and reassessing their values and bring new knowledge or "institute better procedures"[47] to optimize working conditions. These strategies are commensurate with a Lutheran view of a calling, in which one accepts or copes with their station in life.

Job crafting is an adaptive, albeit, temporary solution. However, job crafting alone is not a sustainable solution for living one's calling; nor, by definition, can you use it to "make your job your calling," which I elaborate on in Chapter 8. Job crafting is not sustainable because it focuses on changing outward conditions but does little to address inward conditions that result from the indignities of underemployment or demeaning work; nor does it remedy the soul-depleting effects of doing "fitting" work without adequate resources to be excellent, the moral abrasions of being embedded in an unethical community, or recognizing that one's organization produces harmful goods and services.

Gardner goes beyond "job crafting" to suggest the need to create the conditions for "good work," which involves being morally conscious and taking steps to preserve your dignity and resist tyranny. That may entail seeking reassignment within the organization, taking an overt stand to challenge leaders about work conditions, or leaving. Coincidentally, Max Weber, Richard Baxter, and John Calvin agreed[48] that the calling ethic was subject to exploitation, and that sometimes ethical stewardship of one's gifts means protecting them. As Gardner noted, the problem is: "No one is irreplaceable, and there seems to be an endless supply of willing practitioners who feel no compulsion to honor the tacit contract that binds them to their domains."[49] Someone is more than willing to step into the tyrannical conditions that you vacate.

To illustrate the limits of job crafting and the need to assert one's dignity as part of a calling, Gardner and his colleagues[50] described tensions that Ray Suarez navigated at work. Seasoned journalist Ray Suarez's "heart told him to get out of this line of work, while his bank balance told him to swallow his pride and do his assigned job."[51] The choice became clear when he was asked to compromise his journalistic integrity by sensationalizing and reporting an utterly trivial story that did not serve society. He had a choice between recrafting how he thought about the work or maintaining his integrity by exerting personal agency. He took a stand and lost. Suarez could have complied reflexively and thus violated his personal and journalistic integrity; instead, he continued charting a career transition that led him away from NPR and toward PBS. "If Suarez were insecure and pessimistic, he might conclude that he had no future in journalism . . . But if he were more self-confident and optimistic about the future, he might interpret the boss's words as a wake-up call."[52] Although an average person may not have the reserve of experience, professional networks, and income that Suarez had, he or she might have the inner reserves to take a stand, albeit more incrementally, maintain their dignity, and leave—in service of their calling. Such "spiritedness is the assertion of one's dignity."[53]

Even if your calling is delayed or denied, you can exert spiritedness and agency in subtle or bold ways that enable even the lowliest worker to do good work with integrity. To do so requires soul crafting. Soul obviously focuses on one's interior world. I use the word *crafting*, however, to indicate that more than a random, self-directed, individualized quest is involved. In this context, I define soul crafting as relying on your existing collective cosmologies, which may be professional, cultural, familial, or religious. Cosmologies provide coherence and help you sculpt moral identity; gain perspective; find guidance, wisdom, and insight; solve problems; and acquire emotional and practical resources to be your best and do your best work. Jacob's work challenges illustrate the limits of job crafting, the importance of soul crafting, and the role of guiding cosmologies.

Jacob, a biblical figure (Gen. 31), experienced great personal difficulties and spiritual struggle, which led him in search of a new life—his calling.

On his journey, Jacob noticed a stunning shepherdess named Rachel, whose captivating beauty moved him to tears. She's the one!

Jacob agreed to work for Rachel's father, his uncle Laban, to earn her hand in marriage. The seven years that Jacob spent tending Laban's flock seemed like only days as he imagined marrying Rachel. But on the wedding day, Laban tricked Jacob and gave him Rachel's older sister Leah instead. Knowing Jacob's passion for Rachel, Laban demanded that Jacob work yet another seven years to marry her—which he did.

Jacob worked for his uncle Laban for 20 years—20 years of deception, exploitation, and greed. Even though Laban profited greatly from Jacob's skillful shepherding, he repeatedly cheated Jacob out of his wages. Not surprisingly, Jacob wanted to leave. But Laban said to him, "If now it pleases you, stay with me; I have divined that the Lord has blessed me on your account." He continued, "Name me your wages, and I will give it." But Jacob said to him, "You yourself know how I have served you and how your cattle have fared with me. For you had little before I came and it has increased to a multitude, and the Lord has blessed you wherever I turned. But now, when shall I provide for my own household also?" (Gen. 30:27–30). They agreed on a severance package.

Laban promised to give Jacob all of the speckled and spotted livestock, while he kept the solid-colored animals. True to form, Laban told his sons to gather all of the spotted and speckled flock so that Jacob could not find them. But Jacob outwitted Laban by putting striped sticks near the watering stream so that when the hardy solid-colored livestock saw stripes and spots reflected in the water, they bred spotted and speckled offspring. Meanwhile, Jacob allowed Laban's feeble solid-colored animals to breed as usual. Laban's sons were infuriated as they watched Jacob's wealth increase. The work climate was untenable.

So Jacob sent and called Rachel and Leah to his flock in the field and said to them, "I see your father's attitude that it is not friendly toward me as formerly, but the God of my father has been with me. You know that I have served your father with all my strength. Yet your father has cheated me and changed my wages ten times; however, God did not allow him to hurt me" (Gen. 31:4–7). In a dream, God told Jacob that He saw Laban's chicanery and directed Jacob to go back home to Canaan.[54]

Source: Copyright, GlobaLens case study Calling and Talent Development: Not Your Average Working Joe Case (2011) #1-429-200 by Valerie Myers

Obviously, Jacob engaged in cognitive crafting to motivate himself to work seven more years to marry the woman of his dreams. He tried relational crafting, but it was impossible; Laban and his sons were unethical, exploitative, greedy, and deceptive and showed no signs of stopping. They hoarded rather than shared the profits. By the time

Jacob began using his skills to engage in task crafting, it was to build his bridge to a better future rather than to further enrich his employer. That is where job crafting ended and soul crafting began. Jacob relied on his family and religious cosmologies to make sense of the situation, devise a creative solution, and implement a plan that honored his dignity and gifts. He quit!

According to theologian Michael Novak, the nation's founders left the "daily task of soul-craft" to the leaders of "moral and cultural institutions": families, communities, churches, the press (today, the media), and universities and schools.[55] In Chapter 12, I describe a structured, evidence-based approach to education that can support soul crafting in ways that foster the fulfillment of one's calling to work and other life roles.

In sum, job crafting primarily rearranges the outside world; soul crafting rearranges one's interior world and is a catalyst for positive actions that honor one's gifts and dignity. (In Chapters 7 and 11, I provide case examples of how cultural and religious cosmologies were used in service of callings to ignite positive action at multiple levels.) The idea of soul crafting is aligned with theologies of calling that succeeded Martin Luther; these theologies encourage caring for one's soul and changing one's situation rather than accepting it. Research is needed to examine how soul crafting helps people navigate the vicissitudes of living a transcendent calling.

The Defining Features of Calling

Several assumptions about the defining features of a transcendent calling warrant scrutiny. First, distinctions between an internal or external summons are specious at best. As Weber and others[56] have noted (and Chapters 6 and 8 show), one's calling can come from multiple sources; it is not an either/or proposition. Given that a sense of calling both endures and changes over the life course, it is conceivable that the constellation of internal and external summons varies. A more fruitful research trajectory might be to examine how people interpret and respond to different perceived summons.

Second, the transcendent conversation about calling draws on two career theories, P-E fit plus altruism and the Life-Span, Life-Space Model; putatively, altruism, or making the world better, is the defining characteristic of a calling. Notably, incommensurability between the theories and the idea that calling is alignment, enjoyment, and altruism must be reconciled. Consider the logic statements in Figure 3.1.

As evidence, hobbies and parenting may be fitting roles that are associated with a sense of calling. However, hobbies are for purely

Challenging Assumptions About Calling
IF IT IS TRUE THAT. . .
Calling = PE fit + Altruism *AND* Calling = 'Fitting' roles across the lifespan and life roles
BUT. . .
Not all 'fitting' life roles are altruistic *AND* Not all roles across the lifespan are a blissful fit
THEN. . .
It is logically impossible for altruism, fit or both to be <u>the</u> distinguishing feature of calling.

Figure 3.1 Challenging assumptions about calling.

individual enjoyment, and parenting is a self-interested act in service of one's own gene pool, not primarily the common good. Thus, although fit and altruism may be elements of a calling, they cannot be the defining criteria. What is, then? The answer: good work.

The idea of good work has a theological basis (e.g., Genesis, "and it was good") in Judeo-Christian and other theologies; it also has obvious practical benefits. Work can be good along several dimensions: *enjoyment, enrichment, ethics,* and *excellence*. More specifically, paid or unpaid work can be experienced as intrinsically pleasurable and enjoyable, which is a highly individualized experience that has been the focus of management scholarship (e.g., blissful fit). Fit, however, is a means to an end, not the ultimate aim of a calling.

Third, paid or unpaid work might be individually or socially *enriching*; that is, it may enhance, expand, or ennoble one's own competencies. For example, one might be personally enriched by engaging in leisure and civic activities. Society might be enriched due to a person fulfilling a transcendent purpose through his or her work or volunteering. But enrichment is not the ultimate aim of a calling either. Enrichment and enjoyment are derivative (but still important), as we'll discover in Part II of this book.

For a calling to objectively add value or improve society, one's approach must be ethical *and* excellent. Ethical work refers to subjective goodness and virtue, whereas excellent work refers to objective goodness, continuous improvement (e.g., becoming more skilled in a hobby), and quality. Theoretically speaking, aspiring to excellence and adhering to ethics are the ultimate goals and defining necessary qualities of a calling. Good work was the ultimate transcendent purpose of a calling—working in a way that glorified God.[57] I illustrate the defining and derivative qualities of calling in Figure 3.2. Thus far, management scholarship has focused on derivative rather than primary dimensions of calling.

Figure 3.2 Good work: The goal and defining quality of calling.

Identifying good work as the defining quality of calling helps us reconcile the idea that a calling might enrich others but might not be enjoyable; conversely, a calling might be enjoyable but not socially enriching. But both aim to be good or better. For example, we all have duties that are not particularly enjoyable or gratifying, but they provide deeper levels of satisfaction that result from completing tasks, being virtuous, increasing mastery, doing the right thing, or fulfilling an obligation. On the other hand, the calling to leisure or service activities is solely for personal pleasure or the enjoyment of people who are the immediate recipients of one's gifts (e.g., culinary arts). In either case, the goal is always the ethical pursuit of excellence, by some objective social criteria, and the quest to continuously improve. So, it is not P-E fit or prosocial intentions that define calling, but the *way* that one approaches the work itself—with ethics in one's pursuit of excellence. This was the means by which a transcendent or sacred calling added tangible value to work and curbed individualism.

Author and philosopher Dorothy Sayers wrote about the ethics-excellence duo in *Creed or Chaos?*[58] She explained that the work itself should be central, while individual feelings and intentions recede in importance. This a radical shift away from management scholars' typical conceptualizations; although the *way* of a calling is discussed vaguely, it has not been defined. Instead, the way has been defined by psychologists.

Echoing Weber's notion of specialists with spirit, psychologists Howard Gardner, Mihaly Csikszentmihalyi, and William Damon wrote eloquently about the callings of geneticists and journalists in their book *Good Work: When Excellence and Ethics Meet*. As the title suggests, they offered "good" because of its dual meaning—high quality and social responsibility.[59] They said: "The word calling may sound antiquated today . . . A contemporary way of framing this ancient notion is through the psychological concept of moral identity. When a person thinks about the self, or the self's occupations, in moral terms, the person experiences a sense of moral identity."[60] Situating moral identity at the center of calling makes the concept far more robust and practical. To my knowledge, however, no studies have examined excellence, commitment to excellence, or moral identity relative to a calling.

The Moral Dimension

A major limitation of the transcendent conversation, and indeed all of management scholarship, is that it has made what was once central to calling utterly peripheral. This dilution of calling is particularly perplexing given employers' increasing concern about unethical behavior.[61] In his writings about American culture, John Mizzoni stated: "In a culture of democratic capitalism, ethical traditions are needed to keep the market moral; it cannot become moral on its own."[62] This is true of for-profit and not-for profit organizations, as well as workers at every level of the organizational hierarchy. Hence, a transcendent calling has the potential to add even greater value than a secular individualistic calling because moral identity can curtail the negative effects of specialists *without* spirit.

The term *moral identity* expresses the notion that people use moral principles to define themselves: it "determines not merely what the person considers to be the right course of action but also *why* he or she would decide: 'I myself must take this course.'"[63] Moral identity develops incrementally through education, socialization, many small steps and challenges, feedback, and observation. Therefore, a sense of calling is the ultimate moral identity and it is shaped by moral communities.

Communities exert social influences on one's calling in many different ways. For example, by studying occupational groups (e.g., environmentalists and zookeepers), management scholars found that calling is characterized by adhering to shared professional ethics. These studies were mute, however, about how respondents' sense of moral duty evolved. Beyond the boundaries of management, however, psychologists and philosophers have described informal and formal ways to cultivate the moral identity of one's calling and the call to be accountable to a professional community.

Matthew Crawford, author of *Shopclass as Soulcraft*, described the influence of informal communities this way: "I try to be a good mechanic. This effort connects me to others, in particular to those who exemplify good motorcycling, because it is they who can best judge how well I have realized the functional goods I am aiming at . . . I wouldn't even know what those goods are if I didn't spend time with people who ride at a much higher level than I, and are therefore more discerning of what is good in a motorcycle."[64] So, peers, mentors, and informal information sharing help cultivate standards of ethics and excellence.

Similarly, Gardner and his colleagues described how journalists who were vexed by ethical lapses and declining standards in their profession took formal actions to elevate the calling to journalism: "The most respected journalists have banded together in various ways to stipulate what is central to their calling, document trends, and create models that can guide both rookies on the beat and crusty professionals who may have lost their passion or sense of direction. The very threats to the integrity of the journalistic calling may stimulate leading professionals to dig in their heels, take a stand, and launch a revolution (or counterrevolution) in standards."[65] Veterans who define violations of professional tenets and model appropriate behaviors set a powerful example for budding professionals to emulate. Such actions define what it means to be a *specialist* in the traditional sense.[66]

Specialists, in the traditional sense, recognize admirable and awful traits of their profession. For example, geneticists should be "honest, open, and original; they honor those among their peers who have carried out the most original, path-breaking work. They are most critical of those who are secretive, cut corners, and fail to make a bona fide contribution to knowledge."[67] Similarly, journalists "respect work that is adequately researched, appropriately contextualized, and expressed crisply and vigorously; they disdain work that is derivative, shoddy, biased, and reported clumsily or insipidly."[68] By extension, every profession has a parallel set of positive and negative instrumental values that govern behavior and establish quality standards. Gardner and his colleagues noted that "the power of a religious belief is not easily rivaled, but the mission of a domain—the sense of calling for a profession—can play an analogous role." The question is, do we want it to?[69]

Even the most well-intentioned professionals may have blind spots and biases when evaluating the goodness of their work, which is why society needs objective regulatory bodies. While a professional community is one source of moral identity, it is not the sole source or even the optimal source of moral instruction. In fact, papers from a symposium titled "Understanding Professional Misconduct: A Symposium on the Moral Responsibilities of Professionals" that were published in the *Journal of Business Ethics* decried the failure of professional ethics and attendant dire consequences.[70] One may be part of what sociologist Eliot Freidson[71] called a "delinquent community"—a group of specialists *without* spirit who adhere to their own code of conduct, with little regard for how their behavior negatively impacts their organization, industry, or society. Such a group of "bad apples" can be found in every profession; the problem is magnified when they establish norms for entire organizations and industries. Communitarian standards cease to be standards, in the optimal sense, when a critical mass of professionals and organizations fail to adhere to them or adhere to their opposite.

Social pressures to conform to deviant group, organization, or industry norms can corrupt even good people.[72] To counter negative influences from professions, organizations, leaders, and teams, philosopher John Mizzoni says that "outside influences (non-economic perspectives) are needed to help us see work as a calling."[73] *Weber, Habits*, and Gardner concur: the moral core of calling needs to be cultivated via instruction in traditional institutions that are exogenous to the workplace—that is, the family, community, schools, and religious congregations. Their influence on moral identity can ripple beyond the domain of work to different life roles throughout the life span (e.g., spouse, citizen, or parent). The authors of *Good Work* note that: "In the best of circumstances, these complement one another and add up to a coherent and positive attitude, one that makes sense to the person and to the surrounding community. Of course, such an integrated sense of identity remains an ideal: nearly everyone suffers at times from some fragmentation of identity, some diffusion, some confusion. Nor does identity ever completely coalesce."[74] Indeed, in the best of circumstance, positive moral education has occurred, but we can't assume that it has.

Habits laments that the cultural drift toward individualism has resulted in a so-called sink-or-swim approach to moral development and economic success that is untethered from a moral community and guiding norms.[75] Furthermore, the duty to God and community has been replaced by a duty to self,[76] which is the antithesis of calling. Lacking an anchor to institutions that define moral behavior, or what *Habits* describes as "the moral community of calling,"[77] individual behavior will be guided by idiosyncratic ethics, feelings, or highly variable professional standards—in other words, a secular individualistic calling. In fact, the authors of *Habits* say that "separated from family, religion, and calling as a source of authority, duty, and moral example, the self first seeks to work out its own form of action by autonomously pursuing happiness and satisfying its wants."[78] Other scholars have similarly opined about the negative consequences of individualism. Weiss and his colleagues considered individualized spiritual questing, evident in the proliferation of books on calling, as "an unfortunate consequence of the privatization and compartmentalization of spirituality."[79] Therefore, in order for calling to become more than a ghost of its former self, it must be cultivated in community—communities that define ethics and standards of excellence.

In sum, moral identity and moral communities are essential to a calling; they weave its intertwined threads of ethics and excellence across life roles. This perspective deserves far greater attention in management scholarship because of its obvious practical benefits.

Further, given the very important role of communities, it is worth considering how they may help people interpret their experiences of being *called by* or *called to* as transcendent. More pointedly, how do ideological communities help us make sense of calling? The answer lies in cosmologies.

Cosmologies and Meaning

What is a cosmology? A cosmology is the "ultimate macro perspective"[80] that provides a sense-making framework for interpreting one's identity, purpose, values, behaviors, relationships, and responsibilities.[81] Cosmologies provide a sense of coherence and restore order when the world makes no sense.[82] Management scholars Michael Pratt and Blake Ashforth described cosmologies in nonacademic terms: "In the vernacular, cosmologies foster transcendence by helping individuals find their place within the grand scheme of things."[83]

As Gardner and his colleagues noted: "Every culture that has endured and that has advanced the human condition through art or knowledge has had a coherent view of the universe. The cosmologies that the Chinese, the Indians, the Aztecs, or the Judeo-Christian West invented may appear inadequate or even bizarre in hindsight." Yet, "there is no record of a human group prospering without a coherent set of values based on a cosmology—flawed and preposterous as those guiding frameworks might seem in the 'age of the smart machine.'"[84]

To date, the cosmologies of callings have been implicit or absent in contemporary management research; we need to make them explicit. From a research perspective, we need to understand the explicit cosmologies of calling and what schemas people use to (1) make sense of, identify, or understand their experiences as clues to their calling; (2) impute meanings to work as something more than mundane self-interest; (3) define worthwhile purposes to pursue; (4) identify behavioral standards to which they will adhere; (5) cope with crises and reframe difficulties and drudgery as surmountable and ultimately worthwhile; and (6) to frame the vicissitudes of calling in a larger context. (In Chapters 7 and 11, I use examples to illustrate how one's calling may be anchored and reinforced by various cosmologies.)

Max Weber explored those issues by examining denominational and class differences in cosmologies. Theological inaccuracies aside, Weber gave lengthy interpretations about the ways that the cosmologies of different denominations (e.g., Catholic, Methodist, and Baptist) influenced callings in Chapter 4 of his book, "The Religious Foundations of Worldly Asceticism." He asserted that different cosmologies gave a sense of coherence about work and influenced people's beliefs about their position in the work hierarchy and appropriate behaviors; some were conditioned to be analytic and risk-taking owners and managers, while others were socialized to be compliant laborers and support staff. Rightly or wrongly, he asserted that those different cosmologies reinforced divisions of labor and provided a "solid religious basis for the *ethic of calling*."[85] Whether religious, spiritual, or moral, the cosmologies of calling still matter, but we know little about them. One scholar who has shed light on the topic is Marjolein Lips-Wiersma.

In her recent study of middle-aged workers, Lips-Wiersma identified specific ways that people used spiritual cosmologies to foster sense making at work in general,[86] but these insights have yet to be applied to calling research. Nevertheless, the analytic frameworks and tools to examine cosmologies relative to calling exist,[87] and I will discuss them in greater detail in Chapters 4 & 12. Ultimately, scholars' inattention to the guiding cosmologies of calling is not just a lacuna—it's an abyss. Additional research about cosmologies can elucidate how individuals experience calling and all its attendant meanings at a granular level.

The fact that Hagmaier and Abele found a very weak connection between meaning and calling gives us reason to pause, particularly since calling is routinely referred to and measured as "meaningful," "very meaningful," and "deeply meaningful" work by scholars too numerous to mention here. Most likely, the empirical disconnect between meaning and calling reflects a measurement problem. Studies typically reveal a vague sense of more meaning, rather than specific transcendent meanings related to work activities. For example, in this chapter, studies showed that work toward specific purposes (e.g., caring for people) may be associated with increased task significance. Hence, pursuing ultimate ends such as world peace, beauty, and equality[88] may infuse callings with specific transcendent meanings, but ultimate ends are not a focus in existing research.

Instead, a circular logic, which is highly problematic, is often used to discuss the meaning of calling—the meaning is devoid of any specific content, and the source of meaning is ambiguous. More pointedly, we still don't know *what* work in a calling means! Yet meaning, deep meaning, and meaningfulness are described as main features of calling. The following phrases by scholars illustrate the problem: calling inspires meaning, calling results in meaning, calling is deeply meaningful, calling is deriving meaning, calling leads to meaning in life, the meaning of work as a calling aligns with meaning in life, meaningful work is indicative of a calling, make meaning at work, meaning making at work, and meaning leads to a different approach to work. Some have also said that meaning comes from reframing—but how? For example, if an unemployed person finds employment, even if the work is undesirable, it can be "deeply meaningful"; it means a lot to have income that supplies basic needs. But that doesn't mean it's a calling.

According to *Habits*, calling once meant moral actions and sacred meaning. Likewise, in the Judeo-Christian tradition, a calling meant that ordinary work had *sacred* meaning. Our need to understand what calling means leads us to the last emerging conversation about calling in management—sacred calling.

Advancing the Discourse

Insights about transcendent callings are changing the conversation in management in important ways. Foremost, evidence is mounting to show that transcendence is a defining feature of calling—as it was historically. Transcendence relates to being *called by* inner and outer forces, *called to* a specific transcendent purpose, and *called to behave* in accordance with the ethical and quality standards of one's moral community. The historic and reemerging idea of morals as central to calling expands and strengthens the secular, individualistic perspective in important ways. For example, although one may feel called by internal and external transcendent forces, called to pursue a transcendent purpose, and called to behave in accordance with professional standards, if these summons are not grounded in the ethos of an ideological community outside the workplace, it cannot be a calling in the highest, truest sense. One is at risk of doing social harm rather than social good, regardless of "prosocial intentions," if they are only guided by professional and organizational ethics. Ideally, noneconomic social influences of moral communities, beyond corporate or professional communities, inform one's calling to purposeful action and cultivate one's moral identity. Research is needed to understand the ways in which all communities influence the moral identity, ethics, and performance standards of a calling, as these are its defining qualities.

The conversation about the transcendent calling is promising; hopefully moral duty will become more salient in the management literature and at least equal with "destiny." To do this, scholars must draw on decades of psychological research that measured the Protestant work ethic[89] (e.g., moral duty, diligence, etc.), rather than create new measures. It is worth noting, however, that although the zookeeper study was published in 2009, morals have not been added to subsequent measures of calling in management since. To advance, we need to understand the duty dimension of calling, how *duty* interacts with one's sense of *destiny*, as well as how social forces differentially influence one's calling ethic.

A major oversight in management research to date is that it has progressed under the assumption that one's calling has indeed been cultivated. Little suggests that this is the case (see Chapter 9). Few if any studies have examined which moral communities have influenced one's attitudes about ethics, quality, navigating normal work challenges, and what cosmologies people invoke to cope, make sense of, and live up to their callings. Moreover, how do those cosmologies relate to spiritual well-being? Those are all fruitful lines of inquiry. Rather than reinventing tools to analyze these factors, management scholars can appropriate tools from other disciplines to accelerate the pace of knowledge gains.

Finally, I began this chapter by describing how Hagmaier and Abele's study showed that calling is multidimensional and that transcendence is its most salient dimension, over and above P-E fit. Increasingly, transcendence, spiritual well-being, and ethics are being discussed in emerging management enclaves; empirical studies are amplifying their message. The question remains: Do studies show that a modern calling still has sacred meaning? I explore that question in the next chapter.

NOTES

1. Tamara Hagmaier and Andrea E. Abele, "The Multidimensionality of Calling: Conceptualization, Measurement and a Bicultural Perspective," *Journal of Vocational Behavior* 81, no. 1 (2012): 39–51.
2. Ibid.
3. Bryan J. Dik and Ryan D. Duffy, *Make Your Job a Calling: How the Psychology of Vocation Can Change Your Life at Work* (West Conshohocken, PA: Templeton Press, 2012).
4. Jessica T. Kovan and John M. Dirkx, "'Being Called Awake': The Role of Transformative Learning in the Lives of Environmental Activists," *Adult Education Quarterly* 53, no. 2 (2003): 99–118; T. Conklin, "Work Worth Doing: A Phenomenological Study of the Experience of Discovering and Following One's Calling," *Journal of Management Inquiry* 21, no. 3 (2012): 298; R. Treadgold, "Transcendent Vocations: Their Relationship to Stress, Depression, and Clarity of Self-Concept," *Journal of Humanistic Psychology* 39, no. 1 (1999): 81–105.
5. Dik and Duffy, *Make Your Job a Calling*.

6. J. W. Weiss, M. F. Skelley, J. C. Haughey, and D. T. Hall, "Callings, New Careers and Spirituality: A Reflective Perspective for Organizational Leaders and Professionals," *Research in Ethical Issues in Organizations* 5 (2004): 175–201.
7. B. J. Dik and R. D. Duffy, "Calling and Vocation at Work: Definitions and Prospects for Research and Practice," *The Counseling Psychologist* 37, no. 3 (2009): 427.
8. Dik and Duffy, *Make Your Job a Calling*, 112.
9. D. E. Super, "A Life-Span, Life-Space Approach to Career Development," *Journal of Vocational Behavior* 16 (1980): 282–98.
10. Douglas T. Hall and Dawn E. Chandler, "Psychological Success: When the Career Is a Calling," *Journal of Organizational Behavior* 26, no. 2 (2005): 155–76.
11. Valerie L. Myers, "An Ontology of Calling: Examining Mechanisms and the Transcendent Possibilities of Work Orientation Theory," in *Critical Management Studies Conference Proceedings* (Manchester, UK: Manchester Business School, 2007).
12. Dik and Duffy, *Make Your Job a Calling*, 41.
13. Ryan D. Duffy and William E. Sedlacek, "The Presence of and Search for a Calling: Connections to Career Development," *Journal of Vocational Behavior* 70, no. 3 (2007): 590–601; Dik and Duffy, "Calling and Vocation at Work."
14. S. M. Stowe, "Seeing Themselves at Work: Physicians and the Case Narrative in the Mid-Nineteenth-Century American South," *American Historical Review* 101, no. 1 (1996): 41–79.
15. Kovan and Dirkx, "'Being Called Awake.'"
16. J. Stuart Bunderson and Jeffrey A. Thompson, "The Call of the Wild: Zookeepers, Callings, and the Dual Edges of Deeply Meaningful Work," *Administrative Science Quarterly* 54, no. 32 (2009): 32–57.
17. Kovan and Dirkx, "'Being Called Awake'"; Conklin, "Work Worth Doing."
18. Joanne B. Ciulla, *The Working Life: The Promise and Betrayal of Modern Work* (New York: Times Books, 2000); Treadgold, "Transcendent Vocations."
19. S. Dobrow, "Dynamics of Calling: A Longitudinal Study of Musicians," *Journal of Organizational Behavior* (June 11, 2012). doi: 10.1002/job.1808.
20. Treadgold, "Transcendent Vocations."
21. Kovan and Dirkx, "'Being Called Awake.'"
22. Hall and Chandler, "Psychological Success."
23. Dik and Duffy, *Make Your Job a Calling*, 124.
24. S. Hawks, "Spiritual Health: Definition and Theory," *Wellness Perspectives* 10 (1994): 3–13; R. Banks, D. Poehler, and R. Russell, "Spirit and Human-Spiritual Interactions as a Factor in Health and in Health Education," *Journal of Health Education* 15 (1984): 16–19.
25. Milton Rokeach, *Understanding Human Values: Individual and Societal* (New York: Free Press, 1979).
26. M. G. Pratt and B. E. Ashforth, "Fostering Meaningfulness in Working and at Work," in *Positive Organizational Scholarship: Foundations of a New Discipline,* ed. J. E. Dutton, K. S. Cameron, and R. E. Quinn, 309–27 (San Francisco: Berrett-Koehler, 2003).
27. Rokeach, *Understanding Human Values.*
28. J. Richard Hackman and Greg R. Oldham, "Motivation through the Design of Work: Test of a Theory," *Organizational Behavior and Human Performance* 16, no. 2 (1976): 250–79.

29. I use the term *mundane* as the antithesis of transcendence instead of job, because it is not yet clear that a job is distinct from a calling.
30. Bunderson and Thompson, "The Call of the Wild."
31. Conklin, "Work Worth Doing."
32. Dik and Duffy, *Make Your Job a Calling*, 91.
33. Conklin, "Work Worth Doing."
34. Hall and Chandler, "Psychological Success."
35. Studs Terkel, *Working: People Talk about What They Do All Day and How They Feel about What They Do* (New York: The New Press, 1972).
36. Dik and Duffy recommended the concept, which was developed by Amy Wrzesniewski and Jane E. Dutton, "Crafting a Job: Revisioning Employees as Active Crafters of Their Work," *The Academy of Management Review* 26, no. 2 (2001): 179–201.
37. Max Weber, *The Protestant Ethic and the Spirit of Capitalism* (London: Routledge, 1904/1992).
38. A ProQuest literature search for "Protestant work ethic" (PWE) revealed a prodigious amount of scholarship (March 22, 2008): 177 articles about the PWE that ensued in the 1970s. See James G. Goodale, "Effects of Personal Background and Training on Work Values of the Hard-Core Unemployed," *Journal of Applied Psychology* 57, no. 1 (1973): 1; Patricia Gurin, "Psychological Dimensions of Minorities' Workforce Participation," *Sloan Management Review* 15, no. 3 (1974): 47; John P. Wanous, "Individual Differences and Reactions to Job Characteristics," *Journal of Applied Psychology* 59, no. 5 (1974): 616; Eugene F. Stone, "The Moderating Effect of Work-related Values on the Job Scope–Job-Satisfaction Relationship," *Organizational Behavior and Human Performance* 15, no. 2 (1976): 147; R. A. Buchholz and G. E. Connell, *Business and Society (pre-1986)* 18, no. 1 (1977): 13–20. Scholars generally agree that the PWE, also called the "work ethic" (Buchholz and Connell, *Business and Society*; Larry Reynolds, "America's Work Ethic: Lost in Turbulent Times?" *Management Review* 81, no. 10 [1992]: 20), is an orientation toward work that embodies persistence, purpose, an internal locus of control, hard work, discipline, achievement orientation, dependability, commitment, and sometimes a guiding morality (H. G. Gough, "A Work Orientation Scale for the California Psychological Inventory," *Journal of Applied Psychology* 70, no. 3 [1985]: 505–13). Decades of research have resulted in relatively high but imperfect construct validity (Paula C. Morrow, "Concept Redundancy in Organizational Research: The Case of Work Commitment," *The Academy of Management Review* 8, no. 3 [1983]: 486) and mixed results regarding a relationship between PWE and religiosity. See J. W. McHoskey, "Factor Structure of the Protestant Work Ethic Scale," *Personality and Individual Difference* 17, no. 1 (1994): 49–52; P. E. Mudrack, "Protestant Work-Ethic Dimensions and Work Orientations," *Personality and Individual Difference* 23, no. 2 (1997): 217–25; Adrian Furnham, "A Content, Correlational, and Factor Analytic Study of Seven Questionnaire Measures of the Protestant Work Ethic," *Human Relations* 43, no. 4 (1990): 383; L. K. Waters and Todd Zakrajsek, "The Construct Validity of Four Protestant Ethic Attitude," *Scales Educational and Psychological Measurement* 51, no. 1 (1991): 117; A. Furnham and E. Koritsas, "The Protestant Work Ethic and Vocational Preference," *Journal of Organizational Behavior* (1990)(1986–1998): 1; Jennifer J. Dose, "Work Values: An Integrative Framework and Illustrative Application to Organizational Socialization," *Journal of Occupational and*

Organizational Psychology 70, no. 3 (1997): 219–40; H.G. Gough, "A Work Orientation Scale for the California Psychological Inventory," *Journal of Applied Psychology* 70, no. 3 (1985): 505–13; F. Stanford Wayne, "An Instrument to Measure Adherence to the Protestant Ethic," *Journal of Business Ethics* 8, no. 10 (1989): 793; Thomas Li-Ping Tang and Jen Yann Tzeng, "Demographic Correlates of the Protestant Work Ethic," *The Journal of Psychology* 126, no. 2 (1992): 163–70; L. H. Chusmir and C. S. Koberg, "Religion and Attitudes Toward Work: A New Look at an Old Question," *Journal of Organizational Behavior* 9 (1988): 251–62; W. F. Stanford, "An Instrument to Measure Adherence to the Protestant Ethic," *Journal of Business Ethics* 8, no. 10 (1989): 793–804.

Although the PWE is not linked to occupational or social hierarchies, studies have examined variations in work ethic relative to racial, regional, cultural, and class differences (Gurin, "Psychological Dimensions of Minorities' Workforce Participation"; Wanous, "Individual Differences and Reactions to Job Characteristics"; Rabi S. Bhagat, "Black-White Ethnic Differences in Identification with the Work Ethic: Some Implications for Organizational Integration," *The Academy of Management Review* 4, no. 3 [1979]: 381; Norman Coates, "The 'Confucian Ethic' and the Spirit of Japanese Capitalism," *Leadership & Organization Development* 8, no. 3 [1987]: 17; Kyuhan Bae and Chinsung Chung, "Cultural Values and Work Attitudes of Korean Industrial Workers in Comparison with Those of the United States and Japan," *Work and Occupations* 24, no. 1 [1997]: 80–96; Tang and Tzeng, "Demographic Correlates of the Protestant Work Ethic"; Kevin Cokley, Meera Komarraju, Rachel Pickett, Frances Shen, et al., "Ethnic Differences in Endorsement of the Protestant Work Ethic: The Role of Ethnic Identity and Perceptions of Social Class," *The Journal of Social Psychology* 147, no. 1 [2007]: 75–90), ; as well as religious differences (Chusmir and Koberg, "Religion and Attitudes Toward Work"; Abbas J. Ali, Thomas Falcone, and A. A. Azim, "Work Ethic in the USA and Canada," *The Journal of Management Development* 14, no. 6 [1995]: 26–35). In sum, the PWE literature is cohesive, well developed, and empirically rigorous.

39. Karen Golden-Biddle, Karen Locke, and Trish Reay, "Using Knowledge in Management Studies: An Investigation of How We Cite Prior Work," *Journal of Management Inquiry* 15, no. 3 (2006): 237–54.
40. Dik and Duffy, *Make Your Job a Calling*.
41. R. F. Baumeister, *Work, Work, Work, Work: Meanings of Life* (New York: The Guilford Press, 1991).
42. Weber, *The Protestant Ethic*, 51.
43. Robert N. Bellah, Richard Madsen, William M. Sullivan, Ann Swidler, and Steven M. Tipton, *Habits of the Heart: Individualism and Commitment in American Life: Updated Edition with a New Introduction* (Berkeley: University of California Press, 1996), 71.
44. Ibid., 66.
45. Quist Albertson, *The Gods of Business: The Intersection of Faith in the Marketplace* (Los Angeles, CA: Trinity University Alumni Press, 2007); J. Mizzoni, "Perspectives on Work in American Culture," *Journal of Interdisciplinary Studies* 16, nos. 1/2 (2004): 97–110.
46. Weber, *The Protestant Ethic*.
47. Howard E. Gardner, Mihaly Csikszentmihalyi, and William Damon, *Good Work: When Excellence and Ethics Meet* (New York: Basic Books, 2001), 232.
48. Weber, *The Protestant Ethic*.

49. Gardner, Csikszentmihalyi, and Damon, *Good Work,* 235.

50. Ibid.

51. Ibid.

52. Ibid., 12.

53. Matthew B. Crawford, *Shop Class as Soulcraft: An Inquiry into the Value of Work* (New York: Penguin Press, 2009), 55.

54. Excerpt from Valerie L. Myers, "Calling and Talent Development: Not Your Average Working Joe Case #1–429–200," *GlobaLens Business Case* (2011): 5–6.

55. Michael Novak, *Business as a Calling: Work and the Examined Life* (New York: Free Press, 1996), 113.

56. Baumeister, *Work, Work, Work, Work.*

57. Weber, *The Protestant Ethic.*

58. D. L. Sayers, "Why Work." In *Creed or Chaos? And Other Essays in Popular Theology* (Manchester: Sophia Institute Press, 1948/1999), 63–84.

59. Gardner, Csikszentmihalyi, and Damon, *Good Work*, 257.

60. Ibid., 163.

61. David W. Miller, *God at Work: The History and Promise of the Faith at Work Movement* (New York: Oxford University Press, 2007).

62. Mizzoni, "Perspectives on Work in American Culture," 107.

63. W. Damon, "The Moral Development of Children," *Scientific American* (August 1999): 76.

64. Crawford, *Shop Class as Soulcraft*, 197.

65. Csikszentmihalyi, Damon, and Gardner, *Good Work*, 211–12.

66. Bellah et al., *Habits of the Heart.*

67. Gardner, Csikszentmihalyi, and Damon, *Good Work*, 211.

68. Ibid.

69. Ibid., 89.

70. George E. Panichas, "Introduction," *Journal of Business Ethics* 10, no. 8 (1991): 559–60.

71. E. Freidson, *Doctoring Together: A Study of Professional Social Control* (New York: Elsevier, 1975).

72. Philip Zimbardo, *The Lucifer Effect: Understanding How Good People Turn Evil* (New York: Random House, 2008).

73. Mizzoni, "Perspectives on Work in American Culture," 107.

74. Gardner, Csikszentmihalyi, and Damon, *Good Work*, 11.

75. Bellah et al., *Habits of the Heart*, viii.

76. Baumeister, *Work, Work, Work, Work.*

77. Bellah et al., *Habits of the Heart*, 71.

78. Ibid., 79.

79. Weiss et al., "Callings, New Careers and Spirituality," 181.

80. Karl E. Weick, "The Collapse of Sensemaking in Organizations: The Mann Gulch Disaster," *Administrative Science Quarterly* 38, no. 4 (1993): 628–52.

81. Blake E. Ashforth and Deepa Vaidyanath, "Work Organizations as Secular Religions," *Journal of Management Inquiry* 11, no. 4 (2002): 359.

82. Weick, "The Collapse of Sensemaking in Organizations."

83. Pratt and Ashforth, "Fostering Meaningfulness in Working and at Work," 323.

84. Gardner, Csikszentmihalyi, and Damon, *Good Work*, 237.

85. Weber, *The Protestant Ethic.*

86. M. Lips-Wiersma, "The Influence of Spiritual 'Meaning Making' on Career Behavior," *Journal of Management Development* 21 (2002): 497–520.

87. Valerie L. Myers, *An Interdisciplinary Analysis of Faith-Based Human Services: Analyzing Latent Organizational, Social and Psychological Processes* (PhD diss., University of Michigan, 2003).

88. Rokeach, *Understanding Human Values.*

89. See Buchholz and Connell, *Business and Society*; Goodale, "Effects of Personal Background"; Gough, "A Work Orientation Scale for the California Psychological Inventory"; Gurin, "Psychological Dimensions of Minorities' Workforce Participation"; Reynolds, "America's Work Ethic"; Stone, "The Moderating Effect of Work-related Values"; Wanous, "Individual Differences and Reactions to Job Characteristics." The PWE literature is cohesive, well developed, and empirically rigorous. See, for example, Chusmir and Koberg, "Religion and Attitudes Toward Work"; Dose, "Work Values"; Furnham, "A Content, Correlational, and Factor Analytic Study"; Furnham and Koritsas, "The Protestant Work Ethic and Vocational Preference"; Gough, "A Work Orientation Scale for the California Psychological Inventory"; McHoskey, "Factor Structure of the Protestant Work Ethic Scale"; Mudrack, "Protestant Work-Ethic Dimensions and Work Orientations"; Stanford, "An Instrument to Measure Adherence to the Protestant Ethic"; Tang and Tzeng, "Demographic Correlates of the Protestant Work Ethic"; Waters and Zakrajsek, "The Construct Validity of Four Protestant Ethic Attitude"; Wayne, "An Instrument to Measure Adherence to the Protestant Ethic."

4

Sacred Callings

A purely secular approach distorts our understanding of people's orientations toward work, leaving the false impression that nobody thinks of work in religious terms when, in fact, some people do.

—James Davidson and David Caddell,
"Religion and the Meaning of Work"

All major faith traditions espouse a theology of work or work ethic, even though they may not describe it as a calling. Quist Albertson wrote about them in *The Gods of Business: The Intersection of Faith in the Marketplace*.[1] The results of his research suggest that calling can be construed as a cross-cultural concept that is broader than Christianity. Admittedly, because Weber and Protestant reformers were Christians, and most related research is from a Christian perspective, I draw heavily from that tradition. My goal, however, is to explicate the theoretical foundation of calling and to show how the concepts can be applied across faiths and philosophical traditions. I do this in Chapter 10.

Management scholars that discuss sacred calling attempt to retain religious elements of the concept that were espoused by Protestant reformers Martin Luther and John Calvin in the 1500s. Hence, this conversation is more closely aligned with the transcendent calling than the secular individualistic calling. Yet it differs from both in substantive ways.

First, the lexicon of sacred calling is distinct. Terms such as *religious community*, *cosmologies*, *scripture*, *beliefs*, *individual religiosity*, *gifts*, *faith*, and *sanctification* are pervasive. Although the lexicon is a radical departure from mainstream management scholarship, it is aligned with the grand conversation about calling and can now be interpreted using the tools of social science. Religious language aside, this conversation offers major theoretical insights about calling—how it is cultivated and may be measured.

Second, exploration of transcendence in this context is explicitly religious, not just moral or spiritual. It follows then that, with regard to communitarian influences, scholars seek to understand how religious collectives and cosmologies might relate to one's calling.

Finally, scholars in this conversation blend person-environment (P-E) fit and life-span[2] theories as the foundation for sacred callings, focusing broadly on work as an activity (a verb) rather than solely an occupation (a noun). However, compared to preceding management conversations, very few scholars are engaged in research related to sacred callings, and what exists is rarely published in top-tier journals. Although Davidson and Caddell began the dialogue nearly 20 years ago, only recently have scholars in the secular individualistic and transcendent conversations even acknowledged that the sacred calling might still be relevant for some modern workers.[3] Conceding this point suggests that the dominant conversation about calling is in flux or is amenable to revision based on evidence. In the preceding chapters, I presented evidence which suggests that revisions are in order. This most-marginalized conversation about callings in management—rife with oversights—may, in fact, be highly instrumental in advancing theory construction and research.

Against the prevailing positivist headwinds that reject comingling faith with management,[4] some scholars have embraced calling's inherently religious roots[5] and boldly initiated explicit conversations about sacred callings in modern-era management. Those scholars are James Davidson and David Caddell,[6] James McGee and Andre Delbecq,[7] and Joseph Weiss with his colleagues Michael Skelley, John Haughey, and Douglas (Tim) Hall.[8] Davidson and Caddell examined the relationship between one's religious community and its influence on calling; Weiss and his colleagues provided insights into the religious cosmologies, social construction, and evolution of callings; and McGee and Delbecq apply the concept of calling to business and leadership (which I explore in Chapter 8). Other scholars have since joined this conversation and offered additional insights.

Because relevant management research is so scarce, the format of this chapter is necessarily unique. Rather than exhaustively review management studies, which are quite limited, I refer to several studies about calling and religion that appeared in social science journals or conference presentations. In addition, I draw from developments in other disciplines to highlight knowledge that is easily transferrable to and can accelerate the pace of progress in management. I divide this review about sacred callings into two sections: (1) religious community, which examines affiliation and involvement; and (2) sacred cosmologies that might help a person interpret and live their calling. I summarize the contributions, limitations, and future possibilities of each.

Religious Community and Calling:
Affiliation and Involvement

Max Weber posited that religious affiliation, denomination, and education predicted one's sense of calling. In 1994, sociologists Davidson and Caddell conducted a path-forging study to test this idea by surveying 1,869 affluent people who were members of Protestant and Catholic churches.[9] These researchers were interested in factors that predicted church members' sense of calling. Notably, they defined calling as "My work has special meaning because I have been called to do what I'm doing regardless of how much time it takes or how little money I earn; I was put on this earth to do what I am doing."[10] They also sought to understand how religious affiliation and involvement might relate to a sense of calling by asking about the salience of religion in respondents' lives, religious participation (in public and private acts), and the influence of pastors' sermons on their calling.

Davidson and Caddell found that only 15% of respondents believed that their work was a calling, compared to people who viewed their work as a career (56%) or a job (29%). Factors that predicted a sense of calling included the salience of religion in respondents' lives, as well as their religious participation and religious beliefs related to social justice. Also, as education and income increased, so did the likelihood of viewing one's work as a calling. Interestingly, religious denomination, pastoral influences, and sermons did not predict a sense of calling. These results can be interpreted in several ways and suggest new research trajectories.

Foremost, this study showed that a connection remains between religiosity and calling, even though the percentage is rather modest. This unimpressive finding, however, may reveal more about the research methodology and shifts in institutional practices than the phenomenon that interests us.

First, although Davidson and Caddell inquired about the influence of pastors and sermons on calling, they did not explicitly ask about the content of the pastors' sermons or whether calling was a topic that they addressed. So, the results could indicate that either pastors and their sermons were ineffective regarding calling and work or that those were simply not topics that pastors emphasized through sermons or otherwise. Based on Fox's[11] study of church-based vocational programs during that time, we might deduce that these results reflect a similar inattention to vocation and calling in sermons and in the ideological community more broadly. Other scholars have also noted clergy's inattention to theologies of work.[12] So what Davidson and Caddell actually discovered is that religious affiliation is not synonymous with internalizing specific beliefs. More pointedly, sitting in a congregation does not make you have a calling any more than sitting in a garage makes you a car.[13] Weber hypothesized that religious *education* was instrumental in forming a calling, not just church membership alone. If clergy were ill-equipped to educate their members about theologies of work, or if they avoided the topic altogether, then it is not surprising that members did not espouse a connection between faith and calling.

Second, we now know that Davidson and Caddell's measure of calling was inadequate. In their survey, they defined calling as P-E fit rather than as a transcendent phenomenon that spans multiple life roles. In fairness, however, neither were management scholars, and theirs was a very innovative study at the time. However, the fact that this simple measure dominates the field 20 years later is quite problematic. In addition, their measures of religiosity, although intuitively insightful, were rather blunt. Social science research into religiosity has evolved since then. For example, subjective involvement entails individual attitudes, beliefs, and self-perceptions. Nonorganizational involvement refers to private religious practices such as prayer, consuming religious media, and devotional practices. Conversely, organizational involvement refers to denominational affiliation and attending services. Research has shown that different types of religious involvement predict different outcomes, such as spiritual well-being,[14] which was linked to transcendent calling in Chapter 3. These insights can be used to advance calling scholarship by inquiring about the following: (1) different types of religious involvement, spiritual well-being, and calling; (2) different types of religious involvement and coping; and (3) the specific effects of reading different books on one's sense of calling and spiritual well-being.

Studies since Davidson and Caddell's have similarly shown existing yet weak connections between religion and calling, lending some credence to the notion that calling is a secular construct—but they shouldn't. Unfortunately, during the past two decades, subsequent management studies have used even fewer and less sophisticated religiosity measures than Davidson and Caddell, yielding similar and unremarkable results. Hence, there is no need to list them here. Current nonfindings reveal more about the inadequacy of research methods in management, and the absence or quality of religious education about calling, than about the religious meaning of calling (still printed in books). Because social science has progressed beyond simple measures of religious involvement, and it is becoming clearer that different measures of calling should be used, it is incumbent on management scholars to use the appropriate tools to study the sacred calling, rather than dismiss it as irrelevant. Empirical findings about the transcendent calling, spirituality, and the influence of community suggest that this is a potentially vibrant research trajectory.

Finally, we know empirically from the *National Congregations Study*[15] and from the *Faith Communities Today* report[16] that congregational membership of religious denominations varies by income, race, and occupation. We thus have robust resources to investigate Weber's claims about denominational differences, class, and calling. Weber hypothesized that calling was common across occupational groups and social classes but materialized differently based on one's socioeconomic status and the religious education that one received. Consider the following:

> If we can, at least provisionally, point out any practical consequence of the difference, we may say that the virtues favoured by Pietism were more those on the one hand of the faithful official, clerk, labourer, or domestic worker, and on the other of the predominantly patriarchal employer with a pious condescension (in Zinderdorf's manner). Calvinism, in comparison, appears to be more closely related to the hard legalism and the active enterprise of bourgeois-capitalistic entrepreneurs. Finally, the purely emotional form of Pietism is, as Ritschl has pointed out, a religious dilettantism for the leisure classes. However far this characterization falls short of being exhaustive, it helps to explain certain differences in the character (including the economic character) of peoples which have been under the influence of one or the other of these two ascetic movements.[17]

> Among journeymen, in other words, the Catholics show a stronger propensity to remain in their crafts, that is, they more often become master craftsmen, whereas Protestants are attracted to a larger extent into the factories in order to fill the upper ranks of skilled labour and administrative positions.[18]

> A specifically bourgeois economic ethic had grown up. With the consciousness of standing in the fullness of God's grace and being visibly blessed by Him, the bourgeois business man, as long as he remained within the bounds of formal correctness, as long as his moral conduct was spotless and the use to which he put his wealth was not objectionable, could follow his pecuniary interests as he would and feel that he was fulfilling a duty in doing so. The power of religious asceticism provided him in addition with sober, conscientious, and unusually industrious workmen, who clung to their work as to a life purpose willed by God.[19]

> To be sure, these Puritanical ideals tended to give way under pressure from the temptations of wealth, as the Puritans themselves knew very well. With great regularity we find the most genuine adherents of Puritanism among the classes which were rising from a lowly status, the small bourgeois and farmers.[20]

It would be very interesting to analyze the degree to which and how denominations and communities differ in their attention to work,

work-related messages, and the different cosmologies they use to give members a sense of meaning and coherence about work.

Sacred Cosmologies

> My job of making motorcycles run right is subservient to the higher good that is achieved when one of my customers leans hard through a corner on the Blue Ridge Parkway, to the point of deliberately dragging his well-armored knee on the inside. This moment of faith, daring, and skill casts a sanctifying light over my work.[21]
>
> —Crawford, *Shop Class as Soulcraft*

What does it mean to sanctify something or make it sacred? As Matt Crawford's statement about motorcycles suggests, people can view ordinary roles and activities as sacred. Psychologist Ken Pargament agrees; he has pondered and researched this question for more than 15 years and written prolifically about how people make the ordinary sacred in theistic or nontheistic ways. Pargament contends that when people transform something ordinary into something sacred, they imbue it with divine character and significance. This leads them to invest time and energy; experience emotional attraction, awe, or reverence; and to suffer greater devastation when the sacred is profaned. It does not mean, however, that they worship it.[22]

Any aspect of life can be imputed with sacred significance, including parenting, health, family relationships, and work. Geneticist Francis Collins put it this way: "It's fair to say that my belief in God accentuates my sense that one of the things that we are supposed to do while we are here is to reach out to other people. This contributes to the motivation to try to see genetic research benefit human beings. In the mandates of the long tradition of Judaism and Christianity, one of the things we are to do is to try to heal the sick."[23] Studies have shown that people who view ordinary activities as sacred are more physically and psychologically invested in those activities and experience greater emotional attraction and reverence, higher satisfaction, and extraordinary personal and social resources throughout life. Thus, s*acred meaning*, as opposed to simply meaningfulness, may account for why the sacred calling yielded both tangible and intangible benefits to organizations and society, as Weber hypothesized. He thought that workers' sacred calling increased their commitment, care, and ethics, which enabled them to glorify God with their "good work." Weber believed that the good work of a sacred calling transcended traditionalism, enhanced efficiency, and thereby fueled the ethical expansion of capitalism. Weber warned, however, that the effects of capitalism on the culture in the form of individualism, unrestrained competition, and a focus on winning rather than quality,

Figure 4.1 Hypothesized relationships between calling, capitalism, and specialists without spirit.

would erode the spirit of calling and make it a ghost of its former self. Weber's warning is illustrated in Figure 4.1.

Weber inferred that the combination of sacred meaning cultivated through education; a sense of transcendent purpose; transcendent behaviors (e.g., reverence and adhering to norms); and a guiding cosmology that provides resources for extraordinary insights, emotional renewal, and coping were factors that differentiated calling from ordinary approaches to work and profoundly influenced the growth of capitalism. In fact, he even claimed that religious cosmologies were a source of innovation:

> The ability of mental concentration, as well as the absolutely essential feeling of obligation to one's job, are here most often combined with a strict economy which calculates the possibility of high earnings, and a cool self-control and frugality which enormously increase performance. This provides the most favorable foundation for the conception of labor as an end in itself, as a calling which is necessary to capitalism: the chances of overcoming traditionalism are greatest on account of the religious upbringing.[24]

With regard to religious coping, Pargament built on a century of psychological philosophy to write exhaustively about how people rely on religious cosmologies to cope with crises and loss such as divorce or discrimination after 9/11.[25] He and his colleagues found that some forms of religious coping have resulted not only in resilience but also posttraumatic growth![26] (It is important to note here that crises can also lead to depression and despair. Consequently, Gardner and his colleagues discussed other tactics to create the conditions for good work, which I discuss in Chapter 6.) Thus, the cosmology of one's calling may be a resource to cope with seismic and disorienting events such as layoffs, protracted unemployment, discrimination, harassment, or reentering the workforce. Few, if any, scholars have pondered the notion that one's calling, because of inherent soul-crafting, might be instrumental in fostering posttraumatic growth. One exception is an article by Weiss and his colleagues.[27]

Weiss and his colleagues wrote a most insightful and cogent article about calling from a religious perspective, which expands and refines ideas in the transcendent conversation about calling. Namely, callings are not primarily about blissful alignment and occupational choice but are "part of the developmental process of realizing one's identity— since it is not a 'set task,' it doesn't begin or focus on finding the right 'career' or job choice."[28] Instead, calling is a lifelong process of making choices, coping with change, and the fluctuating salience of various life roles, including work. They note that the work of one's calling may, in fact, be undesirable. It might mean fulfilling a duty that one has the resources or obligation to do, regardless of desire. Furthermore, Weiss and his colleagues view calling through a postpositivist lens and explain that it can evolve in quantum rather than linear patterns, which makes it difficult to discern. Therefore, enacting and advancing one's calling requires more than traditional "career problem-solving and decision-making" skills. Individuals who answer their callings benefit from having a learning orientation, guidance from community helpers who have the individual's and the community's (*not the corporation's*) best interest at heart, and the inner resources to adapt and cope with change.[29] Thus, those who are called need intrapersonal awareness and the ability to adapt, respond to, and manage uncertainty.

Weiss and colleagues also assert that callings are socially constructed, not "excessively individualistic" or driven primarily by inner impulses. They noted that callings are "conducted not only according to one's individual values, but a sense of those global ethical values that are the foundations of human community."[30] They contend that one's religious identity is central to forming a complete identity and that a religious community and its cosmologies can be instrumental in forming identity and fulfilling a calling.

To illustrate their points, Weiss et al. described how spiritual cosmologies influenced the values, choices, and the sometimes circuitous life paths of Mohandas Gandhi, Martin Luther King Jr., and Jesus Christ. They used metaphors and scripture to describe how one discerns the call by being attentive to their gifts, social needs, others' affirmations, and insights from their faith. In addition, they described how spirituality was a resource that helped Gandhi, King, and Christ cope with difficulties and ambiguities as they pursued what would become their life missions—their callings. Although management scholars in the other conversations have cited Weiss's article, few have built on or tested the core claims that it advanced.

Scholarship related to the sacred calling in management is still in a nascent stage. As such, I present examples from my own work, as well as that of scholars who have published in social science journals.

Cosmologies, Sacred Meaning, and Coping

Prior to graduate school, I developed a faith-based vocational educational program to infuse work with sacred meanings, with the hope of cultivating participants' sense of calling.[31] My approach—although I didn't know it at the time—was congruent with Weber's idea that calling is the product of "long and arduous education," principles of intervention design,[32] and evidence-based practices in faith-based curriculum development.[33] I used a Christian cosmology to develop a curriculum intended to help participants discover their gifts and interests and to reframe all types of work, life roles, and transitions (e.g., jobs, career, family obligation, volunteering, civic engagement, and parenting). In addition, it conveyed collective norms about ethics, the use of power, quality, relationships, and suggested ways to cope with the inherent difficulties of work.

To illustrate these points, I used the life of one representative character as a case study. I describe this historical, biblical figure in Chapter 11. The narrative on which the curriculum was based includes his adolescence, various jobs, career aspirations, family and community service, leisure activities, life legacy, and how sacred meaning was actualized throughout his life. It is worth noting that discovering his work "destiny" was of minor importance compared to other aspects of his journey. In addition, I selected verses that were specifically intended to inoculate participants against setbacks at work and to cope with difficulties such as delayed dreams, self-doubt, being different, and structural barriers that people confront because of their social status. The various sacred meanings, as well as norms and coping tactics are summarized in Table 4.1.

Table 4.1 Content of Myers Faith-Based Vocational Educational Program

Sacred Meanings Of	*Norms or Tactics to Cope With*
Work	Relationships
Work Quality and Good Work	Social Status
Jobs	Difficulties
Career Destiny	Being Different
Volunteering	Delayed/Denied Dreams
Gifts and Interests	Self-Doubt
Duty to Family	Transitions
Civic Duty	Opportunities and Success
Leisure Activities	Leaders and Leadership
Legacy	Using Power
Wealth	Structural Barriers
Social Responsibility	Self-Awareness

With the award of a student fellowship,[34] I conducted eight, two-hour, structured, interactive educational sessions with 15 youth (ages 14–22) in Durban, South Africa.[35] To ensure that the content was culturally relevant, I included elements of South African cosmology (e.g., phrases, icons, and historical references). Pre- and posttest measures showed modest but insignificant increases in career and calling orientations (using typical secular P-E fit measures).[36] Respondents were also asked to answer open-ended questions such as "What did you learn about jobs, careers, volunteering, God at work, etc.?" All of the respondents expressed sacred meanings for different types of work (e.g., "Jobs are also part of God's plan" and "Praise the Lord and be involved in His creation") and religious coping themes (e.g., "God can use bad things to achieve good ends"). Results from this pilot study suggested that it is possible to use workers' existing religious and cultural cosmologies to infuse work with sacred meaning and promote active coping.

It is worth noting that the biblical narrative offered theoretical insights about calling that presaged management scholarship. Obviously, the rigor of research that examines sacred callings could be enhanced by drawing on advances in and the application of recent developments in social science.

Religious Cosmologies and Developments in Social Science

The faith-based approach to educational intervention is grounded in a large and rapidly evolving body of knowledge in public health. Faith-based interventions use the target population's existing religious and cultural cosmologies to reframe ordinary activities as sacred. Studies have shown that faith-based educational interventions, when applied to various life domains (e.g., exercise, nutrition, and health screenings), have resulted in statistically significant and sustained positive changes in beliefs and behaviors.[37] Generally speaking, the educational content (1) is derived from religious scriptures; (2) reframes ordinary activities as sacred; (3) inoculates participants against setbacks and offers individual, social, and spiritual strategies to cope; (4) is delivered across a minimum of four to six educational sessions that occur in a community setting; (5) is conducted by laypersons, professionals, or both; and (6) is reinforced with tailored messages from the leader/clergy and culturally relevant social activities. Those tactics are quite similar to the ones that Fox[38] discovered were recommended by scholars from her study to improve vocational education in congregations. Those recommendations have not been heeded, however. If they were, the results have not been published.

Although research about faith-based educational interventions is new, the concept itself is not. One of the first documented faith-based interventions in the United States was the Negro health movement of 1915,[39] which sought to change deplorable societal conditions—high mortality rates and poor sanitation in African American communities. Toward that end, a diverse group of professionals (e.g., clergy, nurses, and educators) collectively used the tools of their trades and shared cosmologies (e.g., faith and culture) to engage in soul crafting. In other words, they created messages about the sacred meaning of health and health behaviors. Initially a local program, this grassroots effort spread across the country and resulted in improved individual health, community sanitation, and system-level changes. The movement culminated in establishing the U.S. Office of Minority Health and became a model for faith-based interventions and theories developed decades later. (Sometimes, theoretical insights and practical advances occur in surprising ways.)

We now know empirically that faith communities have the potential to influence the sacred meaning of ordinary activities that are directed toward transcendent and prosocial goals (e.g., life and health). Moreover, these communities offer a cosmology for sense making and behavior, and can foster change at multiple levels (e.g., individual and community). Management scholars in the sacred conversation, however, have not yet availed themselves of this intervention research and, to date, have not conducted comparable[40] studies that examine the application of religious and cultural cosmologies to work and calling.

Calling and Coping with Role Conflicts

Several studies provide some empirical support for Weiss et al.'s assertions about relationships between calling, life roles, coping, and meaning. For example, in their study of undergraduates, psychologist Isaac Hunter and his colleagues[41] found that students who believed that their calling originated from a guiding force also felt that their calling helped them cope with multiple demands. As such, Hunter and others are gravitating toward the position that calling is a lifestyle rather than just a destiny.

Using more in-depth questions about spirituality, Esperanza Hernandez[42] and her colleagues sought to understand how the religious cosmologies of seven Catholic adults (ages 43–61) influenced their career decisions. Researchers asked about specific resources that people used to discern their calling. Responses from adults led researchers to describe calling as a nonlinear process that unfolds over time, and is located in the context of social and spiritual relationships. Furthermore, respondents indicated that their faith helped them manage ambivalence, doubt, and other difficult emotions related to career transitions. Likewise, Kerris Oates and her colleagues sought to understand the connection between calling, specific roles, and coping in a sample of mothers working in academia.[43] They found that a sense of calling helped women cope with the interrole tensions of being a teacher, mentor, researcher, spouse, and mother; they felt their roles were structured hierarchically. Kerris Oates et al. measured calling as having a comprehensive nature (it spans life domains), being collective (in the context of relationships), involving a sense of conviction about vocation, and seeing one's vocation as meaningful. They considered this combination of activities as sanctifying life's roles and used them to predict the respondents' ability to cope. Their finding sheds light on how cosmologies are a mechanism for sanctifying ordinary activities. Despite these developments, studies that examine sacred calling are limited by the use of overly parsimonious measures of religiosity and P-E fit measures of calling.

Advancing the Discourse

Admittedly, research in the sacred calling conversation is scarce; however, transferrable knowledge from other disciplines is not. Advances in the scientific study of religion and community-based educational interventions provide numerous resources to advance management scholarship about calling.

Calling was and is a theology of work and its multiple sacred meanings. Hence, it is sacred meaning, not meaningfulness, that is the substantive meaning of calling. Sacred meaning offers infinite possibilities for education and research. As previous examples have shown, it is possible to transform secular things into sacred things and yet have no religious attachment. The converse is also true, and this is what appears to have happened to the sacred calling in the hands of most management scholars.

Aforementioned studies, although embryonic, are important because they diverge from positivist approaches in management that seek only to measure whether or not people express a sense of calling (fit) or the feeling of having been summoned. Indeed, positivistic approaches in the secular individualistic conversation have overestimated the degree to which instruction about calling has occurred in traditional institutional settings—a trend that concerns both theologians and academics. Before measuring the absence or presence of calling, we first need to examine how—*and indeed whether*—calling has been cultivated. Toward this end, it essential to use new refined measures of religious involvement to analyze community influences on calling and to draw on faith-based intervention research to analyze the educational impact of religious cosmologies on calling. More specifically, rather than creating new measures, management scholarship can be advanced by using established methods to (1) measure religiosity; (2) analyze how different forms of religious involvement influence one's sense of calling; and (3) examine denominational, occupational, and sociodemographic differences in the meanings of calling. Furthermore, few, if any, studies have used control groups and intervention methods to analyze the degree to which tailored religious or cultural messages influence one's perceptions of, search for, and enactment of calling. Advances in social science and faith-based intervention planning and research provide the necessary tools to infuse various life domains with sacred meaning in a systematic way.[44] Since faith-based education has been effective in other life domains, why not apply it to work? In Chapter 12, I explore systematic educational approaches that could be used to cultivate sacred callings in emerging and established adults. For example, congregations and their leaders reach all levels of the social and occupational hierarchy, span sociodemographic groups, and are located worldwide. As such, they are ideally situated to educate their members about calling, soul crafting, and work. And, because the majority of people around the globe (80%) embrace some religious ideology or philosophy, the forthcoming analysis will help us understand how a theory of calling can be adapted and applied across cultures to reach large segments of the global population.

Another contribution of the conversation about sacred calling, and its obvious gaps, is that it elucidates variables that may be missing—theoretical links between what people believe, how they behave, and why callings might have positive implications for organizations and society. Research is limited, however, by overly parsimonious measures, lack of rigor, and the fact that scholars in the sacred conversation have been shouted down or dismissed by scholars in the secular individualistic conversation. Increased attention to the mechanisms of a sacred calling can yield interesting new trajectories for research in management and beyond.

In sum, although marginal and emerging in a management context, the conversation about sacred callings retains themes that are part of *the* larger conversation about calling. Due to advances in other disciplines beyond management, the conversation about sacred callings can now be advanced in ways that were impossible decades ago. Once it is, will other management scholars listen?

NOTES

1. Quist Albertson, *The Gods of Business: The Intersection of Faith in the Marketplace* (Los Angeles, CA: Trinity University Alumni Press, 2007).
2. D. E. Super, J. O. Crites, R. C. Hummel, H. P. Moser, P. L. Overstreet, and C. F. Warnath, *Vocational Development: A Framework for Research* (New York: Teachers College Press, 1957).

3. B. D. Rosso, K. H. Dekas, and A. Wrzesniewski, "On the Meaning of Work: A Theoretical Integration and Review," *Research in Organizational Behavior: An Annual Series of Analytical Essays and Critical Reviews* 30 (2010): 91–127; Douglas T. Hall and Dawn E. Chandler, "Psychological Success: When the Career Is a Calling," *Journal of Organizational Behavior* 26, no. 2 (2005): 155–76.

4. James E. King, "(Dis)Missing the Obvious: Will Mainstream Management Research Ever Take Religion Seriously?" *Journal of Management Inquiry* 17 (2008): 214.

5. Joanne B. Ciulla, *The Working Life: The Promise and Betrayal of Modern Work* (New York: Times Books, 2000).

6. J. C. Davidson and D. P. Caddell, "Religion and the Meaning of Work," *Journal of Scientific Study of Religion* 33, no. 2 (1994): 135–47.

7. J. J. McGee and A. L. Delbecq, "Vocation as a Critical Factor in Spirituality for Executive Leadership in Business," in *Business, Religion and Spirituality: A New Synthesis*, ed. Oliver F. Williams, 94–110 (Notre Dame, IN: University of Notre Dame Press, 2003).

8. J. W. Weiss, M. F. Skelley, J. C. Haughey, and D. T. Hall, "Callings, New Careers and Spirituality: A Reflective Perspective for Organizational Leaders and Professionals," *Research in Ethical Issues in Organizations* 5 (2004): 175–201.

9. Davidson and Caddell, "Religion and the Meaning of Work."

10. Ibid., 138.

11. Lori A. Fox, "The Role of the Church in Career Guidance and Development: A Review of the Literature 1960–Early 2000s," *Journal of Career Development* 29, no. 3 (2003): 167–82.

12. Lake Lambert III, *Spirituality Inc.: Religion in the American Workplace* (New York: New York University Press, 2009); Miroslav Volf, *Work in the Spirit: Toward a Theology of Work* (Eugene, OR: Wipf & Stock Publishers, 2001).

13. Thanks to my editor, Leslie Wilhelm, for suggesting this analogy.

14. L. M. Chatters, "Religion and Health: Public Health and Practice," *Annual Review of Public Health* 21 (2000): 335–67; L. M. Chatters, J. S. Levin, and R. J. Taylor, "Antecedents and Dimensions of Religious Involvement among Older Black Adults," *Journal of Gerontology* 47, no. 6 (1992): S269–S278.

15. Mark Chaves, *National Congregations Study*. Data file and codebook (Tucson, AZ: University of Arizona, Department of Sociology, 1998).

16. Carl S. Dudley and David A. Roozen, *Faith Communities Today: A Report on Religion in the United States Today* (Hartford Institute for Religion Research, 2001), http://www/hartsem.edu.

17. Max Weber, *The Protestant Ethic and the Spirit of Capitalism* (London: Routledge, 1904/1992), 139.

18. Ibid., 39.

19. Ibid., 176–77.

20. Ibid., 174.

21. Matthew B. Crawford, *Shop Class as Soulcraft: An Inquiry into the Value of Work* (New York: Penguin Press, 2009), 196.

22. Kenneth I. Pargament and Annette Mahoney, "Sacred Matters: Sanctification as a Vital Topic for the Psychology of Religion," *International Journal for the Psychology of Religion* 15, no. 3 (2005): 179–98.

23. Howard Gardner, Mihaly Csikszentmihalyi, and William Damon, *Good Work* (New York: Perseus Books Group), 89.

24. Weber, *The Protestant Ethic*, 63.
25. Kenneth I. Pargament, *The Psychology of Religion and Coping: Theory, Research, Practice* (New York: Guilford Press, 1997).
26. Kenneth I. Pargament, Gina M. Magyar, Ethan Benore, and Annette Mahoney, "Sacrilege: A Study of Sacred Loss and Desecration and Their Implications for Health and Well-Being in a Community Sample," *Journal for the Scientific Study of Religion* 44, no. 1 (2005): 59–78; Hisham Abu-Raiya, Kenneth Pargament, and Annette Mahoney, "Examining Coping Methods with Stressful Interpersonal Events Experienced by Muslims Living in the United States Following the 9/11 Attacks," *Psychology of Religion and Spirituality* 3, no. 1 (2011): 1–14; Elizabeth J. Krumrei, Annette Mahoney, and Kenneth I. Pargament, "Divorce and the Divine: The Role of Spirituality in Adjustment to Divorce," *Journal of Marriage and Family* 71, no. 2 (2009): 373–83; Lawrence G. Calhoun and Richard G. Tedeschi, eds., *Handbook of Posttraumatic Growth: Research and Practice* (Mahwah, NJ: Lawrence Erlbaum, 2006).
27. Weiss et al., "Callings, New Careers and Spirituality."
28. Ibid., 197.
29. Ibid., 188–89.
30. Ibid., 189.
31. The self-published manual titled "Stir up the Gift Within You: A Christian Perspective of Work" was first used in the United States with working adults and teens.
32. Lawrence W. Green and Marshall W. Kreuter, *Health Promotion Planning: An Educational and Ecological Approach* (Mountain View, CA: Mayfield, 1999).
33. Valerie L. Myers, *An Interdisciplinary Analysis of Faith-Based Human Services: Analyzing Latent Organizational, Social and Psychological Processes* (PhD diss., University of Michigan, 2003).
34. This graduate student research was funded by an award from the Office of South Africa Initiative's Charles Moody Fellowship. It was conducted with the help of Rev. Fred Mayakiso pastor, and assistant pastor Nesta, of St. Francis A.M.E. Church in Chesterfield Township, Durban, South Africa. It was supported by Rev. David Jarrett pastor of Smith Chapel A.M.E. Church Inkster, MI, donations and pilot study participation from the church family, my family, and friends.
35. Leoneda Inge-Barry, "Career Lessons from the Biblical Joseph," *Michigan Today* 32, no. 2(2000); V. L. Myers, "Cultivating Calling: A Faith-Based Approach to Work Orientation and Spirituality at Work," paper presented at the Symposium at the Society of Industrial Organizational Psychologists Annual Conference, Dallas, Texas, May 2006.
36. Amy Wrzesniewski, Clark McCauley, Paul Rozin, and Barry Schwartz, "Jobs, Careers, and Callings: People's Relations to Their Work," *Journal of Research in Personality* 31, no. 1 (1997): 21–33.
37. Mark J. DeHaven, Irby B. Hunter, Laura Wilder, James W. Walton, and Jarett Berry, "Health Programs in Faith-Based Organizations: Are They Effective?" *American Journal of Public Health* 94, no. 6 (2004): 1030; Myers, *An Interdisciplinary Analysis of Faith-Based Human Services*; B. R. Johnson, R. B. Tompkins, and D. Webb, *Objective Hope—Assessing the Effectiveness of Faith-Based Organizations: A Review of the Literature* (Baylor Institute for Studies of Religion, 2002).
38. Fox, "The Role of the Church in Career Guidance and Development."

39. Roscoe C. Brown, "The National Negro Health Week Movement," *The Journal of Negro Education* 6, no. 3 (1937): 553–64.

40. Bryan J. Dik and Michael F. Steger, "Randomized Trial of a Calling-Infused Career Workshop Incorporating Counselor Self-Disclosure," *Journal of Vocational Behavior* 73, no. 2 (2008): 203–11. However, their two-session workshop is not comparable to multisession (6–8) programs founded and derived from intervention planning theory. Despite the growing number of workplace ministry programs, they have not been subject to rigorous design or evaluation. The strength and endurance of Holland's model is that it has been tested.

41. I. Hunter, B. J. Dik, and J. H. Banning, "College Students' Perceptions of Calling in Work and Life: A Qualitative Analysis," *Journal of Vocational Behavior* 76, no. 2 (2010): 178–86.

42. Esperanza F. Hernandez, Ben K. Beitin, and Pamela F. Foley, "Hearing the Call: A Phenomenological Study of Religion in Career Choice," *Journal of Career Development* 38, no. 1 (2011): 62–88.

43. Kerris Oates, M. Elizabeth Lewis Hall, and Tamara Anderson, "Calling and Conflict: A Qualitative Exploration of Interrole Conflict and the Sanctification of Work in Christian Mothers in Academia," *Journal of Psychology and Theology* 33, no. 3 (2005): 210–23.

44. Johnson, Tompkins, and Webb, *Objective Hope*; DeHaven et al., "Health Programs in Faith-Based Organizations"; Myers, *An Interdisciplinary Analysis of Faith-Based Human Services*.

5

Calling in the Iron Cage

Scholars have resurrected the concept of calling in management, suggesting new meanings and yielding interesting insights into its relevance in modern organizational life. Conceptual and empirical work has propelled calling scholarship forward; different worldviews are reflected in three conversational streams: secular individualistic callings, transcendent callings, and sacred callings. Each conversation increases our understanding about core dimensions of calling, whether it's alignment, emotions, prosocial intent, transcendence, or faith. Given the contradictions and lingering questions generated within each conversation, however, I suspect there is even more for us to discover beyond the iron cage of management.

The *iron cage* is a metaphor that Max Weber used to describe a collective rationality that, once established by powerful actors, becomes "taken for granted as correct." In the face of uncertainty, others turn to the collective rationale for guidance, are rewarded for conforming to it, and thereafter sit happily perched in an iron cage of certainty and similarity. But conformity is not synonymous with efficacy; conformists aren't necessarily more effective than their deviant peers. Still, once in place, the collective rationale is very difficult to change—despite compelling reasons to do so.[1]

The age-old idea of a sacred calling now sits in the iron cage of modern management as the secular individualistic concept of person-environment (P-E) fit. It bears only a faint resemblance to theologians' 500-year-old idea or Weber's 100-year-old idea. The fact that management scholars drifted toward a secular individualistic definition of calling is completely rational. After decades of dormancy, a few scholars boldly attempted to revive and define calling in earnest in the 1990s, but considerable confusion and uncertainty arose about its meaning, which is typical in the early years of researching a concept. This uncertainty was compounded by a social context that was far more individualistic, grappling with rapidly changing technology, and sculpted by the forces of capitalism. After the idea of a secular individualist calling became established in the literature, it became resistant to change, even by scholars in emerging conversations who tacitly desire to shift the conversation. It is now clear that the dominant, taken-for-granted definition of calling is not the best definition.

From a sociological perspective, the evolution of calling scholarship is quite rational. What is not rational, however, is that after 20 years, management scholars are *still* wandering in the wilderness without a concrete definition of calling or a comprehensive theory to guide it. (In the spirit of an interdisciplinary conversation, I am purposefully mixing metaphors.)

When the Israelites escaped bondage in Egypt and journeyed toward the Promised Land, they wandered in the wilderness for 40 years, subsisting on manna from heaven, before arriving at their destination. The actual distance they traveled, however, could have been traversed in 11 days! Why did they make the journey so much longer and harder than it had to be? And, indeed, why have we? In both cases, the meandering can be attributed to an iron cage of conforming to dysfunctional, habitual routines.[2]

Habitual routines provide stability and certainty but rarely lead to innovation. One dysfunctional habit among management scholars who study calling is the new taken-for-granted-as-correct practice of acknowledging at the outset of their publication that there is no agreed on definition or theory of calling; this acknowledgment garners a pass to publish more research based on nontheories! Consequently, we've seen a dizzying pace of publications that offer new definitions, new variables, new measures, and new language, but there is little theory building. If management scholars continue on this trajectory, we will wander in the wilderness for another 20 years before arriving at the Promised Land of a theory. So, how did we get where we are? And, more important, where do we go from here?

We arrived here by conforming to habitual routines of academia that have forestalled progress, including (1) gap-spotting research, (2) careless citation patterns, and (3) intellectual insularity. Several scholars have written quite eloquently about these problems, so I begin this chapter by summarizing habitual routines that have enabled management scholars to wander so long without a theory of calling. Then, I draw on institutional theory to suggest a path to the Promised Land—a theory that I propose in Chapter 10. I must emphasize that my theory is *a path* and not the Promised Land itself. My modest goal is to lay a theoretical foundation that accelerates the pace of academic progress, not to present an ultimate theory. I hope and fully expect that with testing, my proposed theory will be modified, refined, and expounded on. But, as a scholar myself who has also wandered in search of a theory of calling, I think it is time to offer one.

As I have indicated, the evolutionary pattern of calling scholarship is not surprising—but the pace of progress is. Larry Laudan wrote brilliantly about *Progress and Its Problems*[3] and the tedious, deliberate, incremental steps that are needed to achieve it. Before progressing to Part II of this book, I believe it's important for us to understand the routines and practices that have prevented management scholarship from advancing this discourse—even though they are accepted norms in academia—as well as what steps are needed to rise above them.

Gap Spotting

It is customary for scholars to begin an article by identifying knowledge gaps in existing literature to verify that what they are studying is a legitimate topic of research in their discipline, presumably because others have studied it; demonstrate that they have a firm grasp of the topic; imply that their research will make a contribution by filling the gap; and meet prerequisites for being published in top-tier journals. Mats Alvesson and Jörgen Sandberg call this "gap-spotting" research and contend that it rarely leads to theoretical developments.[4]

One reason that gap spotting impedes progress is that scholars fill so-called gaps without questioning whether "there is something more fundamentally problematic with existing literature or whether the data really are valuable indicators of the phenomena supposedly addressed."[5] As I have shown, the fundamental problems with the secular individualistic definition of calling are that (1) it is not socially relevant for 80% of the world's population who have some religious faith; (2) a vibrant book market indicates a popular thirst for how to link calling and faith, but may be insufficient in terms of how to do so (based on research results); (3) it is denuded of elements that have actual practical utility in organizations and society (ethics and quality); and (4) it is unclear that existing studies measure the phenomenon that interests us because they lack a transcendent dimension. Nevertheless, scholars have continued to measure the presence or absence of something that is not yet well defined, as if people just naturally possess a calling. Instead, we need to conduct research on the front end to understand how one's sense of calling is constructed in the modern era. So, the fundamental problems that management scholarship needs to address include defining calling, identifying its antecedents, understanding the conditions under which it flourishes, and understanding the reasons it became a toothless tiger in an individualistic yet religious culture that threatens its extinction.

Another reason that gap spotting doesn't result in theoretical development is that the practice either reinforces or incrementally revises (rather than challenges) influential perspectives.[6] Hence, gap spotting relative to the secular individualistic calling is not likely to result in real progress. In the quest to fill gaps in the dominant conversation, scholars have yet to address—in a serious way—the voluminous literature and layers of meaning that have been woven into the definition of calling over hundreds of years. Instead, the accepted taken-for-granted routine is to cite Martin Luther, John Calvin, and Max Weber, as if no other philosophers or practitioners have engaged or informed the dialogue between or since these works.

Elements and insights that can truly fill gaps in calling scholarship are scattered all about us in other disciplines—like manna from heaven. We have the arduous task of collecting them. Granted, perusing 500 years of philosophy is not trivial, yet such writings can shorten an already tedious journey toward a theory. This crucial yet missing step is what Laudan contends is essential for academic progress. Although it is impossible to conduct a thorough analysis of that voluminous literature here, in Part II of this book, I present highlights from philosophers across the centuries and through the 21st century. The real gap to be filled is not within management alone but among management, philosophy, and theology. My hope is to create a bridge across these disciplines by increasing understanding, proposing a theory, and providing some different references on which we can build. Hopefully, different references will encourage scholars to stop mimicking existing yet ineffective citation patterns.

Mimicry of Citation Patterns

Academic progress requires analyzing, critiquing, and refining existing theories before introducing new ones.[7] Therefore, we must comprehensively materialize ideas that are in original works.[8] Few researchers, however, have undertaken this task. For example, rather than comprehensively materializing and dissecting theologians' or Weber's central claims, as many sociologists have done, management scholars have dismissed Weber's major claims (particularly that calling is moral and sacred) or selectively materialized incidental claims. This problem is exacerbated by peripheral citations of incidental claims that are least likely to preserve Weber's original ideas.

Peripheral citations make simple generalizations without considering prior work, selecting a concept but inadequately operationalizing or testing it, and giving disproportionate attention to one component or dismissing ideas that are germane to the seminal work. One peripheral citation that management scholars routinely use is "Beruf, a task set by God,"[9] which appears in *The Protestant Ethic and the Spirit of Capitalism*. *Beruf*, however, was not Weber's main point, and the quote has been taken out of context. Weber used this clause to introduce the chapter titled "Luther's Conception of the Calling" and to explain how ideas about calling evolved beyond it to a Calvinist view. Midway through the chapter, Weber wrote:

> *Thus the mere idea of the calling in the Lutheran sense is at best of questionable importance for the problems in which we are interested* . . . It is thus well for us next to look into those forms in which a relation between practical life and a religious motivation *can be more easily perceived than in Lutheranism.* We have already called attention to the conspicuous part played by Calvinism and the Protestant sects in the history of capitalistic development . . . . And Catholicism has to the present day looked upon Calvinism as its real opponent . . . . *without Calvinism his work could not have had permanent concrete success.*[10]

Italicized phrases of the preceding quote indicate that Weber was simply recognizing *beruf* as the historical basis of calling but it was not important to his argument. Instead, he was interested in and developed Calvin's perspective, which advanced Luther's idea. Routinely citing *beruf* completely misses and misrepresents Weber's point. Weber mentioned *beruf* to demonstrate his adherence to the academic norm of comprehensively materializing Luther's core claim so that he could contrast it with Calvinism. Weber simply showed how he was building on prior work. Note that my goal here is not to litigate Weber's theological claims; that task is beyond the scope of this book. Instead, I want to show how the peripheral idea of *beruf* has been taken for granted as a central claim in management scholarship when it was never meant to be a central claim. Nevertheless, scholars routinely cite *beruf,* and then that citation is deemed acceptable by the people who cited it before them!

Peripheral citations are exacerbated by secondary and tertiary citations, which are the most egregious. Secondary citations involve scholars citing what other scholars claim that Weber has said rather than reading Weber's own words. It becomes tertiary when other scholars cite that secondary citation. Like a game of telephone, the original message degenerates until it is comically unrecognizably. In management scholarship, references to Weber are usually tertiary. He is not exhaustively or correctly cited, and scholars rarely cite the original words of the religious reformers, preferring to rely on Weber's (mis)interpretations instead.

Such citation patterns are then reinforced by normative and mimetic isomorphism.[11] What management scholar writes about calling without referring to Weber? Leading authors cite *Weber* and *Habits* in similar ways, advancing lopsided points of view.[12] Their citation patterns and practices then become taken for granted as correct and normative. Junior scholars then mimic citation patterns their mentors used because, once established, social forces demand and reward conformity and punish deviance. Alvesson and Sandberg articulate this best: "pigeonholing helps to boost their productivity and to meet academic performance criteria in the sense that: one knows the literature, goes to the right conferences, cultivates a network of people that matters, is familiar with the norms and rules of the journals in the sub-area, and therefore is capable of successfully publishing incremental contributions regularly. But the likelihood of generating frame-bending and high-impact research through such pigeonholing is typically low."[13]

As a result, a group of scholars circuitously cites each other, creating an echo chamber in academia rather than exploring vast literatures that can add substance and texture to theorizing. And yet these scholars have done precisely what is expected and rewarded. They are "winning" the publication race toward tenure, producing a prodigious number of "new" definitions that have little grounding in history or contemporary reality, and developing "new measures" that capture something different in every study. This gap spotting, novelty-based strategy leads to publications and lines on one's curriculum vita but adds little to theory construction. This approach to scholarship is not true of all scholars, but it is particularly apparent among management scholars who study calling. Eminent management scholars Bob Sutton and Barry Staw[14] contend that this lapse has occurred because doctoral programs do not teach classes in how to construct theory; instead, they teach statistical skills that are often rigorously applied to oversimplified "ideal types"[15] and nontheories. The result is management scholars that have used sophisticated statistical tools to analyze something that falls short of a complete theory of calling. Gap spotting, peripheral citations, and normative isomorphism have resulted in an insular approach to constructing knowledge that probably has Max Weber turning in his grave.

Mad Max and Intellectual Insularity

Management conversations reveal important aspects of calling and frame them as revolutionary, when in fact, they are not new. Whether management scholars know it or not, many gaps in scholarship could be filled easily by inserting core claims that Weber espoused more than 100 years ago. He is cited as the authoritative voice that scholars claim has influenced them. But, like a brilliant yet senile old uncle, scholars have politely dismissed Weber's core claims with fleeting, obligatory citations.[16]

A similar problem has occurred in sociology. Scholars cite Weber, presumably because his work represents good theorizing, yet they then contradict his major claims.[17] If Weber is still worth citing—despite his theological inaccuracies—then it must be because he has made lasting theoretical contributions.[18] Weber has indeed offered theoretical contributions that answer questions still perplexing management scholars about the essence, antecedents, and core characteristics of calling. I can only imagine Weber's displeasure about being dismissed in the discourse that he started.

For example, how is it that management scholars have marginalized "spirit" when "spirit" was in the title of Weber's book? When Weber combined the study of religion and work to describe calling, he retained its sacred meaning and used each chapter of *The Protestant Ethic and the Spirit of Capitalism* to describe elements that could be combined into a coherent theory.[19] At the end of his book, he lamented the secularization of calling in the context of capitalism: "The idea of duty in one's calling prowls about in our lives like the ghost of dead religious beliefs."[20] This was not an indictment against religion, but against the forces of capitalism that might dilute its influence on work. Yet, the secular individualistic conversation has achieved dominance in its ideological stance, albeit a wavering one, without critically examining the reasons for, or the implications of shifts in the idea of calling and the practical implications for modern organizations.[21]

Weber's core claims are not the only ones that have been overlooked. Management scholars have also politely dismissed other credible contemporary voices, even though these voices are resounding in their respective areas of study. Robert Bellah and his colleagues, Joseph Weiss and his colleagues, and Howard Gardner and his colleagues have all authored path-forging publications about calling, yet they are peripherally cited or not cited at all. This is due in part to prevailing citation patterns and because what they've written—their core claims—doesn't conform to the dominant management idea of a calling. Moreover, the management conversation elides large swaths of historical and contemporary literature that could potentially aid theory construction. This approach to scholarship falls short of the calling to be an intellectual, which Andrew Shanks writes about in his book *The Other Calling: Theology, Intellectual Vocation and Truth*.[22] That calling demands honesty and pursuit of truth, wherever it resides, even if it disturbs our preexisting ideas and theoretical preferences. Theory is built across literatures, disciplines, and eras. Thus, gap spotting must proceed at a much higher level, a field level, in order for management to advance.

A Field of Calling Scholarship and Practice

Fields only exist to the extent that they are institutionally defined. The process of institutional definition, or "structuration" consists of four parts: an increase in the extent of interaction among organizations in the field; the emergence of sharply defined inter-organizational structures of domination and patterns of coalition; an increase in the information load with which organizations in a field must contend; and the development of a mutual awareness among participants in a set of organizations that they are involved in a common enterprise.[23]

— DiMaggio and Powell, "The Iron Cage Revisited"

Thus far, I have used the word *conversation* as a metaphor for the field of philosophy related to calling and the many different actors in it who are engaged in their own side conversations. I have presented evidence that the field is well established, yet in flux. Once primarily defined by theologians and philosophers, management scholars and consultants that have recently entered the field are proposing new definitions.

At a macro level, there is renewed interaction between ecumenical, business, and academic institutions and their agents. (I discuss their historical interactions in Chapter 9.) There are also more interorganizational structures among them. Coalitions composed of clergy, management scholars, consultants, corporations, and universities are evident in established workplace ministries. And, organizations such as the Management, Spirituality, and Religion interest division of the Academy of Management; student organizations such as Coram Deo; university centers for religion/ethics and work; and scholarship that examines spirituality and work are all evidence that the field is becoming more structured. Calling philosophy is embedded within these coalitions and structures. Based on these coalitions, we can surmise that all actors in the field of calling philosophy are aware of each other.

The final hurdle toward structuring the field has yet to be overcome: managing the information load and increasing mutual awareness among diverse actors that they are involved in a common enterprise. More specifically, although new and different actors are interacting with greater frequency and forging new partnerships, it is not clear that they are engaged in a common enterprise. To raise this awareness, they will need a common language and shared understanding to contend with voluminous bodies of knowledge that they did not author. However, management scholars and theologians have limited tools for crossing those boundaries.[24] Consequently, rather than managing the information load, management actors are reinventing the wheel, and ecumenical actors are unaware of new developments in wheel technology! Clearly, this moment presents a great opportunity for the entire field to advance.

To do so, ecumenical actors must now consider decades of social science research that can enhance their practice, even though they tend to be uninitiated to management and psychological theories. Conversely, academic actors (particularly those in management) must contend with a voluminous theological body of knowledge that is inaccessible, alien, off-putting, or intriguing depending on one's particular world-view. However, by not engaging the theological literature, management scholars in the dominant conversation about calling remain oblivious to theoretical insights that reside in other disciplines and documents. We don't have to wander through the wilderness of trial and error to discover them. Management scholars in emerging conversations have started to discuss some latent elements of theory, but there may be even more to discover in conversations beyond the boundaries of management.

As a management scholar, my goal is to wade into the information overload and increase awareness of the philosophical discourse that unites all actors, highlight interesting developments, point out the implications of mindless shifts, and offer a path forward with theory. I do not seek to advance one perspective over another, but instead to think critically about what each perspective contributes to an ongoing and highly relevant conversation about calling. While I discuss developments in religion and the social sciences, my goal here is not to proselytize, but to elucidate evidence-based practices that are relevant for the majority of the working population and that can also strengthen management theories, practices, and outcomes across cultures. Given the breadth of theological writings about callings, it is impossible to survey them all here. Instead, I highlight elemental nuggets that may contribute to a coherent theory of calling—or at least the beginning of one. Management scholarship cannot advance without some consensus about the meaning and measurement of calling. Hopefully, this book will create a space for listening across conversations to occur.

Thus far, I have highlighted the competing ideologies within management and how they have not capitalized on knowledge and advances in other social sciences, primarily sociology, psychology, and health behavior research. Practitioners such as consultants and clinicians are at the interstices and are, therefore, uniquely poised to bridge the divide between management scholars, ecumenical actors, and the general population. Because they are at the interstices, practitioners traverse boundaries, fluently speak the language of several disciplines, and are closest to people in the quest for their calling. Given this position, they understand which conversations are socially relevant and how to translate them. Hence, their perspectives will be particularly useful for grappling with the information overload and making sense of it.

In the spirit of social science, it is important to triangulate perspectives about calling by confirming, disconfirming, or enhancing them with knowledge from practitioners and theologians. I do this in Part II, where I explore modern practitioner perspectives of calling and compare them to historic theological writings.

Advancing the Discourse

The discordant cacophony of competing perspectives about calling is impeding real progress. Yet the knowledge we seek is not 20 years away; it is as close as other disciplines and as distant as a history lesson. To overcome inertia and liberate calling from the iron cage of the dominant management perspective, we must suspend rigid notions about what constitutes valid knowledge and step outside of our discipline to gain new insights. Throughout the balance of this book, I seek

Table 5.1 Summary of Insights about Calling from Preceding Chapters

What we think we know about calling . . .	*Lingering questions . . .*
Secularization and individualism denude calling of important features that have practical utility in organizations and society.	How might other social forces further diminish calling?
It is transcendent or religious for some; but, the summons may be internal or external.	To what extent do traditional institutions educate people about calling?
Calling spans one's life and life roles; there may be multiple calls or one major call.	How and when do transitions occur? What are the individual and organizational factors that facilitate change?
Calling is a sense of destiny, duty, or both; the difference is desire versus responsibility.	Why did duty disappear and how do we to reclaim it?
The unifying thread across all roles is a commitment to ethical and excellent delivery, which entails giving one's best at the time.	Why did ethics and quality disappear from calling and how do we reclaim them?
Calling is sustained by collective cosmologies that are disseminated through traditional and contemporary institutions (e.g., the media) and informal networks. Cosmologies:	What role can traditional and contemporary institutions and informal networks play in reconstituting the cosmologies of calling?

- Inform one's ethical commitments and standards of excellence
- Provide a coherent, interpretive framework that facilitates clarifying values, sense-making, and coping with detours
- Foster spiritual well-being, renewal, and wisdom
- Are learned over time by education, not affiliation
- Complement and correct work cosmologies

to shorten the journey toward a theory by presenting select insights from the vast terrain of scholarship about calling over the centuries. My approach, however, is not theological. I am a social scientist who recognizes that knowledge resides beyond the boundaries of my discipline; I am willing to cross those boundaries to access it.

Thus far, we have identified several theories that help us measure calling, namely, P-E fit,[25] the Life-Span, Life-Space Model,[26] psychological success,[27] sanctification,[28] religious coping, and moral development,[29] to name a few. The question remains: Are there more? Table 5.1 summarizes what we've learned about calling from the preceding chapters, as well as lingering questions.

In Part II, I explore conversations outside the boundaries of management to assess the degree to which others confirm, refute, or complement conversations about calling in management.

NOTES

1. P. J. DiMaggio and W. W. Powell, "The Iron Cage Revisited: Institutional Isomorphism and Collective Rationality in Organizational Fields," in *The New Institutionalism in Organizational Analysis*, ed. W. W. Powell and P. J. DiMaggio, 63–82 (Chicago: University of Chicago Press, 1991).
2. Connie J. G. Gersick and J. Richard Hackman, "Habitual Routines in Task-Performing Groups," *Organizational Behavior and Human Decision Processes* 47, no. 1 (1990): 65–97.
3. Larry Laudan, *Progress and Its Problems: Toward a Theory of Scientific Growth* (Berkeley: University of California Press, 1977).
4. Mats Alvesson and Jörgen Sandberg, "Has Management Studies Lost Its Way? Ideas for More Imaginative and Innovative Research," *Journal of Management Studies* (2012). doi: 10.1111/j.1467-6486.2012.01070.x.
5. Ibid., 6.
6. J. Sandberg and M. Alvesson, " Routes to Research Questions: Beyond Gap-Spotting," *Organization* 18 (2011): 22–44.
7. Laudan, *Progress and Its Problems*; Colin Campbell, "Do Today's Sociologists Really Appreciate Weber's Essay *The Protestant Ethic and the Spirit of Capitalism*?" *The Sociological Review* 54 (2006): 207.
8. Karen Golden-Biddle, Karen Locke, and Trish Reay, "Using Knowledge in Management Studies: An Investigation of How We Cite Prior Work," *Journal of Management Inquiry* 15, no. 3 (2006): 237–54.
9. Max Weber, *The Protestant Ethic and the Spirit of Capitalism* (London: Routledge, 1904/1992), 79.
10. Ibid., 86–87.
11. DiMaggio and Powell, "The Iron Cage Revisited."
12. E. A. Shils and H. A. Finch, *Max Weber on the Methodology of the Social Sciences* (Glencoe, IL: Free Press, 1949).
13. Alvesson and Sandberg, "Has Management Studies Lost Its Way?" 7.

14. Robert I. Sutton and Barry M. Staw, "What Theory Is Not," *Administrative Science Quarterly* 40, no. 3 (1995): 371–84.

15. Shils and Finch, *Max Weber on the Methodology of the Social Sciences*; S. Kalberg, "Should the 'Dynamic Autonomy' of Ideas Matter to Sociologists?: Max Weber on the Origin of Other-Worldly Salvation Religions and the Constitution of Groups in American Society Today," *Journal of Classic Sociology* 1 no. 3 (2001): 291–327.

16. Valerie L. Myers, "An Ontology of Calling: Examining Mechanisms and the Transcendent Possibilities of Work Orientation Theory," in *Critical Management Studies Conference Proceedings* (Manchester, UK: Manchester Business School, 2007); Valerie L. Myers, "What Did Weber Say?: A Comprehensive Materialization of His Implicit Theory of Calling," in *Academy of Management Annual Conference—Management, Spirituality and Religion Division* (Chicago, IL: 2009).

17. Campbell, "Do Todays Sociologists."

18. Hartmut Lehmann and Guenther Roth, eds., *Weber's Protestant Ethic: Origins, Evidence, Contexts* (Cambridge: Cambridge University Press, 1987).

19. Myers, "An Ontology of Calling"; Myers, "What Did Weber Say?"

20. Weber, *The Protestant Ethic*, 182.

21. Kalberg, "Should the 'Dynamic Autonomy' of Ideas Matter to Sociologists?"; S. R. Barley and G. Kunda, "Design and Devotion: Surges of Rational and Normative Ideologies of Control in Managerial Discourse," *Administrative Science Quarterly* 37, no. 3 (1992): 363–99.

22. Andrew Shanks, *The Other Calling: Theology, Intellectual Vocation and Truth* (Hoboken, NJ: Wiley-Blackwell, 2007).

23. DiMaggio and Powell, "The Iron Cage Revisited," 65.

24. J. J. McGee and A. L. Delbecq, "Vocation as a Critical Factor in Spirituality for Executive Leadership in Business," in *Business, Religion and Spirituality: A New Synthesis*, ed. Oliver F. Williams, 94–110 (Notre Dame, IN: University of Notre Dame Press, 2003).

25. J. L. Holland, *Making Vocational Choices: A Theory of Careers* (Englewood Cliffs, NJ: Prentice-Hall, 1973).

26. Donald E. Super, "A Life-Span, Life-Space Approach to Career Development," *Journal of Vocational Behavior* 16, no. 3 (1980): 282–98.

27. Douglas T. Hall and Dawn E. Chandler, "Psychological Success: When the Career Is a Calling," *Journal of Organizational Behavior* 26, no. 2 (2005): 155–76.

28. Kenneth I. Pargament and Annette Mahoney, "Sacred Matters: Sanctification as a Vitaltopic for the Psychology of Religion," *The International Journal for the Psychology of Religion* 15, no. 3 (2005): 179–98.

29. Lawrence Kohlberg, *The Psychology of Moral Development: The Nature and Validity of Moral Stages, Essays on Moral Development*, vol. 2 (San Francisco: Harper & Row, 1984).

Part II

Other Conversations about Calling 1520–2012

6

Practitioner Perspectives (1980s–2012): The Essence of Calling

> Not everybody has a calling. I know you disagree . . . I just had to work to support myself and my family and in doing so, I had a lot of good luck as well. I think, on behalf of the people who are not born with a calling, some of us have to find our way, some of us have to work hard, some of us have to make a living. I think it's great if you have a calling—but not everybody does [audience applause] . . . I don't think that everyone is born, as Oprah was, "knowing what I was born to do."
>
> —Barbara Walters, cohost of ABC's *The View*

Surprisingly, internationally acclaimed journalist and television producer Barbara Walters, whose career continues after 50 years, does not feel that she had a calling. Walters's quote conveys several important points that are central to the practitioner conversation about calling. First and foremost, her understanding of a calling and the belief that she didn't have one indicate just how diluted the word *calling* has become in some segments of modern culture. What Walters described is actually quite similar to the Protestant work ethic and the sense of duty and obligation that practitioners recognize as an essential part of a calling.

Second, Walters's quote echoes a tension that is embedded deeply in Western notions, particularly American notions of destiny. Presumably, democracy creates the conditions for boundless opportunities that are energized by individual desire, determination, and devoted actions. But circumstances remind people that their plans are contingent, vulnerable, and subject to social injustices and human limits that constrain choices.[1] The tension between notions of democracy and contingency indicate that a calling is composed of far more than finding "it." Moreover, you can't—and don't—always get what you want. Some people rely on their faith or other cosmologies to make sense of and manage that tension. Hence, the practitioner conversation explores the ways that people manage the bounded nature of human choice and control relative to calling. Compared to the P-E fit paradigm in management, a majority of practitioners are far less deterministic in their view of calling. Instead, they focus on how people compose their callings over a lifetime and the cosmologies that people use to give their calling coherence.

Third, Walters's quote crystalizes what practitioners have said about the organic nature of calling: it forms and unfolds in messy, uncertain, and serendipitous ways. Consider the audience applause to her comment about not having a calling, for example. It suggests that many people do not have a clear guiding vision of their destiny, a smooth career path, or opportunities to engage in "fitting" work. Is it still possible for them to have and fulfill a calling? Many practitioners argue that yes, they have a calling.[2] So, what hinders people's ability to discern or enact their calling? Practitioners offer hopeful insights to answer this question too. More importantly, they caution against recent cultural trends that threaten to further dilute calling.

Finally, of all the conversations discussed thus far, the practitioner conversation is the most incisive, pragmatic, and solution focused; practitioners concentrate on *understanding* calling, not *measuring* it. Practitioners inject a strong dose of realism into the discourse about the four dimensions of calling that have guided us thus far (e.g., alignment, emotions, prosocial intent, and transcendence). They describe what alignment is not, why a calling isn't always enjoyable, why prosocial concerns should not dictate one's path, practical steps to take when callings are denied, and the internal work needed to actually live one's calling. Hence, this conversation echoes and elaborates main points in the transcendent conversation about calling in management and adds texture to emerging management perspectives. In addition, practitioners lead us beyond destiny and duty to a third dimension of calling that is largely overlooked in management conversations. This chapter focuses on that essential missing dimension.

Unlike preceding chapters, in which I summarized empirical data, in this chapter my primary data sources are narratives, stories, archival information, and popular books written by practitioners—psychologists, psychiatrists, clergy, management consultant/scholars,[3] journalists qua consultants, career counselors, philosophers, and theology professors. Given the array of voices in this conversation, the lexicon used to describe calling is quite broad. Nevertheless, social science provides a prism through which we can identify the theoretical contributions of practitioners' claims.

Rather than simply stating parallels between the claims of practitioners and management scholars, I use this chapter to highlight distinct practitioner insights that advance the conversation about calling. I begin by describing the core elements that they have identified thus far: the meaning of calling, transcendence, antecedents, destiny, duty, and denied callings. Next, I present an additional dimension of calling and illustrate how the core dimensions interrelate in a conceptual model.

Becoming Barbara: An Alternative View of Calling

In her memoir, *Audition*,[4] Walters described pivotal moments in her life beginning with a sense of responsibility for her older, mentally impaired sister Jackie. It was a responsibility that Walters knew would ultimately be hers completely. Throughout her life, Walters wrestled with intense emotions toward her sister that vacillated between sisterly love, guilt, embarrassment, resentment, and even hatred.

Both of Walters's parents were Jewish. She said, however, "I'd never felt any special religious or spiritual connection to the Jewish state, perhaps because my parents and I were not religious and none of our relatives lived there."[5] Walters's family didn't attend temple, observe Jewish festivals, or engage in religious practices. Walters's mother was a practical woman who sold men's ties; her father was a risk-taking entertainment entrepreneur—a booking agent and theater and club owner. Every holiday, birthday, and special occasion was celebrated in one of her father's clubs. Consequently, young Walters was routinely exposed to legendary celebrities and privy to their offstage personae. Due to Lou Walters's various ventures, the family relocated multiple times—sometimes unpredictably. The combination of risky business deals and gambling debts created a financial roller coaster of luxury, upheaval, and ruin for the family. Walters saw him lose it all and rebound. Her early years were juxtaposed by celebrity and entertainment on one hand and personal sacrifice, struggle, and economic uncertainty on the other.

Although she was a diligent student, when Walters went to Sarah Lawrence College, she had no clue what she wanted to do with her life. (Ironically, she lied about attending Sunday school in her college essay to improve her chances for admission.) After discovering a class called "Theater," she bypassed academic subjects in favor of something that was familiar; it made sense to become an actress. In her book, she even states, "I had found my calling."[6] But when faced with an opportunity to audition, Walters was too timid and feared failure: "I had the pull because of my father's prominence in show business, but I didn't have the push."[7]

After graduation, Walters's career path was still uncertain; she stepped into the unknown while her friends stepped into their chosen careers. She enrolled in a speed-writing course and finally found something at which she excelled—typing and shorthand. Walters worked as a secretary in an ad agency, then left after being sexually harassed. A friend helped her get her next job—in television.

Ironically, the same industry that threatened her father's entertainment business proved propitious for Walters. With a little help and a few "small" lies, she was hired to assist the director of the publicity department, where she learned the craft of journalism by writing press releases. In time, she launched her journalism career, but not without significant twists and turns, both personally and professionally. Walters chose a mate as pragmatically as she chose her college major, but then divorced. Her decisions to be an actress and to marry a sexy but boring beau that her friends liked, demonstrates that you can't just choose it, dream it, or do it and make it fit.

As the years progressed, Walters had the wherewithal to help her father financially after yet another failed venture. She fought mightily against sexism in her field; she endured sexual harassment and open professional animus in the male-dominated television industry; she was fired and rebounded; and she cared for her sister Jackie. Driven largely by her family obligations and the quest for financial stability, Walters strove for excellence, seized opportunities, and willingly performed lowly jobs that expanded her skills and assisted her ascent. She wrote openly about her personal failings, challenges, victories, and myriad relationships. Upon reflection, Walters said: "Was all this, in a strange way, my destiny? I guess it's really impossible to know the answer about the whole destiny business. But my feeling is that the answer is yes. Very definitely yes."[8] Walters arrived at her fervent "yes" with the benefit of decades of hindsight to make sense of her experiences: "How lucky I was. How lucky! Perhaps I have made it a little easier for some of the women who followed in my footsteps—maybe even for some in other careers. Television is no longer a man's world. Perhaps, too, I helped to change that. If so, I am very grateful. I am blessed seven times over."[9]

I detail Walters's story because it is closely aligned with practitioners' perspectives about calling. First, calling is transcendent and, in most cases, spiritual; people can imbue secular situations with sacred meaning *as they define it*. Second, destiny is defined broadly and is perhaps best understood retrospectively across one's life span and with regard to legacy, rather than prospectively as something for which one searches. Third, moral duty and a commitment to "good work" (e.g., ethics and excellence) are central to a calling. Fourth, difficulties are an inherent part of the path, just as work has inherent burdens. Finally, practitioners note that it is very difficult to miss your calling because it is unfolding every day. I describe those insights in the sections that follow.

Calling: Spiritual, Transcendent, and Sacred

Although Walters considered herself somewhat spiritual, she is not religious. Spirituality is not the guiding cosmology of her calling. Instead, she used terms such as *fate*, *luck*, *fortunate*, *blessed*, *timing*, and *destiny* to express her understanding of her path. Walters's lexicon echoes that of her entrepreneurial and gambling father. Based on her lack of faith, some practitioners might contend that her experience is not a calling. But psychotherapist Robert Furey is not one of them. According to Furey, "One of the most common misconceptions about callings is that a person must be 'spiritual' in order to hear one. This is erroneous . . . The truth is that callings have *brought* many people to a spiritual life."[10]

Prolific author and philosopher C. S. Lewis is one such example; his life illustrates how various callings can occur at any time in one's life yet be connected by a single thread. Lewis's love of literature defined his life. At 10 years old, Lewis found solace in books after his mother died, which is when he decided to become an atheist. Twenty years later, Lewis's literary colleagues and career pursuits created the intellectual platform that launched his spiritual transformation to Christianity—from the seat of a motorcycle. Lewis wrote about his experience in his autobiography, *Surprised by Joy*.[11] For years, Lewis had struggled as a poet, but after his spiritual experience, he changed directions and started writing fiction and Christian nonfiction, which resulted in a legendary literary career. Lewis lived modestly, despite increased wealth, which enabled him to fund numerous charitable causes. At age 59, Lewis was surprised by a woman named Joy who enjoyed reading his books and ultimately became his wife.

Lewis's motorcycle epiphany and late-in-life romance are captured in Parker Palmer's sentiments about vocation: "we awaken one day to find that the sacred center is here and now—in every moment of the journey."[12] Lewis's life is an example of how one's situation can be sanctified[13] to become part of one's calling and how sacred meaning sanctifies the ordinary and makes it good and noble.[14] (To be clear, a situation is not a calling, but it can be part of one's calling.)

Indeed, calling is a transcendent or spiritual phenomenon,[15] and for some it is sacred.[16] Even practitioners who write from a secular perspective or are not particularly theological have described how the religious and spiritual traditions of Native Americans, Muslims, Buddhists, Taoists, Jews, and Christians helped them understand their callings. Psychologist and theology professor John Neafsey put it this way, "My understanding of vocation is based on the assumption that the intuition of a sacred purpose for our lives is a universal or archetypal human phenomenon. In other words, *everyone* has a vocation. This includes Catholics and Protestants, Christians and non-Christians, the religious and non-religious, those who use God-talk and those who don't. For many people, referring to God (by any of many names) is the only way to adequately express the profound sense of depth and sacredness they feel in connection with their life's work or purpose."[17] Naturally, some practitioners disagree.

Gordon Smith, a theology professor and consultant, argued that a "secular calling" is an oxymoron; according to Smith, calling comes from God and is inherently sacred. To support his position, Smith referred to Ecclesiastes 2:24 to confirm that work is from God and Colossians 3:23 to affirm that it should be for God: "Whatever your tasks, put yourselves into it, as done for the Lord and not for your masters." Of course, the source of one's calling is scientifically unknowable;[18] human beings may identify the source as God, a higher power, spirit, or their own inner voice depending on their guiding cosmology. And, since calling spans a lifetime, there may be multiple sources. Yet the phrase "whatever your tasks," is congruent with how many practitioners describe destiny and calling.

Destiny, Fit, and the Life Span

A majority of management scholars, and some practitioners, use the language of industry to describe calling; they seek to "fit" people into jobs and careers like cogs in a wheel (described in detail in Chapters 2 and 3). In contrast, many practitioners have written metaphorically about calling and how people need a compass to find their way, lessons to sing their own song, sunlight to help them grow in their own direction, to surrender or flow with the current, or signals to tune in to their own radio frequency. The notion of fitting versus finding and following is a major source of contention among practitioners and between practitioners and management scholars.

Some practitioners still advance an occupation-focused view of calling that emphasizes fit, gifts, and career, relying on Holland's model and gift assessments as a means to discover one's calling.[19] This is especially true of recent Christian publications about calling; there are numerous detractors, however. For example, Paul Stevens, professor of marketplace theology, criticized the "guidance mania" of evangelical Christians as a continuation of the *What Color Is Your Parachute?* movement.[20] Similarly, Gordon Smith insists that calling is more than aligning one's gifts and talents with occupational and employment opportunities; indeed, personality, temperament, and emotions also play a part.[21] Nor can it be found in a book or assessment.[22] More pointedly, Parker Palmer said, "The willful pursuit of a vocation is an act of violence toward ourselves—violence in the name of a vision that, however lofty, is forced on the self from without rather than grown from within."[23] In other words, we cannot impose a life path on ourselves, based on external criteria, without experiencing considerable dissatisfaction or worse.[24] Walters learned this lesson the hard way, having chosen a career because of her father's work and a husband because of her friends' approval.

Rather than a select occupation, many secular and religious practitioners think of calling holistically, as a vocation in the traditional sense—the call to a way of life.[25] This holistic view of calling can be theoretically supported by Super's[26] life-span model and interpreted as a call to different roles, a new occupation, higher-quality work, or even reordering your priorities.[27] The vocational view of calling is always more than aligning one's strengths and interests with a job. Rather than a "fit," these practitioners view calling as ultimate self-knowledge of one's strengths, temperament, and foibles.[28] It is a commitment to continuous growth and the willingness to endure spiritual discomfort;[29] it may also result in a slow burning passion that lasts a lifetime,[30] which was certainly the case for C. S. Lewis. For him, literature was the slow burning passion that radiated throughout most aspects of his life including childhood, family crisis, education, career, marriage, philanthropy, and faith.

Smith suggests that the vocational perspective has several advantages. First, it is personally liberating because in the quest of becoming oneself, there is no need for social comparison, people pleasing, adhering to externally imposed timelines, or being inordinately subject to the caprices of praise and criticism. Indeed, the fit, so to speak, is with oneself. Furthermore, experiences that once might have been considered insignificant, "wasted,"[31] or "false starts"[32] are ennobled and valued as relevant in the larger context.[33] In fact, many people live their fundamental calling "outside of or alongside gainful employment, possibly as homemakers, volunteer workers, or a wide variety of other roles."[34] For these people, employment may simply be a way to provide for basic needs—a job. As Walters said, and others know, it is a blessing to fulfill your fundamental calling through a fitting occupation, but a calling is fulfilled through a variety of roles.

Theoretically, calling as a traditional vocation erases distinctions between job, career, unpaid work, and other life roles; each can have transcendent or sacred meaning, depending on one's worldview. Thus, a calling is not a career; one may be called to a job, career, or other uncompensated role. The difference is the transcendent or sacred meaning that is imputed to those roles, however one defines it. For example, C. S. Lewis's spiritual epiphany led him to impute sacred meaning to his literary work and its pervasiveness across his life span and life roles, even the mundane act of riding a motorcycle.

Mundane Work and Moral Duty

> Mundane tasks simply refer to the earthworks needed to shape a world, and boredom doesn't necessarily mean you picked the wrong path.[35]
>
> —Levoy, *Callings*

The practitioner conversation does not describe moral duty, per se. Instead, practitioners frame mundane and less desirable tasks as inherent aspects of calling that one is simply obliged to undertake as part of the burden of work.[36] That obligation implies a moral duty to work in a way that is ethical and leads to excellence, but it need not have some lofty purpose. Gordon Smith described it this way, "Some things are obvious: . . . If the downspout around my house is loose and water is pouring into the foundation of my home, I do not go on a prayer retreat to determine if fixing this is my calling! Rather I put on rain gear and head out into the stormy weather to do what needs to be done!"[37] Similarly, we need to do jobs well, not because it is our chosen work, but because it is our work—an obligation to fulfill at this moment. And, if we are living a calling, that work is sacred because it fits into a larger transcendent scheme. Moreover, just as it is in our own self-interest to fix the downspout carefully and correctly, the same is true of mundane work.

With a calling, we are obligated, even when work goes against our "grain," to invest in it enough to meet its demands. When that is impossible, we are also obliged to choose a different path or find another solution. Sometimes however, there is no alternate path or solution readily available. In that instance, Palmer, Richard Leider, his co-author David Shapiro, and Gregg Levoy all suggest that if you can't get out of it, get into it. The idea of getting into it is congruent with the notion of job crafting—rearranging how one thinks about the work, the tasks, or relationships.

The bounded nature of choice, situational demands, and getting into it are comically illustrated in the film *The Devil Wears Prada*.[38] In the film, Andrea, a recent college graduate, had difficulty finding work as a serious news journalist. In desperation, she accepted a job at the fictional equivalent of *Vogue* fashion magazine. But Andrea thought fashion was frivolous and that her skills were grossly underutilized as the receptionist for an extremely demanding and demeaning editor-in-chief. Miserable, Andrea shared her frustrations about the job with a senior colleague who told her: "Wake up! The place where you only deign to work, others would die to work."[39]

So, Andrea got into it. Cognitively, she changed the way she thought about the meaning of fashion and working there; she also reconsidered what it meant to her personally. By investing in daily activities and relationships, she learned to value the magazine's aesthetic mission, its influence on the larger culture, and what a truly extraordinary opportunity it was to work for Miranda Priestly (Meryl Streep). She also enhanced her personal life by cultivating her fashion, beauty, and design aesthetic and dramatically changing her appearance. Andrea approached her tasks, lowly though they were, with enthusiasm, diligence, and graceful forbearance of catty coworkers and a passive-aggressive, perfectionist boss. Andrea even began to speak like them; they noticed her changes. As Levoy noted, "any calling requires a certain affection for drudgery."[40] It entails investing in the minutia that makes progress possible.

Andrea was rewarded for her efforts with greater responsibility, more opportunities, and more perks. Indeed, she achieved public recognition and career advancement. Managing the mundane and doing the morally right thing at work paid off.

Yet, despite her investments, Andrea still wasn't doing work that she wanted to do; she couldn't make her job at that magazine fit. Nor could a pay increase or more perks change that reality. This is congruent with Weber's point, that calling "cannot be evoked by low wages or high ones alone."[41] Andrea reflected on how this work fit into her life, holistically. She realized that success at work had adversely affected her closest relationships; essentially, she became a different person in both desirable and undesirable ways. She could increase the meaning and make work *more* meaningful, but ultimately the meaning of working at the fashion magazine was misaligned with her identity and values. The cutthroat fashion business and its hyperaesthetic focus went against her grain. So, although she tried to craft the job, the job was crafting her spirit and, in some ways, doing violence to her soul.

When Andrea quit, she left with an enhanced skill set, a more refined aesthetic sensibility, and positive recommendations for having fulfilled her duties at a job that some would covet as a career. Getting into it ultimately helped her to get out of it. Fulfilling a duty can similarly move us toward destiny and fitting roles.

Andrea's story reveals several insights about calling and job crafting. First, calling focuses on *how* you work, not whether you are doing fitting work; this is a vital yet underexamined dimension of calling, perhaps because it is not always "enjoyable." Nevertheless, one's moral responsibility should be honored; it has ethical and practical significance. Ethically, it shows that we recognize and want to satisfy behavioral norms of the community, objectively (quality) and subjectively (correct actions). From a practical standpoint, fulfilling obligations may be instrumental in fulfilling one's destiny, as it was for Andrea. Job crafting offers a way to meet that moral obligation—in the short term.

Second, although you may rearrange aspects of the work, your skill level, enjoyment, or "fit" may not improve. In such cases, some soul crafting is needed at work and in other areas of your life. Your job may forever be just your duty, and the obligation still exists to do your job ethically, with nobility, and to the best of your ability. That too is part of a calling.

Third, while Andrea had a moral duty to behave in a certain way, she also had a moral duty to herself—to honor her nature rather than work against it. As she adapted and conformed to industry norms, Andrea realized that she was also violating her own core values. As Jiddu Krishnamurti[42] stated, "It is no measure of health to be well adjusted to a profoundly sick society." Allowing your soul to be damaged at work is in fact, antithetical to a calling, which I will describe in Chapter 9. Andrea realized that no amount of job crafting could erase the fact that her work was not aligned with her career aspiration (news journalist) and temperament. She still thought the industry was superficial and shallow. And she was simultaneously inspired, demoralized, and vexed by her unethical boss. With introspection (soul crafting), she found the courage to assert her dignity and leave! Leaving is rarely discussed with regard to calling in the management literature, because management's goal is to promote employee commitment and retention. The practitioner conversation, however, discusses the importance and appropriateness of leaving, as well as other tactics to deal with delayed and denied callings, which I discuss later in this chapter.

The practitioner's emphasis on the moral duty to do mundane work well makes an enormous theoretical contribution. The mundane is not currently part of our theorizing about or measures of calling, but it should be. Practitioners posit that a causal link exists between duty and one's destiny, such that fulfilling one's duty can be a step toward one's destined roles (e.g., Walters and the public relations department). Further, "getting into it" can cultivate skills and traits that are beneficial in a variety of future roles. Indeed, practitioner's insights about duty highlight the obvious inadequacy of Frederick Buechner's often-cited quote about calling being "the place where your deep gladness and the world's deep hunger meet."[43] The truth is you aren't always glad; you can't let duty dictate; and sometimes, you're just grateful for a job and obliged to do it well. In those instances, you don't need job crafting, you need soul crafting to manage the duty and drudgery of calling on a much deeper level.

In fact, practitioners caution against a misguided sense of duty[44] and note that your destiny can be derailed by duty and excessive demands, thereby suggesting yet another causal link. We are neither equipped nor called to meet every need in the world. Fulfilling one's calling requires being reflective, not reflexive, to all of the situations and circumstances that surround us. We needn't feel obliged to continue on a path simply because it is expected or we were educated for it. For example, Walters exited the path to become an actress; introspection helped her recognize that despite her training and family background, it wasn't a good fit and changed course. Similarly, we needn't feel obligated or committed to an organization beyond what is appropriate, because the place is rarely the calling. Smith described it this way: "Rarely is an individual called to make a commitment to a company, a school, a religious organization or a movement that would qualify as a lifelong covenant commitment . . . .We should not be capricious in our commitments. But neither should we overstay when God calls us to move on."[45] As an example, he cited public expectations for Jesus to visit Capernaum; he went to other villages instead: "Jesus did not ignore the needs around him. He was filled with compassion and responded generously as he was able. But he was not derailed from his vocation."[46] Misguided commitments, excessive demands, and an overly developed sense of duty are among the many reasons that people miss or undermine their vocational callings.

Discernment and Missed Messages

The ultimate prerequisite for discerning one's calling is being awake. To be awake means to be fully present in the moment, not only to the transcendent but also to an internal voice that elucidates what delights us and what troubles us, and not only to the "other world" but also to the real world of situations, other people, and our social environment. Practitioners have described the transcendent awakenings of "Jesus, Moses, Muhammad, Zororoaster, and the Buddha, who all sought wilderness experiences to discover major visions."[47] For C. S. Lewis, the wake-up call occurred during an ordinary motorcycle ride. How one interprets, attributes the source of, and responds to the summons depends on their cosmology. The wake-up call may even come through difficulty, as John Neafsey suggests: "We get sick in one way or another when we are living in a way that is out-of-sync with who we really are. At such times, the painful physical or emotional symptoms we experience can be interpreted as a wakeup call, as a kind of cry for help from our soul."[48] It's important to note that although pain can awaken and bring out the best in us, it can also have many negative effects; pain is transformative but may not always be redemptive. Whether we are awakened by a situation, a spiritual experience, or physical or emotional pain, practitioners contend that the ability to discern and interpret those existential nudges requires intrapersonal intelligence and social interactions.

Intrapersonal Understanding

Foremost, discerning one's calling requires retrospection and introspection that increase intrapersonal insight. Walters shows how, retrospectively, it is essential to ponder one's disposition and how one's family of origin, community, and life experiences have influenced the contours of their habitus. *Habitus* is our predisposed ways of being in the world, taken-for-granted beliefs and behaviors, and responsiveness to new information, the environment, and opportunities.[49] The idea that calling is a product of habitus is aligned with Weber's notion that calling is first cultivated in the "home community." Such experiences may constrain or enhance the ability to discern one's trajectory. For example, Walters grew up immersed in entertainment and thought that her calling was to become an actress; she was wrong. It wasn't discernment that led her to acting, but limited early exposure to different alternatives. Nevertheless, it was that same background that enabled her to transition to a different entertainment medium and gracefully interact with celebrities; she had been around them all of her life. Retrospection also reveals insights into early interests and personality traits that may have been forgotten.

Discerning a calling also requires the capacity for introspection—that is, intrapersonal understanding of one's current preferences, strengths, limitations, and issues that are burdensome. Discernment occurs in moments of stillness, attentiveness, listening, and responsiveness, qualities that are usually cultivated in solitude, meditation, or prayer.[50] During moments of reflection and introspection, one can perceive new possibilities and envision new prospects for the future and the potential for new or different kinds of social experiences.

Social Awareness and Influences

Social awareness and influence are highly instrumental in the discovery, formation, maturation, and calibration of one's calling. More specifically, since calling is putatively about contributing to society and making the world a better place, ideally its evolution is guided by an awareness of and responsiveness to the social world. It stands to reason, then, that someone with a calling is actually socially aware and responsive. (But research to date has not examined that assertion.) Neafsey suggests that social discernment involves analysis, a sort of practical wisdom, which results from critically reflecting on the world in which one lives and one's place in it—that is, where we fit in the "web of economic, political and cultural systems"[51] and whether we are advantaged or disadvantaged, a resource for others or in need of resources. Such examination helps us to discern what responsibilities might be morally and tactically best for us to assume. A socially aware calling requires us to observe, judge, and act in accordance not only with social needs, but also with our abilities and responsibilities.

The social world also influences our ability to listen and detect the calling for our lives. Toward those ends, practitioners stress the importance of community in discerning one's calling, whether to obtain feedback, guidance, and mentoring or by providing unexpected opportunities or other forms of help. As an example, Neafsey described the ritual of "vision quest," which is part of the Native American Lakota culture, during which people seek a vision or dream for their life:

> The word for the vision quest ritual is *hanblecheya*, which translates into English as "crying for a vision" or lamenting for a dream: The "crying" or "lamenting" suggests that visions do not come easily. The vision must be earned by a humble person with a sincere heart through the ordeal of fasting and suffering. The seeker must recognize his or her need for help and direction and guidance from a power beyond the self.[52]

Palmer also described a need for connection, which is congruent with spiritual well-being described in Chapter 3—connection to oneself, others, God, and the universe.

Social forces can nudge us to fit in, climb the ladder, meet family expectations, or conform to other people's timing and expectations. In fact, although other people can help with discernment, they can also be an impediment. Manipulative, unsupportive and self-interested others[53] highlight the fact that callings are both socially constructed and destructed.

Impediments to Discernment

Given the need for reflection, being distracted or dazed are the foremost impediments to discerning one's calling. Even more than the individualistic 1980s, the 21st-century's distractions of hyperconnected work and personal lives, a media culture that glorifies sensation rather than substance,[54] and the pride of busyness[55] and excessive demands all threaten the utter extinction of calling—except for those who can disconnect and set their own pace.

At the other end of the continuum are somnambulants[56]—people who sleepwalk through life like dazed zombies. I contend that there are at least two kinds of somnambulants. The first type includes people whose perceptions are dulled by mindless routines, soul deadening and alienating labor, psychological or spiritual trauma, or substance abuse. The second type of sleepwalker includes people who are amoral zombies, oblivious to their lack of moral development or conscience. For the former, there is job crafting and counseling; for the latter, Gardner and his colleagues suggest the universal mirror test: "What would it be like to live in a world if everyone were to behave in the way that I have?"[57]

Myriad other factors hinder the discernment and fulfillment of one's calling as well. As examples, Levoy mentioned that messages are missed due to overanalyzing the call, waiting for the perfect moment, being unwilling to make adjustments needed to follow through, self-sabotage, lowered expectations, and fear of failure. To these reasons, Smith added workaholism, not resting, and the deification of work. Furey added shame, abandonment, ignorance, greed, need for control, intellectualizing, and refusing to believe. Levoy summarized impediments this way: "Sometimes, it isn't even that we consciously *say* no to our calls but that we're stuck in a position of negating ourselves. Our calls are just swallowed up in the same black hole as all our soul's other petitions. The very self that receives calls is injured, fouled with surrender, lamed by the injured souls who raised us and their poor estimation of themselves."[58]

Finally, a person may stand in their own way and resist the summons, as biblical figures Jonah and Moses did. Thus, while many impediments to calling are social and situational, some individuals may miss or delay their calling due to perceived limitations, lack of confidence, and defiance.

In sum, numerous individual, social, situational, and cultural factors may interfere with the ability to discern one's calling, leading to inertia or destruction. But calling is always a summons to generativity, creation, contribution, and renewal. Whether distracted, dazed, or defiant, many people must first be awakened before they can perceive or pursue their calling. While awakening may require intervention; overcoming impediments and advancing will require a certain disposition.

Disposition: An Added Dimension of Calling

Practitioners, management scholars and Max Weber frequently refer to calling as a disposition or way of working. However, practitioners go further by explaining the "way" as a blend of character and coping skills. Together, character and coping foster the goodness, generativity and renewal that are inherent in a calling; they enable its ascent and prevent its decline.

Character

In their groundbreaking handbook, *Character Strengths and Virtues*,[59] positive psychologists Chris Peterson and Martin Seligman described 6 virtues and 24 character strengths that are essential for a "good life" and to solve life problems. The virtues are (1) knowledge and wisdom, (2) courage, (3) humanity, (4) justice, (5) temperance, and (6) transcendence. The 24 character strengths that constitute these virtues are listed in Table 6.1. The authors acknowledged that the list is not exhaustive but provides a broad foundation for empirical research.

Table 6.1 Contrasts in Character Traits

Virtues and Character Strengths	*Undesirable Opposites*
Wisdom and Knowledge: Cognitive strengths that entail acquiring and using knowledge such as creativity, curiosity, open-mindedness, love of learning, perspective/wise counsel.	Dull, boring, insipid, monotonous, unimaginative, and uninspired; disinterest, ennui, world-weary; inflexibility, rigidity, dogmatic, prejudiced, intolerant, ethnocentrism, authoritarianism, stereotypes;intellectual resistance and inertia, foolishness, thoughtlessness, idiocy
Courage: Strength to exercise will to accomplish goals in the face of opposition, internal or external. Honesty, bravery, persistence, integrity, vitality.	Cowardice, spinelessness, laziness, sloth, giving up, not trying, losing heart, losing interest, taking shortcuts, cutting corners, gong for the quick fix and vacillation, deceitfulness, lying, insincerity, phoniness, pretentiousness, and falseness; sluggish, depressed, subdued, dull, jaded, listless, limp, lethargic, and lifeless
Humanity: Interpersonal strengths that involve tending and befriending others such as kindness, love, social intelligence, + empathy	Alienation, estrangement and loneliness, hatred, loathing, spite and abhorrence; clueless, self-deceived, lacking insight, stereotyping; selfishness, stinginess, mean-spiritedness
Justice: Civic strengths that underlie healthy community life, including citizenship, fairness, leadership, + teamwork	Selfishness, self-centered, egotism; prejudice, caprice, bias, poorly guides, neglects tasks, + abdicate responsibilities
Temperance: Strengths that protect against excess, including forgiveness and mercy, humility/modesty, prudence, self-control	Unforgiving, spiteful, punitive, vengeful, merciless, and hard-hearted; arrogance, pride, pomposity, grandiosity and self-centeredness; recklessness, foolishness, thoughtlessness and irresponsibility; undisciplined, out of control, impulsive, explosive, wild, raging; a root of all emotional disorders
Transcendence: Strengths that forge a connection to the larger universe and provide meaning. This includes appreciating beauty and excellence, hope, gratitude, humor, faith/spirituality	Oblivious, unmoved, unmindful, philistine, ignorant, or insensible. Crude, coarse, prosaic, clichéd, shallow, uncultured, trivial; pessimism, hopelessness, gloom, helplessness; humorless, grim, sour, dour, tedious or boring; spiritually empty, godless, profane, life of quiet desperation, fidgeting until death, anomie, alienation; entitled, rude, ungrateful, unappreciative, unthankful

Source: Material is derived from Christopher Peterson and Martin E. P. Seligman, *Character Strengths and Virtues: A Handbook and Classification* (New York: Oxford University Press, 2004), 29–30, ff. (*Note:* + denotes a strength that I've added.)

Several features of character strengths are noteworthy. First, they may be "tonic" (constant) or "phasic" (they wax and wane), which means they typically vary across situations and over time. These strengths can be examined, therefore, across life roles and throughout the life span. Second, through exhaustive research, Peterson and Seligman found that these traits are common across many cultures, as well as Eastern and Western religious traditions. Their insights reveal yet another way that calling can be a cross-cultural construct that is not limited to adherents of a particular religious faith or any faith. Third, unlike a perceived destiny, everyone can aspire to achieve character strengths, even if they can't achieve their career aspirations or other desired roles. Character strengths ennoble the work of being human rather than work in a specific job or profession. This perspective is congruent with the democratic ideal of calling—everyone can have one. Lastly, Peterson and Seligman described the "nonfelicitous opposites" to acknowledge undesirable character traits and vices. I have juxtaposed strengths and their opposites in Table 6.1.

Given the potential for distortion and lapses in character, standards are needed against which one can examine and recalibrate their motivations—a collective cosmology. Peterson and Seligman described several collective cosmologies that influence character development: "Our common sense tells us that enabling conditions include educational and vocational opportunities, a supportive and consistent family, safe neighborhoods and schools, political stability and (perhaps) democracy. The existence of mentors, role models, and supportive peers—inside or outside the immediate family—are probably also enabling conditions."[60] Lessons about character strengths and vices may also be embodied in and disseminated through collective "stories, parables, creeds, mottoes, pledges, songs, and poems that feature people who compellingly demonstrate a given positive trait."[61] (These dissemination mechanisms are described more in Chapters 7 and 9.) The breadth of potential influences on character reveals the socially constructed nature of calling and suggests that it may be cultivated in ways that are not solely dependent on religious institutions and their doctrines, although it may be.

Practitioners have identified select character strengths that they believe are essential to advance in one's calling, although they did not use the specific term *character strengths*. The general consensus seems to be that courage is the most essential character strength. In his book, *Courage and Calling*, George Smith listed others as well, including the quest for excellence, generosity, truth, honesty, diligence, discipline, focus, good judgment, and the willingness to take risks. Conversely, conformity, timidity, inflexibility, and hubris undermine fulfilling a calling. As a caution, Smith also noted the shadowy side of strengths and how they can become distorted: "The pursuit of excellence can become perfectionism, the pursuit of truth bigotry, diligence nothing more than hectic activity and even generosity can be misguided."[62] Thus, while character strengths, and perhaps even vices, foster the progression of a calling, it is not without requisite coping skills.

Coping Skills

Psychologists Richard Lazarus and Susan Folkman defined coping as "constantly changing cognitive and behavioral efforts to manage specific external and/or internal demands that are appraised as taxing or exceeding the resources of the person."[63] Coping is a process by which individuals reappraise situations and then draw on internal, external, social, or transcendent resources[64] such as experience, social support, material resources, or practices such as prayer to manage a challenging situation. Thus, coping activities may focus on the problem, emotions, or both.

Coping skills are learned as a result of individual experiences and social interactions. Hence, coping may be an individual or collective (e.g., subcultural group) strategy that people use to meet situational demands.[65] Those experiences and interactions may expand one's repertoire of coping skills and result in greater adaptability over time. However, inflexibility can result in maladaptive coping.[66] Our repertoire of coping skills and how we use them determines whether we will have a productive response to uncertainty, difficulties, suffering, sacrifice, and disappointments, as well as denied and delayed callings.

Levoy described circumstances that can result in delayed or denied callings: "poverty, imprisonment, disease or disability, being responsible for children and aged parents, geographical isolation, lack of any education or any talent—are very real obstacles and exceptionally difficult to surmount."[67] Like management scholars, practitioners have described social inequality and discrimination as impediments to a calling, but in greater detail. According to Neafsey,

> Various forms of discrimination also painfully complicate the vocational picture for people who are "different" in one way or another because of their race, social class, religion, ethnicity, gender, sexual orientation, or any other category of difference that may affect their chances in life. Many people are denied the right or opportunity to pursue their callings and fulfill their God-given potential simply because they are different, i.e., they are the "wrong" skin color or religion, or poor, or members of an unpopular ethnic group, or women, or gay, or whatever. The frustrated callings and deferred dreams that result from such discrimination are the cause of widespread emotional and social misery.[68]

Not to mention lost contributions to society.

Job crafting, quitting, and taking a personal stand based on conscience have been proposed as tactics to cope with denied and delayed callings. With these coping skills, however, responsibility for change rests completely on the individual. Furthermore, those tactics do not ameliorate the real human toll against one's soul that results in depression, despair, and worse. So, while job crafting, quitting, and taking a stand may be effective in the short term, the crucial question is this: then what? These tactics do little to address the root cause of delayed and denied callings or the role that organizations and their leaders play in producing those impediments.

To address root causes, Howard Gardner and his colleagues recommended collective and structural actions as tactics to cope with conditions that do not enable an individual to pursue or fulfill their calling in an ethical or psychologically safe environment. They advocate for creating new institutions, adding new functions to existing institutions, reconfiguring membership, and reaffirming the values of existing institutions.[69] These empowering suggestions greatly expand the repertoire of possible actions that one may take to pursue a calling. Not only do these strategies dictate the need for a social response to unfavorable conditions, but they might also be the seeds of social change. Institutional and collective actions that foster calling will require a great deal of courage, wisdom, creativity, and leadership. I provide a case example of such collective coping in the next chapter.

In summary, the combination of character and coping constitute a third, new dimension of calling. Together, those attributes are instrumental in managing the quantum nature of calling; they facilitate and determine the quality of life transitions and one's trajectory. Character is the missing dimension that transforms the idea of moral duty into the right actions that can result in good work. For example, we need perseverance to fulfill moral duty, grace and humility to accept personal limitations, courage to take risks and change course, wisdom to know how and when to pause or proceed, creativity to excel, and fortitude to overcome character deficits. Whereas coping skills enable one to manage the vicissitudes of a calling such as eustress related to progress, distress from setbacks, and gain equilibrium in the midst of solution finding. Character deficits and maladaptive coping can and do forestall or undermine a calling. Conversely, character, strengths, and coping energize each step up and help us persist in the climb. They constitute the disposition or way of working that, heretofore, was a missing yet essential element of calling.

The Essential Core of Calling

The practitioner conversation reveals that calling is in fact a system composed of three core dimensions—destiny, duty, and now disposition, as illustrated in Figure 6.1. Interlocking circles denote that destiny, duty,

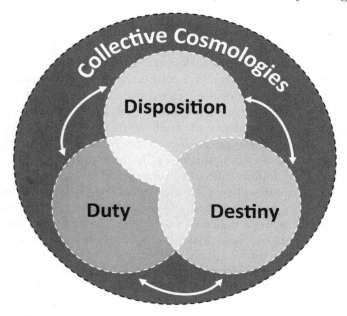

Figure 6.1 The interdependent core elements of calling: Cosmologies that influence duty, destiny, and disposition.

and disposition are also interdependent. The bidirectional arrows denote causal relationships among the elements; the following examples clarify the relationships. Regarding duty and destiny, ideally one satisfies subjective or ethical standards of work and objective standards of excellence in order to advance toward their destiny (as opposed to advancing merely in political, hypercompetitive, or unethical ways). When best efforts do not result in a high quality outcome or show continued improvement, the role is likely a duty, but not your destiny, due to suboptimal fit. Regarding disposition and duty, one's character strengths, deficits, and coping skills link personality and collective standards to actions—in other words, one's individual will and capacity to fulfill their duty. Regarding disposition and destiny, a person's character shapes and is shaped by chosen roles. Similarly, chosen roles can heighten or undermine one's sense of duty depending on contextual and social factors. In sum, a person may discover their destiny to fulfill different roles by performing duties, demonstrating character strengths and coping with different situations. Conversely, work in various roles might cultivate character strengths, heighten moral awareness and add to one's repertoire of coping skills.

Each core dimension of calling is therefore individually and socially constructed. These dimensions are the product of personality and social influences from nurturing and moral communities that: (1) identify, affirm, and cultivate gifts and interests (destiny); (2) define obligations and the value of excellence (duty); and (3) reinforce virtuous behaviors and teach adaptation strategies (disposition). In the early years, those communities include family, neighborhood, religious organizations, schools, and peer networks—all of which define the contours of one's habitus. Thus, destiny, duty, and disposition are analogous to a habitus that is, specifically related to calling and cultivated in one's "home community."

The home community influences habitus and calling through formal and informal education by which socially constructed cosmologies are disseminated among members of a sociocultural group. Fundamentally, a cosmology provides a coherent worldview. It imputes meaning, provides a framework for sense making, defines relational and behavioral norms, defines worthwhile goals, and suggests schemas and strategies for coping with uncertainty, loss, crisis, and surprise. Most importantly, a cosmology provides coherence across the arc of one's life. Figure 6.1 depicts the way in which core dimensions of calling are embedded in, cultivated in, and informed by cosmologies of the home community.

Cosmologies are acquired from the home community from youth through young adulthood—for better or worse. The substance of cosmologies may be conveyed through stories, songs, personal narratives, icons, rituals, and informal interactions. Since those mediums are germane to religious, cultural, and educational institutions, they are uniquely suited to disseminate cosmological messages about calling. Moreover, because participation in such institutions is voluntary, members might be more receptive to their messages.

Ideally, the multiple cosmologies of one's home community are mutually reinforcing and communicate similar positive messages about calling. Hence, an individual has multiple opportunities to cultivate core dimensions of their calling in contexts that are exogenous to the workplace. Practitioner's insights lead us to conclude, therefore, that while workplace cosmologies (e.g., professional and organizational norms) may reinforce, expand, or undermine the foundational cosmologies of one's calling, they are not the primary source.

Advancing the Discourse

Practitioners have injected a much-needed dose of realism into modern conversations about calling by seeking to understand it rather than measure it. In doing so, they have greatly expanded notions of what it means to have a calling from a management perspective, both theoretically and practically.

Theoretically, practitioner insights about disposition as a core dimension of calling are a major contribution. Disposition is the spirit that animates the work; it offers insights into catalytic forces that drive the fulfillment of destiny and duty and the causal relationships among them. Until now, no causal relationship has been proposed. Hence, calling is far less deterministic than destiny and more a matter of integration among three core dimensions. Therefore, any attempts to measure calling must include measures of character and coping.

The addition of disposition makes previously implicit assumptions about calling explicit.

- The inherently secular elements of disposition are universal constructs that reveal *how* calling can be applied across cultures and ideologies.
- Because of the socially constructed nature of character and coping skills, it becomes easier to see the role that traditional institutions played in the cultivation of calling—it is not an individualistic phenomenon.
- Tonic and phasic qualities of character and the iterative development of coping skills helps us understand *how* calling is manifest and changes across life roles and the life span.
- A clearer understanding of the meaning of sacred and sanctification helps us understand *why* a transcendent calling may be secular, spiritual, or sacred—it depends on one's guiding cosmologies.
- Not all cosmologies serve a calling. Rather than asking if religion influences calling, researchers might inquire about positive and negative cosmologies that have influenced character, coping, a sense of destiny, and duty. That would provide insights about necessary educational interventions.

By now it should be obvious that character strengths and coping skills enhance a worker's calling in ways that benefit organizations, society, and expanded capitalism. They make a woefully diluted calling (Chapter 2) more robust and relevant, particularly given ethical challenges in modern organizations. Therefore, there is no compelling theoretical or practical reason for continuing to omit them in research.

In fact, Claudia Harzer and Willibald Ruch[70] studied the number of character strengths that predict positive experiences at work and found that calling and positive experiences were greater when respondents reported four character strengths. Insights from the practitioner conversation indicate that a more fruitful path might be to measure specific character strengths to assess factors that inhibit or enhance fulfilling one's calling, particularly courage.

In addition, no research, to my knowledge, has measured various coping skills beyond job crafting, even though practitioners recommend a more expansive repertoire that includes social action and institutional activism to create the conditions for "good work." To this, I would add entrepreneurship, since it is a path that people might pursue when they leave work that goes against the grain.

Practically speaking, disposition restores the democracy and dignity of calling, making it attainable and ennobling for all, not just a fortunate few who have the material and social resources to pursue their destiny. Everyone can aspire to strengthen their character. Moreover, as we cope with challenges in adaptive ways, it can further refine our character, cultivate new skills, and possibly elicit new commitments that, in turn, become destiny. Thus even drudgery has merit in the grand scheme of a calling. In this way, practitioners have tempered the inordinate focus on specialization as fit and directed us toward specialization as careful methods and ways of working. This is important because, as Barbara Walters's opening quote suggests, many people may have no inkling about their ideal occupation, but they can still live their calling through their disposition and duty. Rather than focusing keenly on purpose, fit, and destiny, it may be more important for people to experience calling as being purposive, idealistic, true to one's inner nature in whatever roles, and trusting that destiny will unfold as it should. As Walters's and Lewis's lives suggest, destiny is perhaps best understood retrospectively. Thus, today's task is not to fit or find it, but to focus on the way we engage the tasks before us.

A practical concern revealed in this chapter is the problem of discerning one's calling and the conditions that are needed to nurture it or that impede it. "Rich lives include continuing internal conversations about who we are, what we want to achieve, where we are successful, and where we are falling short."[71] Thus, discerning and responding to a transcendent summons requires continuously reflecting and recalibrating one's disposition (and duties) in real time. However, being dazed, distracted, increased individualism, and weakened traditional institutions have made it more difficult, not only to discern a calling but also to cultivate its requisite character strengths. Messages from traditional institutions about virtues and character strengths have been eclipsed by irrelevant messages from the popular culture, mass media, and perhaps social networks.[72] That cultural noise, hyperconnectivity, and the dumbing down of mass media threaten to further erode calling—as much as, or even more than, individualism.

From the 19th to the 20th century, we have seen a major shift in traits that are considered culturally valuable, with a strong trend away from character and toward "personality." In her book *Quiet: The Power of Introverts in a World that Can't Stop Talking*,[73] Susan Cain's research revealed that popular manuals of the 19th century promoted cultivating citizenship, duty, work, golden deeds, honor, reputation, morals, manners, and integrity; these readily accessible traits were culturally valued. But with Dale Carnegie's[74] 20th-century advice on winning friends and influence, however, more elusive qualities such as being magnetic, fascinating, stunning, attractive, glowing, dominant, forceful, and energetic became culturally valued. Furthermore, in the West, where extroversion is highly valued, such traits are expressed at an increasingly high volume. Reality television, for example, absolutely shouts forceful and fascinating—in a train wreck sort of way! Calling is not anti personality, but it is pro character.

Those shifts lead me to wonder what traits will be of highest cultural value in the 21st century and what that portends for calling? Will the highest cultural values include the hyperfocus on "quantitative bigness," winning and counting that Weber feared? Will friendship be measured quantitatively by the number of one's Facebook friends and other electronic connections? Will the spread of tweets become the metric for influence, above transcendent ideals? If that is the case, what is culturally valued will erode rather than enrich one's calling.[75] In this digital age, it may be wise to heed Albert Einstein, who said, "Not everything that counts can be counted and not everything that can be counted counts."

Interestingly, practitioner perspectives espoused throughout this chapter were written during the same era that management scholarship about calling gained momentum. Despite being embedded in the same cultural context, those enclaves arrived at very different conclusions about calling. Many practitioners have retained Weber's core ideas, even though most don't cite him; management scholars cite Weber but dismiss his core claims. Nevertheless, insights from practitioners suggest that emerging conversations in management, particularly the transcendent and sacred conversations about calling, deserve a more prominent platform. Only by examining other practitioner perspectives, which I do in Chapter 8, and comparing them all to theological perspectives can that assessment be made.

In the next chapter, I provide a case example of people trying to live their callings under extraordinary circumstances, as well as how destiny, disposition, and duty interrelated and were informed by collective cosmologies. In Chapter 8, I suggest ways in which leaders and organizations can create the conditions for such individuals to flourish.

NOTES

1. Mark R. Schwehn and Dorothy C. Bass, eds., *Can I Control What I Shall Do and Become: Leading Lives That Matter: What We Should Do and Who We Should Be* (Grand Rapids, MI: W. B. Eerdmans, 2006).
2. John Neafsey, *A Sacred Voice Is Calling: Personal Vocation and Social Conscience* (Maryknoll, NY: Orbis Books, 2006); Robert J. Furey, *Called by Name: Discovering Your Unique Purpose in Life* (New York: Crossroad, 1996).
3. I have included management consultant/scholars in the section because, in addition to research, their applied work connects them with a population beyond the classroom, through consulting and popular books.
4. Barbara Walters, *Audition: A Memoir*, Kindle edition (Random House, 2008).
5. Ibid., 4433–37.
6. Ibid., 1154
7. Ibid., 1265–66.
8. Ibid., 1769–75.
9. Ibid., 11257–60.
10. Furey, *Called by Name*.
11. C. S. Lewis, *Surprised by Joy: The Shape of My Early Life* (Orlando, FL: Harcourt, Brace, Jovanovich, 1955).
12. P. J. Palmer, *Let Your Life Speak: Listening to the Voice of Vocation* (San Francisco: Jossey-Bass, 2000), 18.
13. Paul R. Stevens, *The Other Six Days: Vocation, Work, and Ministry in Biblical Perspective* (Grand Rapids, MI: Wm. B. Eerdmans Publishing Company, 2000), 74.
14. Gordon T. Smith, *Courage and Calling: Embracing Your God-Given Potential* (Downers Grove, IL: InterVarsity Press, 2011), 45.
15. Furey, *Called by Name*.
16. Smith, *Courage and Calling*; Travis Collins, *Directionally Challenged: How to Find and Follow God's Course for Your Life* (Birmingham, AL: New Hope Publishers, 2007).
17. Neafsey, *A Sacred Voice Is Calling*, xi.
18. Furey, *Called by Name*.
19. Richard J. Shapiro and David A. Leider, *Whistle While You Work: Heeding Your Life's Calling* (Williston, VT: Berrett-Koehler Publishers, 2001); Jane A. G. Kise, David Stark, and Sandra Krebs Hirsh, *Lifekeys: Discover Who You Are* (Minneapolis, MN: Betheny House, 2005); Kevin Brennfleck and Kay Marie Brennfleck, *Live Your Calling: A Practical Guide to Finding and Fulfilling Your Mission in Life* (San Francisco, CA: Jossey Bass, 2005).
20. Stevens, *The Other Six Days*.
21. Smith, *Courage and Calling*.
22. Furey, *Called by Name*.
23. Palmer, *Let Your Life Speak*, 4.
24. Shapiro and Leider, *Whistle While You Work*.
25. Po Bronson, "What Should I Do with My Life, Now?" *FastCompany* (2009), http://www.fastcompany.com/1130055/what-should-i-do-my-life-now.
26. Donald E. Super, "A Life-Span, Life-Space Approach to Career Development," *Journal of Vocational Behavior* 16, no. 3 (1980): 282–98.
27. Neafsey, *A Sacred Voice Is Calling*.
28. Palmer, *Let Your Life Speak*; Smith, *Courage and Calling*; Gregg Michael Levoy, *Callings: Finding and Following an Authentic Life* (New York: Three Rivers Press, 1997); Furey, *Called by Name*.

29. Neafsey, *A Sacred Voice Is Calling*.
30. Shapiro and Leider, *Whistle While You Work*.
31. Ibid.
32. J. W. Weiss, M. F. Skelley, J. C. Haughey, and D. T. Hall, "Callings, New Careers and Spirituality: A Reflective Perspective for Organizational Leaders and Professionals," *Research in Ethical Issues in Organizations* 5 (2004): 175–201.
33. Smith, *Courage and Calling*; Furey, *Called by Name*; Neafsey, *A Sacred Voice Is Calling*.
34. Smith, *Courage and Calling*, 50.
35. Levoy, *Callings*, 278.
36. Bronson, "What Should I Do with My Life, Now?"; Joanne B. Ciulla, *The Working Life: The Promise and Betrayal of Modern Work* (New York: Times Books, 2000).
37. Smith, *Courage and Calling*, 43.
38. Levoy, *Callings*, 278; David Frankel, dir., *The Devil Wears Prada* (Beverly Hills, CA: 20th Century Fox, 2006).
39. Frankel, *The Devil Wears Prada*.
40. Levoy, *Callings*, 278.
41. Max Weber, *The Protestant Ethic and the Spirit of Capitalism* (London: Routledge, 1904/1992), 62.
42. Jiddu Krishnamurti (1895–1986) was an Indian theosophist philosopher who wrote *The Future of Humanity: Songs of Life, Kingdom Happiness*. This is likely (although not certain) from one of his "Talks in Europe, 1967." These were recorded interviews that I found at http://www.jkrishnamurti.org.
43. John L. Holland, *The Self-Directed Search* (Palo Alto, CA: Consulting Psychologist Press, 1970); Palmer, *Let Your Life Speak*.
44. Smith, *Courage and Calling*.
45. Ibid., 139.
46. Ibid., 76.
47. Furey, *Called by Name*, 145.
48. Neafsey, *A Sacred Voice Is Calling*, 112.
49. Edward K. Strong, *Vocational Interests of Men and Women* (Stanford, CA: Stanford University Press, 1943), 112; Paul Sweetman, "Twenty-First Century Dis-Ease? Habitual Reflexivity or the Reflexive Habitus," *The Sociological Review* 51, no. 4 (2003): 528–49; Pierre Bourdieu, *Distinction: A Social Critique of the Judgement of Taste* (London: Routledge, 1984).
50. Furey, *Called by Name*; Palmer, *Let Your Life Speak*; Smith, *Courage and Calling*.
51. Neafsey, *A Sacred Voice Is Calling*, 49.
52. Ibid., 91.
53. Howard Gardner, Mihaly Csikszentmihalyi, and William Damon, *Good Work: When Excellence and Ethics Meet* (New York: Basic Books, 2001).
54. Tim Kreider, "The 'Busy' Trap," *New York Times*, June 30, 2012.
55. Shapiro and Leider, *Whistle While You Work*.
56. Gardner, Csikszentmihalyi, and Damon, *Good Work*, 12.
57. Shapiro and Leider, *Whistle While You Work*; Smith, *Courage and Calling*; Levoy, *Callings*.
58. Levoy, *Callings*, 223.
59. Christopher Peterson and Martin E. P. Seligman, *Character Strengths and Virtues: A Handbook and Classification* (New York: Oxford University Press, 2004).
60. Ibid., 11.
61. Ibid., 24.

62. Smith, *Courage and Calling*, 111.
63. Richard S. Lazarus and Susan Folkman, *Stress, Appraisal, and Coping*, Kindle edition (New York: Springer, 2010).
64. Kenneth I. Pargament, *The Psychology of Religion and Coping: Theory, Research, Practice* (New York: Guilford Press, 1997).
65. Lazarus and Folkman, *Stress, Appraisal, and Coping*.
66. Albert K. Cohen, "A General Theory of Subcultures [1955]," in *Subcultures Reader*, ed. Ken Gelder and Sarah Thornton, 44–54 (New York: Routledge, 1997).
67. Levoy, *Callings*, 207.
68. Neafsey, *A Sacred Voice Is Calling*, 49.
69. Gardner, Csikszentmihalyi, and Damon, *Good Work*.
70. Claudia Harzer and Willibald Ruch, "When the Job Is a Calling: The Role of Applying One's Signature Strengths at Work," *The Journal of Positive Psychology* 7, no. 5 (2012): 362–71.
71. Susan Cain, *Quiet: The Power of Introverts in a World That Can't Stop Talking* (New York: Crown-Random House, 2012).
72. Gardner, Csikszentmihalyi, and Damon, *Good Work*.
73. Cain, *Quiet*.
74. Dale Carnegie, *How to Win Friends and Influence People* (New York: Simon and Schuster, 1936).
75. By this, I do not mean that technology should be avoided. Especially in the process of writing this book, I've come to appreciate how the digital age may facilitate living one's calling in new, exciting, and more effective ways. However, hyper-connectivity does pose a threat to reflection and meaningful dialogue that is essential to cultivating a calling.

7

Case Example: Unthinkable

In his book *The Age of the Unthinkable*,[1] Joshua Cooper Ramo described the increasing likelihood of unpredictable events in the 21st century and the need for tools to adapt to them: airplane terrorism of office buildings was *unthinkable*; near collapse of the global financial system was *unthinkable*; landing a disabled airplane on the Hudson·River was *unthinkable*; rapid economic expansion of Brazil, Russia, India, China, and South Africa was *unthinkable*; and inventions such as the iPod and iPad were *unthinkable* just over a decade ago. When the unthinkable occurs, we need tools to manage, make sense of, and adapt to life-altering existential events,[2] particularly when it comes to living one's calling.

Throughout one's life, many unthinkable events can occur that influence the ability or opportunity to live one's calling. For Barbara Walters, the unthinkable was her sister's disability, her family's financial vicissitudes, and her own experiences with career uncertainty. Indeed, she grasped an opportunity that led to an unthinkable career marked by sexual harassment, gender discrimination, professional animus, as well as unparalleled longevity, success, and influence. For C. S. Lewis, the unthinkable was the death of his mother and resulting crisis of faith. For others, it may be unemployment, underemployment, dislocation due to plants closing, financial hardship, betrayal by colleagues, being passed over for a promotion, a health crisis, or a shocking corporate scandal that ripples throughout an industry or the economy. But there is nothing more unthinkable in the history of work than the enslavement of Africans throughout Europe, the Caribbean, and the United States of America, or the unthinkable two-time election of an African American to the highest job in the land—President Barack Obama.

An overlooked resource to manage the unthinkable and to understand the relationship between cosmology and calling is the history and culture of African Americans. It is not just a history of trauma and tragedy; it is a story of positive organizing, culturally specific sense making, extraordinary creativity, and coping that resulted in posttraumatic growth (PTG) that advanced the callings of millions! The African American narrative of faith at work, now centuries old, illustrates how collective cosmologies are foundational in cultivating destiny, duty, and disposition across life roles, the life span, and generations. It also shows how collective soul crafting in response to denied callings can lead to extraordinarily positive organizational and social change.

Historical Background

The sociopolitical environment of denigration and segregation led African Americans to create their own institutions to sustain social life. The first antebellum institution that African Americans created was the Black church. However, it functioned as a multipurpose institution that influenced every sphere of life including family, economic, civic, social, educational, health, social welfare, arts, entertainment, and most notably political activisim.[3] By necessity, work was a primary concern. From the church, other institutions emerged and developed programs to support those life domains.[4] These institutions achieved remarkably positive outcomes with the support of a cultural cosmology that was widely disbursed, powerfully reinforced, and that emphasized faith, perseverance, excellence, duty, and above all, justice.

A recent national study, *Faith Communities Today*, showed that black churches across the country still have a portfolio of programs that reflect their historic roots, focusing on spiritual growth, education, artistic expression, economic development, developing youth, parents, and families, and political activism.[5] Thus, although it has changed some with time, this institution's foundational cosmology of faith, work, and the hope of living a calling in the new world has guided a community for generations.

Before I provide examples of the African American cosmology of faith and work, it is important to clarify several points. First, African Americans are not a monolithic group. However, shared experiences that resulted from slavery and segregation created some common cultural understandings and beliefs about the role of religious organizations, work, and ideas in community life, but not everyone in the community holds those same views. Furthermore, there are subcultures within African American culture that adapted the cosmology to their circumstances, for example, by education level and occupation. The specific role of faith in shaping one's habitus also differed by denomination, regional community, and congregation.[6] Nevertheless, the rich cultural history is a resource to gain insights about a cosmology that was diffused and adopted nationally.

Second, functions that the Black church served in the community parallel that of other religious and community organizations in diverse ethnic communities. While my focus is on the Black church, because it is very well documented and one with which I am familiar, insights about cosmology, community, organizations, and calling are relevant to other cultures and community organizations. For example, other cultures that have multifunctional institutions at the heart of their community may identify parallel organizing principles or opportunities. In addition, even when a central organization is not multi-institutional in nature, this example highlights the importance of common and reinforcing cosmologies across an institutional landscape. Toward that end, this example may reveal leverage points and possibilities for organizational partnerships.

Third, even though I use the experience of African Americans to contemplate the intersection of trauma, spirituality, and posttraumatic growth in pursuing one's calling, I am by no means suggesting that everyone who encounters trauma will grow, nor that trauma should be inflicted to promote growth. Society, organizations, and their agents are morally obligated to create safe and humane working and living conditions; I explore the calling of leaders and organizations in Chapters 8 and 9. Fully exploring traumatic historical events is beyond the scope of this chapter. Instead, I take an appreciative approach to show how a cosmology provided the foundation for living callings that lead to extraordinary and surprising results.

My goal here is to illustrate how a shared cosmology yielded astoundingly positive individual and collective outcomes (for some), relative to living one's calling against horrific odds. The following historical vignettes of notable African Americans yield theoretic insights into neglected topics in management. They illustrate the transformational power of a cosmology that is reinforced by various nonwork institutions in ways that enabled people to manage the *unthinkable*, cope with delayed and denied aspirations, and excel. I use these vignettes to illustrate (1) the role of song in a culturally constructed and socially distributed cosmology that anchors a calling; (2) the importance of defining one's own destiny and the confluence of cosmology and good work to achieve it; (3) higher education as a cosmology carrier that simultaneously builds character, communicates duty, and cultivates an array of tactical, professional and psychological skills; and (4) song as a job-crafting and soul-crafting tool that enables one to fulfill work duties and cope with drudgery.

How I Got Over

"How I got over, how I got over my Lord, my soul looks back and wonders how I got over."

—Clara Ward, 1951

"How I Got Over" is a gospel song that was composed and recorded by Clara Ward and the Ward Singers of Philadelphia, "one of the most famous and influential groups of what is considered the golden age of gospel singing."[7] The title and lyrics are illustrative of the historic role of spiritual songs in the collective cosmology of African Americans that were enslaved in the United States, as well as their descendants, the community, and those who escaped or avoided slavery.[8]

The Ward Singers traveled around the world and across the United States, including the racially segregated South; one of those trips inspired Clara Ward to write "How I Got Over." En route to work in Atlanta, in 1951, a group of white men in a pickup truck blocked the road and surrounded their Cadillac; the men were suspicious and incredulous that black women traveled in such luxury. Racial taunts and threats ensued. During that era, it was common for such encounters to result in the murder of African Americans. A terrified but determined Mother Ward "got a desperately brilliant inspiration and proceeded to put it into action."[9] She slumped down, feigned demon possession, and shouted curses at the men, which scared them away. *That* is one example of how they got over: problem-focused coping[10] and improvisation. The song is also a reminder of the importance of retrospection and sense making[11] along one's journey. "How I Got Over" became such a cultural icon that Mahalia Jackson sang it at the 1963 Civil Rights march on Washington, D.C.[12] Fifty years later, it is still performed by contemporary gospel artists. "How I Got Over" is one of hundreds of songs that convey an African American cosmology of agency, reflection, and hope in a hostile environment.

Songs were often the mechanism for diffusing the collective cosmology; core themes were adapted by and reinforced through education in traditional institutions (e.g., family, churches, schools, and universities). Recent empirical research now reveals the processes by which this cultural cosmology may have promoted both psychological success and existential success.[13] African American spirituals likely promoted short cycles of learning, coping, and adaptation.[14] More specifically, lyrical content conveyed a cosmology that defined destiny, duty, and disposition counterculturally rather than promote acceptance of the status quo, socially prescribed identities and roles. Further, communal singing provided a form of social support.[15] Thus, lyrical content, communal singing, and broad diffusion of core themes throughout the community were likely a catalyst for collective PTG.

According to the *Handbook of Posttraumatic Growth*,[16] trauma is characterized by a disruptive seismic event that radically alters one's personal narrative; the event becomes the marker of before and after in one's story. Despite profoundly negative and stressful after effects of trauma, such as depression, lost relationships, crisis of faith, heightened vulnerability, and shaken worldview, trauma can also result in positive effects. Positive effects of trauma may include greater clarity, awareness of one's strengths, new relationships, deeper meaning, spiritual growth, and new skills. PTG is distinct from resilience in its transformative properties; resilience is a return to the baseline or prior state, while PTG is growth beyond the baseline. Surprisingly, posttraumatic stress and PTG are not mutually exclusive; research shows that they can and do coexist under certain conditions.[17] Increasingly, PTG research suggests that for many African Americans, the cosmology communicated through song, literature, and the culture more broadly created the conditions to manage trauma, stress, and promote growth.

Slavery, segregation, and their discriminatory repercussions were (and are) life-quaking events. Africans who integrated their existing yet diverse cultures and shared experiences of trauma in a strange land forged a cosmology that made sense of the new context that was first expressed in spiritual songs.[18] Historian Lawrence Levine noted that "as valuable as secular songs are as a record of slave consciousness, it is the spirituals that historians must look to comprehend the antebellum slaves' world view, for it was in the spirituals that slaves found a medium which resembled in many crucial ways the cosmology they had brought with them from Africa and afforded them the possibility of both *adapting to and transcending their situation*."[19] Levine continued, "For all their inevitable sadness, slave songs were characterized more by a feeling of confidence than of despair. There was a confidence that contemporary power relationships were not immutable: " 'Did not old Pharaoh get lost, get lost, get lost, . . . get lost in the Red Sea?'; confidence in the possibilities of instantaneous change: 'Jesus make de dumb to speak' . . . confidence in the rewards of persistence: Keep a' inching along like a poor inchworm: . . . confidence that nothing could stand in the way of justice they would receive: 'O no man, no man, no man can hinder me'; and confidence in the prospect of the future: 'We'll walk de golden streets.' "[20]

The cosmology expressed in slavery songs was instrumental not only in coping with social dislocation, workplace brutality, drudgery, and discrimination, but based on recent empirical research, also providing cognitive and communal properties that were the impetus for PTG. Specifically, not only were songs hopeful, but the lyrical content promoted coping styles that have been associated with PTG by abetting "management of emotional distress, rumination, self-disclosure, distal and proximal sociocultural influences, narrative development and life wisdom."[21] Some songs were hopeful; others sought divine help in times of distress, while still others simply or humorously commented on reality (see example p. 130).

Lyrical themes were disbursed and interwoven throughout the culture and powerfully reinforced by multiple traditional institutions, including schools and universities, religious congregations, community and fraternal organizations, the workplace, and informal involvement in arts and entertainment (e.g., poetry, literature, and sports). Growth is evident in African Americans' subsequent individual and collective accomplishments despite unimaginable trauma.

Obviously, it is impossible to survey the entire history of music or accomplishments here, nor is that the point. Instead, I provide select examples from the late 1800s to 1964 to illustrate how elements of the cosmology were evoked to cultivate destiny, disposition, and duty in service of a calling and across life roles.

Unthinkable Destiny and Extraordinarily Good Work

Max Weber wrote: "The ability of mental concentration, as well as the absolutely essential feeling of obligation to one's job, are here most often combined with a strict economy which calculates the possibility of high earnings, and a cool self-control and frugality which enormously increase performance. This provides the most favorable foundation for the conception of labor as an end in itself, as a calling which is necessary to capitalism: the chances of overcoming traditionalism are greatest on account of the religious upbringing."[22] His belief is embodied in the extraordinary life of George Washington Carver.

Carver's life was unthinkable from the beginning.[23] He was born a slave in Missouri in 1861 to a slave woman whose husband was killed in the Civil War. Southern raiders stole her and infant George from farmer Carver's property; farmer Carver pursued and overtook the raiders, then bartered an old horse to secure baby George's return. His mother was never found. Baby George was stricken with whooping cough and grew up as a delicate child; as such, he was exempted from vigorous labor on the farm. Instead, young George was allowed to pursue his natural interests, which led him into the woods with plants, insects, and flowers. He was also intellectually curious and learned to read.

Liberated from slavery, Carver earned a scholarship to Simpson College in 1890, the same school where his father was enrolled before enlisting in the military. He later transferred to Iowa State College, where he earned bachelor's and master's degrees in science. Carver's exemplary scholarship earned him a faculty position and charge over the bacteriological laboratory, green house, and department of systematic botany. These alone were remarkable accomplishments for a former slave during that era; Carver's inauspicious origins gave little hint of the destiny that followed.

Carver's scholarship resulted in public notoriety. Booker T. Washington offered Carver a job at the historically black Tuskegee University, in the state of Alabama. But Carver "would not reply until he had gone out into the woods alone and talked it over with God."[24] Carver accepted the job and was given a meager laboratory, in which he improvised laboratory tools from bottle tops, hub caps, and things from "the junk heap"; he called the place "God's Little Workshop."[25] Carver had an unconventional way of working that was guided by his worldview. He told his biographer, "I never grope for methods. The method is revealed the moment I am inspired to create something new . . . After my morning's talk with God I go into my laboratory and begin to carry out His wishes for the day."[26]

Though Carver may have seemed quirky to some, his way of working literally saved Alabama's agricultural industry. He recognized that soil was greatly depleted from farming cotton and tobacco; the devastating economic effects on sharecroppers and the regional economy were *unthinkable*. Moreover, the soil problem was spreading throughout the southern United States. Carver perceived that crop rotation was the answer and began planting peas, sweet potatoes and peanuts. To determine what to do with the abundance, he talked to "Mr. Creator."

> I went into my laboratory and said, "Dear Mr. Creator, please tell me what the universe was made for?" The great Creator answered, "You want to know too much for that little mind of yours. Ask for something more your size." Then I asked, "Dear Mr. Creator, tell me what man was made for." Again the great Creator replied, "Little man, you still are asking too much. Cut down the extent of your request and improve the intent." So then I asked, "Please, Mr. Creator, will you tell me why the peanut was made?" "That's better, but even then it's infinite. What do you want to know about the peanut?" "Mr. Creator, can I make milk out of the peanut?" "What kind of milk do you want, good Jersey milk or just plain boarding-house milk?" "Good Jersey milk." And then the great Creator taught me how to take the peanut apart and put it together again.[27]

After that conversation, an inspired Carver "discovered 300 new uses for the peanut and 150 new uses for the sweet potato. Before he was through, he had rebuilt the agriculture of the South."[28]

Because of Carver's renowned work, he regularly communicated with his community of inventors and leaders of the era including Henry Ford (of Ford Motor Company), who was intrigued by Carver's work on biofuels; Thomas Edison, who unsuccessfully tried to hire Carver away from "God's Little Workshop" in Alabama; and Mohandas Gandhi, for whom Carver worked on "a new kind of soy bean food" for vegetarians. Carver recounted how he, Edison, and Gandhi discussed issues of faith, science, and work: "It is not we little men that do the work, but our blessed Creator working through us."[29]

Unthinkable Disposition and a Legacy of Good Work

> Labor must, on the contrary, be performed as if it were an absolute end in itself, a calling. But such an attitude is by no means a product of nature. It cannot be evoked by low wages or high ones alone, but can only be the product of a long and arduous process of education.[30]
>
> Max Weber

In *Folk Songs of the American Negro* (1915),[31] John Wesley Work captured the lyrics and history of songs from the slaves who sang them. His classification of songs in the table of contents shows that character strengths were vitally important and communicated through songs of joy, sorrow, sorrow with notes of joy, faith, hope, love, determination, adoration, patience, courage, and humility. To preserve and perpetuate cultural teachings about character, journalist Steven Barboza compiled an anthology, comprising more than 900 pages of 19th- and 20th-century sentiments about character in *The African American Book of Values*;[32] essay themes are remarkably similar to Work's table of contents nearly 100 years earlier. Barboza collected essays about individual conduct and how one should relate to others. He then divided them into two books: the *Book of Self-Mastery* includes essays about self-discipline, courage, honesty, self-esteem, work, tenacity, creativity, and faith; and the *Book of Empathy* includes essays about family, community, love, friendship, compassion, responsibility, respect, loyalty, and survival humor. These traits were promoted, not only through song but also by educational institutions—grade schools, colleges, and universities. Sociologist W. E. B. DuBois described the importance of such a holistic education in *The Souls of Black Folk* (1903): "The final product of our training must be neither a psychologist nor a brickmason, but a man. And to make men, we must have ideals, broad, pure, and inspiring ends of living—not sordid money-getting, not apples of gold. The worker must work for the glory of his handiwork, not simply for pay; the thinker must think for truth, not for fame. And all this is gained only by human strife and longing; by ceaseless training and education; by founding right on righteousness and truth on the unhampered search for truth."[33]

Songs and educational institutions, particularly historically black colleges (many of which were founded by religious organizations), elaborated on and reinforced the importance of character education. One example of how the cultural cosmology influenced disposition and excellence in higher education is Professor Melvin Tolson's work with the famous debate team that he coached at Wiley College in Marshall, Texas, during the 1920s and 1930s.

Tolson earned a master's degree in English and comparative literature from Columbia University and was an accomplished poet. He was named poet laureate of the nation of Liberia and his published works were recognized by his contemporaries of the Harlem renaissance, including Langston Hughes. Despite his literary accomplishments, Tolson is probably best known for his 10-year undefeated streak as coach of the Wiley College debate team (forensic representatives) and their social impact.

As the Wiley team excelled, they toured the country to compete with other historically black colleges including Fisk University, Morehouse College, Virginia Union University, Lincoln University, Wilberforce University, and Howard University. Having bested peer competitors, Tolson broke new ground by arranging a nondecision debate with law school students at the predominantly white University of Michigan in 1930. This was perhaps the first interracial debate at a Northern university. The Wiley team engaged in numerous other interracial debate events at predominantly white colleges, among them the University of Oklahoma City, Texas Christian University, and the University of New Mexico. "Tolson viewed the interracial debates, which consistently drew larger audiences than segregated ones, as a breakthrough in the troubled race relations of the country. When the finest intellects of black youth and white youth meet, the thinking person gets the thrill of seeing beyond the racial phenomena the identity of worthy qualities."[34] The team's crowning victory was against the University of Southern California in 1935. Their story was captured in the film *The Great Debaters*,[35] which, although fictionalized, provides historical accounts from interviews with living team members.

Despite their intellectual abilities and character, the Wiley teams were treated as inferior. They excelled even though they confronted challenges that their white competitors did not—threats of lynching as they toured the country to compete in debates. In addition, Jim Crow segregation laws prohibited the Wiley team's lodging in hotels and prevented them from eating at restaurants. Nevertheless, the team members maintained their composure, competed, and won against some of the best minds in the nation. How did they do it? Their exceptional performance was the confluence of disciplined and rigorous intellectual preparation, demanding expectations for excellence, character education, spiritual education, clearly defined obligations to the African American community, an array of coping skills, social support, and guiding cosmologies. Messages of character strength, courage, and

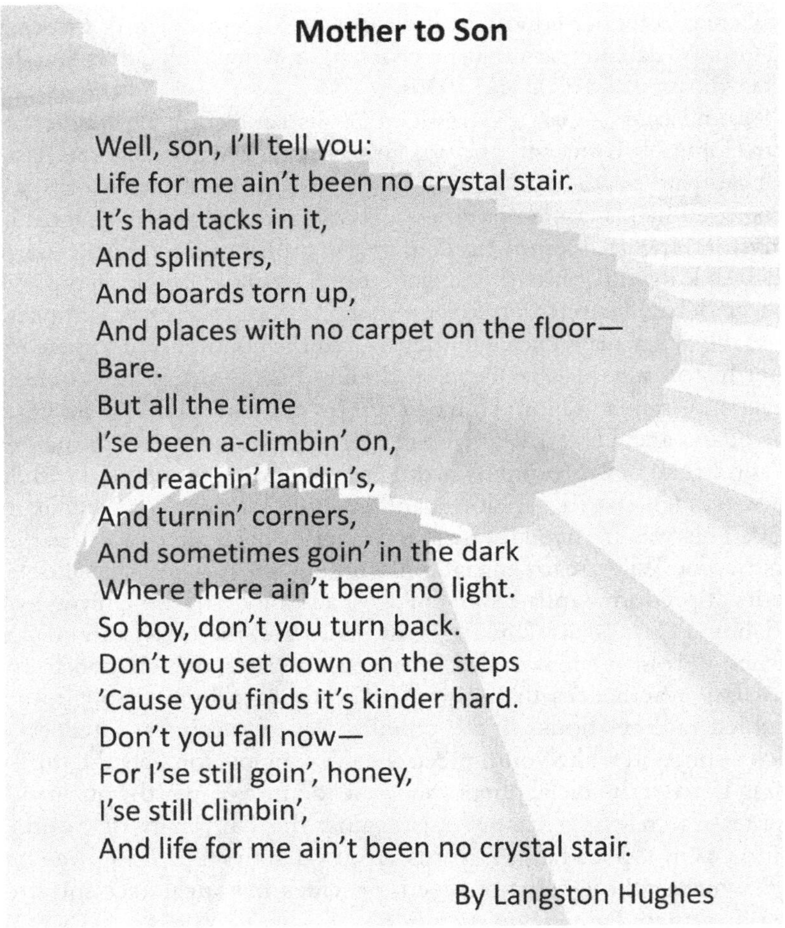

Mother to Son

Well, son, I'll tell you:
Life for me ain't been no crystal stair.
It's had tacks in it,
And splinters,
And boards torn up,
And places with no carpet on the floor—
Bare.
But all the time
I'se been a-climbin' on,
And reachin' landin's,
And turnin' corners,
And sometimes goin' in the dark
Where there ain't been no light.
So boy, don't you turn back.
Don't you set down on the steps
'Cause you finds it's kinder hard.
Don't you fall now—
For I'se still goin', honey,
I'se still climbin',
And life for me ain't been no crystal stair.

By Langston Hughes

Figure 7.1 "Mother to Son," by Langston Hughes.

coping were communicated through song and expressed eruditely or colloquially in poems such as this one by Langston Hughes in Figure 7.1.

Many Wiley debate team members were inspired by these lessons and went on to earn doctoral degrees and excel in their chosen careers—but not everyone. One 1935 team member, Henry Heights, was an older student compared to most and came from a less than supportive home. Still, his teammates said that he was the brightest debater and even "intellectually arrogant."[36] Heights, because of his age, partied and drank alcohol in ways the other students couldn't (or didn't). He dropped in and out of school. In fact, when the film's producers searched for living team members, neither Heights nor records of him could be found. As psychologist Robert Furey said, "It's as if the seed were called by the sun. This seed becomes what it is to become. In the process it finds its own true nature. Some seeds never grow. Some seeds grow magnificently."[37] Heights's unknown fate and blend of virtues and vices highlights the fact that educational institutions (and the workplace) *build on* existing cosmologies from one's parental home and community. Moreover, sometimes foundational cosmologies must be corrected. Nevertheless, Heights blossomed for a time and was part of a historic winning team—one wonders what might have been.

The team's legacy of winning, however, is not their most important achievement. Their debate preparation and involvement proved to be the incubator in which winning arguments against racial segregation and for civil rights were nurtured. James Farmer Jr., the youngest team member and son of a Wiley College professor, went on to found the Congress of Racial Equality, led early freedom rides in the South, and played a central role in the civil rights movement, working with Reverend Martin Luther King Jr. and President Lyndon Johnson. Together, they improved the "disposition" and "good work" of the nation. Farmer did not use his education, in all of its forms, just to pursue a career. "A career seeks to be successful, a calling to be valuable. A career tries to make money, a calling tries to make a difference."[38] Farmer made a difference.

Farmer, his Wiley teammates, and others like them were fortunate indeed. Not everyone was equipped for or had access to a college education in such a supportive community. Some people simple had to fulfill their duty to work.

Unthinkable Duty and Hard Work

African American work songs have been a vital tool for dealing with drudgery at work. The origins of work songs can be traced to the songs that slaves sang to cope with forced labor[39] and have been well documented.[40] According to historical accounts, Levine said:

> Slaves, then, had frequent recourse to their music, and they used it in almost every conceivable setting for almost every possible purpose. The accounts of contemporaries, white and black, and the numerous interviews with former slaves are filled with evidence that the variety

of nonreligious songs in the slaves' repertory was wide. There were songs of in-group and out-group satire, songs of nostalgia, nonsense songs, children's songs, lullabies, songs of play and work and love.[41]

Work songs were a blend of job crafting and soul crafting that Levine says "may not have been able to change the external conditions under which black laborers worked, but they did help them survive those conditions both physically and psychically. In songs like these, workers sought a shared remedy for a common plight. They comforted each other and themselves by memories of the past or projections of the future. Together they transcended the present, however briefly."[42] Because workers had little autonomy to change the task, songs were instrumental in getting the work done, dealing with drudgery, and critiquing relationships that they couldn't change. The following example, captured by history professor Levin, illustrates these points:

> *Captain, O captain, you must be cross,*
> *It's six o'clock an' you won't "knock-off!"*
> *Captain, O captain, you must be blin'*
> *You keep hollerin' "hurry" and I'm darn near flyin'.*[43]
>
> *Trouble in my mind, I'm blue*
> *But I won't be blue always,*
> *For the sun will shine in my back door some-day*[44]

Work songs were used to reframe work tasks and pass the time. Laborers also used the rhythms to punctuate movements needed to coordinate group work. Levine explained that "in both form and function, then, the work song was a communal instrument. It allowed the workers to blend their physical movements and psychic needs with those of other workers; it provided an important outlet for communication, commiseration, and expression; and, as Bruce Jackson suggested, it well may have affected subtle shifts in the meaning of the work experience itself: The songs changed the nature of the work by putting the work into the worker's framework," Jackson has hypothesized. "By incorporating the work with their song, by in effect, co-opting something they are forced to do anyway, they make it theirs in a way it otherwise is not."[45]

By the middle of the century, however, work songs went silent. As the nature of work changed and African Americans' economic conditions improved somewhat, work songs were rejected as an "old-timey" cultural tradition. More mechanized work meant more individualistic work, so communal songs receded in importance and gave rise to solo songs about work—"the blues."

The cultural cosmology disseminated through socialization, song, education in institutions, and the arts remained part of the Black church, which played a central role in the civil rights movement of the 1960s. Community songs were revived to inspire and sustain collective actions once again. This time, the effort was not in service of work, but of a social movement that would improve work and living conditions for millions. Songs of the church, and indeed the culture, reaffirmed a cosmology of hope, determination, justice, and freedom. Through song, the cosmology became a resounding collective voice for positive social actions that created the conditions for millions more to live their callings.

It is *unthinkable* that tens of millions did not.

Still Unthinkable: Implications of Exclusion

People who sang slave songs gave birth to people like George Washington Carver, and some people who sang work songs gave birth to people like the Great Debaters. More important, many people who sang such songs had potential that was comparable to Carver and the debaters but lacked the education, opportunities, economic support, and social support that they needed to overcome barriers to living their calling. Although some barriers are internal, as discussed in Chapter 6, no amount of individual job crafting and soul crafting can overcome rigid, external structural barriers. Cosmologies and coping will only go so far; sometimes collective action and structural changes are needed, as recent statistics show.

Statistics from the National Urban League reveal major impediments to callings for people of color in the United States—persistent structural barriers to participating fully in the economic system. Even in 2012, compared to whites, African Americans (71.5%) and Latinos (76%) had unequal outcomes on five indicators. The only metric in which whites did not significantly excel compared to any other group was the health of Latinos (104%) and the civic engagement of African Americans (98.3%). On every other indicator, however, compared to whites, blacks and Latinos fared far worse on economic equality (56.3% and 61%, respectively), health (African Americans, 76.5%), education (79.7% and 76%, respectively), social justice (56.8% and 61%, respectively), and civic engagement (Latinos, 67%). The inequalities are illustrated in Figure 7.2. Furthermore, the Institute for Women's Policy Research report, "The Gender Wage Gap: 2011,"[46] showed that compared to white men, women earn 82% less income. The gap also differs by race: white women earn 70.6% less, African American women 69.5% less, Latino women 60.5% less, and Asian women 87.7% less than white men. While these statistics reveal inequality in the United

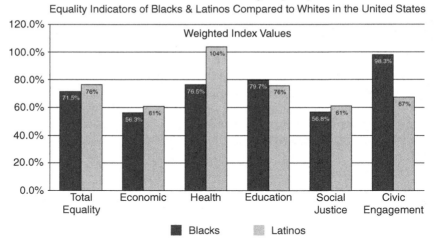

Figure 7.2 Statistics from the *State of Black America 2012 Report.*
Source: http://www.iamempowered.com/node/23900.

States, other countries may also have lingering structural inequalities that prevent large segments of the population from living their calling.

According to policy advisor Michael Novak, "Inequality of outcomes is at the core of two pivotal American concepts: freedom and opportunity. Differential success is a crucial measure of freedom. 'Created equal' means that nothing in one's class status at birth prevents one from seizing opportunity. It does not mean that everyone begins with the same family inheritance at birth or that what we have achieved during our lifetime must be limited to what we began with at birth."[47] He goes on to say that *equal* is "wrongly defined to signify fairness as equality of incomes,"[48] which he feels is socialist and un-American. But equality data indicate that class status at birth and race do indeed prevent or enable opportunities. Furthermore, based on Novak's argument, because inequality is essential for "some" to ensure their freedom and opportunity, there is an inherently perverse incentive for "some" to maintain structures that perpetuate inequalities at others' expense. As Parker Palmer noted, "It is important to distinguish between two kinds of limitations: those that come with selfhood and those that are imposed by people or political forces hell-bent on keeping us 'in our place.'"[49]

Too often, the erroneous perception is that success must come at the expense of others. In her book, *Fear of Falling*, author Barbara Ehrenreich put it this way, "The nervous, uphill financial climb of the professional middle class accelerates the downward spiral of the society as a whole: toward cruelly widening inequalities, toward heightened estrangement along lines of class and race, and toward the moral anesthesia that estrangement requires."[50] The notion that there is a fixed pie with limited slices of opportunity leads not only to a dulled social conscience but also to being oblivious about how our own self-interested behavior contributes to social problems. In the long run, however, no one is served. Structural inequalities are impediments, not only to the people who encounter them, but also to organizations and societies that do not benefit from the talents of people who are prevented from fulfilling their calling to do "good work"!

In his book *The Difference,* political scientist and economist Scott Page[51] demonstrated empirically why "different" people add value to organizations. Specifically, when "different" people possess task-relevant knowledge, and they apply their "different" heuristics and perspectives to the task of solving complex problems, they will actually outperform a group of similarly trained "experts." The reason is that the experts' common backgrounds yield redundant heuristics and perspectives that add little value; it is the principle behind crowd sourcing.[52] Increased diversity, therefore, can result in solutions that expand the pie for everyone. George Washington Carver is an example of a different heuristic and perspective at work. Carver was college educated, as were other agricultural chemists of his time. However, no chemists before Carver had solved the soil depletion problem that adversely affected farmers, sharecroppers, and the regional economy. Carver's leisure activities in nature and his ritual of talking to "Mr. Creator" about his work gave him a different perspective and heuristic tools to solve the soil depletion problem. Carver's perspective, heuristics, and an extraordinary commitment to his craft yielded a novel solution with *unthinkably* positive practical and economic consequences. It not only solved the original problem but also created new inventions and opportunities. So, whether including women, people of color, differently abled people, or creating multicultural teams, when differences are well-managed, people can live their callings and make a positive difference.

Advancing the Discourse

In the 21st century, organizations worldwide confront myriad complex challenges, as well as unique opportunities. Based on Page's work, different people living their calling can help solve the many issues our world faces. How many George Washington Carvers and Great Debaters has your organization excluded? What structural barriers obstruct their climb and impede their ascent? How can structural barriers be removed so that more people can live up to their callings and do good work? What role can traditional institutions play to prepare people with cosmologies that guide and support callings? These are questions that leaders, policy makers, and organizations must answer.

Contextual factors related to calling have received very little attention. Even when scholars and practitioners acknowledge structural barriers to calling, they do so in abstraction; neither organizations nor their leaders are implicated or discussed. Conversely, little attention has been given to the ways that organizations and leaders enable calling as well. This is remarkable because callings are not lived in isolation. Organizations and their agents create the conditions for individuals to flourish or flounder in their calling. In the next chapter, I discuss the role that leaders and organizations play in the calling conversation. Ultimately, because calling means making the world a better place, and the world is increasingly complex, leaders and organizations need to create the conditions for *everyone* to work together to make it better.

NOTES

1. Joshua Cooper Ramo, *The Age of the Unthinkable: Whey the New World Disorder Constantly Surprises Us and What We Can Do About It* (New York: Little, Brown and Company, 2009).
2. Karl E. Weick, "The Collapse of Sensemaking in Organizations: The Mann Gulch Disaster," *Administrative Science Quarterly* 38, no. 4 (1993): 628–52.
3. C. Eric Lincoln and Lawrence H. Mamiya, *The Black Church in the African American Experience* (Durham, NC: Duke University Press, 1990); John Hope Franklin and Alfred A. Moss Jr., *From Slavery to Freedom: A History of African Americans* (New York: Random House, 1994); James E. Blackwell, *The Black Community: Diversity and Unity*, 3rd ed. (New York: Harper Collins, 1991).
4. Lincoln and Mamiya, *The Black Church*.
5. Quist Albertson, *The Gods of Business: The Intersection of Faith in the Marketplace* (Los Angeles, CA: Trinity University Alumni Press, 2007).
6. Barry A. Kosmin, Egon Mayer, and Ariela Keysar, "American Religious Identification Survey" (2001); Barry A. Kosmin and Ariela Keysar, with Ryan Cragun and Juhem Navarro-Rivera, "American Nones: The Profile the No Religion Population 2008" (2009), http://commons.trincoll.edu/aris/files/2011/08/NONES_08.pdf.
7. Dennis Hevesi, "Willa Ward, Gospel Singer, Dies at 91," *New York Times*, August 12, 2012, http://www.nytimes.com/2012/08/23/arts/music/willa-ward-gospel-singer-dies-at-91.html.
8. As Henry Louis Gates Jr. documented in *Life Upon these Shores: Looking at African American History 1513–2008* (New York: Knopf, 2011), note that not all Africans in what became the United States were enslaved. Some were explorers, others gained their freedom, while others were born free. Still, they were connected by shared experiences and cosmologies.

9. Willa Ward-Royster and Toni Rose, *How I Got Over: Clara Ward and the World-Famous Ward Singers* (Philadelphia: Temple University Press, 1997), 102.
10. Kenneth I. Pargament, Kavita M. Desai, and Kelly M. McConnell, "Spirituality: A Pathway to Posttraumatic Growth or Decline?" in *Handbook of Posttraumatic Growth: Research and Practice,* ed. Lawrence G. Calhoun and Richard G. Tedeschi, 121–37 (Mahwah, NJ: Lawrence Erlbaum Associates, 2006).
11. Weick, "The Collapse of Sensemaking in Organizations."
12. See http://www.youtube.com/watch?v = TALcOreZi0A.
13. Douglas T. Hall and Dawn E. Chandler, "Psychological Success: When the Career Is a Calling," *Journal of Organizational Behavior* 26, no. 2 (2005): 155–76.
14. Ibid.
15. Richard S. Lazarus and Susan Folkman, *Stress, Appraisal, and Coping* (New York: Springer, 1984).
16. Lawrence G. Calhoun and Richard G. Tedeschi, eds., *Handbook of Posttraumatic Growth: Research and Practice* (Mahwah, New Jersey: Lawrence Erlbaum, 2006).
17. Ibid.
18. Lawrence W. Levine, *Black Culture and Black Consciousness: Afro-American Folk Thought from Slavery to Freedom* (New York: Oxford University Press, 1977).
19. Ibid., 19, emphasis added.
20. Levine, *Black Culture and Black Consciousness,* 40–41.
21. Lawrence G. Calhoun and Richard G. Tedeschi, "The Foundations of Posttraumatic Growth: An Expanded Framework," in *Handbook of Posttraumatic Growth: Research and Practice,* ed. Lawrence G. Calhoun and Richard G. Tedeschi, 121–37 (New York: Psychology Press, Routledge Taylor & Francis Group, 2006), 9.
22. Max Weber, *The Protestant Ethic and the Spirit of Capitalism* (London: Routledge, 1904/1992), 63.
23. Glenn Clark, *The Man Who Talks with Flowers: The Life Story of Dr. George Washington Carver* (Austin, MN: Macalester Park Publishing Company, 1939).
24. Ibid., 54.
25. Ibid., 14.
26. Ibid., 21.
27. Ibid., 34.
28. Ibid., 11.
29. Ibid., 25.
30. Weber, *The Protestant Ethic,* 62.
31. John Wesley Work, *Folk Songs of the American Negro* (Nashville, TN: Tennessee Press of Fisk University, 1915).
32. Steven Barboza, ed., *The African American Book of Values: Classic Moral Stories* (New York: Doubleday Dell, 1998).
33. Ibid., 275.
34. Gail Beil, "Wiley College's Great Debaters Excerpted from an Article That Originally Appeared in the East Texas Historical Journal"(February 2008), http://www.humanitiestexas.org/news/articles/wiley-colleges-great-debaters.
35. Denzel Washington, dir., *The Great Debaters* (Los Angeles, CA: Genius Products, 2007).
36. Ibid.

37. Robert J. Furey, *Called by Name: Discovering Your Unique Purpose in Life* (New York: Crossroad, 1996), 41.
38. William Sloan Coffin (2004). *Passion for the Possible: A Message to U.S. Churches*, 2nd ed. (Louisville, KY: Westminster/John Knox press), 77.
39. Levine, *Black Culture and Black Consciousness*.
40. A. Lomax, *Afro-American Spirituals, Work Songs, and Ballads* [sound recording, 1933–1939] (Cambridge, MA: Rounder Records, 1998).
41. Levine, *Black Culture and Black Consciousness*, 15.
42. Ibid., 213.
43. Ibid., 215.
44. Ibid., 230.
45. Ibid., 215.
46. Claudia Williams, Ariane Hegewisch, and Anlan Zhang, "The Gender Wage Gap: 2011" (2012), http://www.iwpr.org/publications/pubs/the-gender-wage-gap-2011.
47. Michael Novak, *Business as a Calling: Work and the Examined Life* (New York: Free Press, 1996), 56–57.
48. Ibid., 57.
49. P. J. Palmer, *Let Your Life Speak: Listening to the Voice of Vocation* (San Francisco: Jossey-Bass, 2000), 42.
50. Barbara Ehrenreich, *Fear of Falling: The Inner Life of the Middle Class* (New York: Harper Perennial, 1990), 250.
51. Scott E. Page, *The Difference: How the Power of Diversity Creates Better Groups, Firms, Schools, and Societies* (Princeton, NJ: Princeton University Press, 2007).
52. Jeff Howe, *Crowdsourcing: Why the Power of the Crowd Is Driving the Future of Business* (New York: Three Rivers Press, 2008).

8

Practitioner Perspectives (1980–2012): Callings in Business

The unthinkable case example in Chapter 7 showed how a social system, through its organizations and their agents, erected barriers to calling and the extraordinary efforts that people had to take to overcome them. By creating new institutions, adding new functions to existing institutions, reconfiguring membership, reaffirming the values of existing institutions,[1] and disseminating a transcendent cosmology, millions of people have been able to fulfill their callings, albeit to varying degrees. Sadly, others never did. But what would happen if those barriers didn't exist? How much more talent might be discovered and leveraged to promote the common good? What would it look like if organizations, their leaders, and entrepreneurs behaved as though they had a calling? A small group of practitioners pondered these and similar questions as they wrote about the calling to a specific discipline—business.

Management consultant Jane Kise, who earned an MBA in finance, and her colleague David Stark, a pastor and career consultant, wrote about the calling to business,[2] as did Michael Novak,[3] a theologian and public policy advisor. Others wrote about the calling to business-related roles; for example, management professors and consultants James McGee and Andre Delbecq[4] wrote about the calling to leadership, and Gordon Smith wrote about entrepreneurship.[5] While the call to specific occupations has been a topic of management research, the notion that an organization has a calling has not. Here, practitioners specifically link transcendent purposes, moral duty, and ideas about what is sacred to the business enterprise. Themes that emerge in this practitioner conversation are not unique however; they are the focus of theories and subdisciplines in management such as corporate social responsibility, business ethics, and value-based leadership. What is unique however, is that in this conversation practitioners specifically used the word *calling* to address those topics.

In this chapter, I begin by building on practitioners' assertion that business is a fundamentally noble activity that begins and expands with entrepreneurship. I show how the confluence of disposition, duty, and destiny, grounded in a cosmology and expressed through entrepreneurship and multiple life roles, is one integrated calling. Next, because entrepreneurial activities have the potential to morph into large corporations, I summarize practitioner insights about the calling to business in general and to leadership specifically. This practitioner conversation is important because heretofore, the focus has been on individuals. Here, we shift our attention to the intersection of organizations, leaders, society, and individual employees.

Calling and Entrepreneurship

In *Spirituality Inc.*,[6] Lake Lambert described people who felt called to entrepreneurship and whose self-described spiritual enlightenment was instrumental in the founding and governance of their companies. These entrepreneurs did not see spirituality as inconsistent with business and have written about their philosophies, among them are Howard Schulz, CEO of Starbucks; Ben Cohen and Jerry Greenfield, founders of Ben & Jerry's Ice Cream; Tom Chappell, the CEO of Tom's of Maine personal care products; Max DePree, former CEO of furniture maker Herman Miller; and Mel and Patricia Ziegler and Bill Rosenzweig, who founded the Republic of Tea beverage company. But a calling to entrepreneurship may be one of several calls in the context of a whole life. To illustrate that point, Gordon Smith described the life of a historic female entrepreneur.

Smith described the "virtuous woman" from Proverbs 31:10–31 in the Bible as an example of the occupational calling to entrepreneurship and a general life calling to multiple life roles. This point-in-time narrative about the virtuous woman reveals the confluence of destiny, duty, and disposition that are grounded in a cosmology, and how they are woven throughout one's life. The virtuous woman is a paragon of "good work"—ethical and excellent in all regards. The fecundity of her calling is evident in words used to describe her: she excels, is excellent, and is praiseworthy. She is indeed the calling ideal. Specific verses that describe the substance of her calling are listed in Table 8.1.

Destiny

Smith said, "This woman is celebrated as a merchant because of her capacity to produce wealth, to provide a solid economic foundation for her household and community, and for her generosity toward those in need. Her 'genius' is an economic intelligence."[7] The virtuous woman manufactured and distributed linen garments (v. 24); she distributed men's belts (v. 24); she had a profitable real estate enterprise (v. 16); she was involved in agriculture (v. 16); she was able to provide for the

Table 8.1 An Entrepreneur's Integrated Calling across Life Roles

Cosmology	30 Charm is deceitful and beauty is vain, But a woman who fears the Lord, she shall be praised.
Excellence	10 An excellent wife, who can find? For her worth is far above jewels. 31 Give her the product of her hands, And let her works praise her in the gates.
Relationship Destinies (ethics & excellence)	11 The heart of her husband trusts in her, And he will have no lack of gain. 23 Her husband is known in the gates, When he sits among the elders of the land. 12 She does him good and not evil All the days of her life. 28 Her children rise up and bless her; Her husband also, and he praises her, saying: 29 "Many daughters have done nobly, But you excel them all."
Leisure, Fitness & Fashion	13 She looks for wool and flax And works with her hands in delight.17 She girds herself with strength And makes her arms strong. 19 She stretches out her hands to the distaff, And her hands grasp the spindle. 22 She makes coverings for herself; Her clothing is fine linen and purple.
Occupational Destiny (ethics & excellence)	14 She is like merchant ships; She brings her food from afar. 24 She makes linen garments and sells them, And supplies belts to the tradesmen. 16 She considers a field and buys it; From her earnings she plants a vineyard. 18 She senses that her gain is good; Her lamp does not go out at night.
Disposition	25 Strength and dignity are her clothing, And she smiles at the future. 26 She opens her mouth in wisdom, And the teaching of kindness is on her tongue.
Mundane Duty, Moral Duty, and Industry	15 She rises also while it is still night And gives food to her household And portions to her maidens. 21 She is not afraid of the snow for her household, For all her household are clothed with scarlet. 27 She looks well to the ways of her household, And does not eat the bread of idleness.
Volunteer/ServiceDestiny	20 She extends her hand to the poor, And she stretches out her hands to the needy.

Source: Text is from Proverbs 31:10–31 (New American Standard Bible); the number preceding each statement is the relevant verse.

material needs of her household (v. 18); and she was aware of her considerable skills (v. 18). We know that business was part of her occupational destiny because she excelled at it! Increased mastery over time is one hallmark of a calling.

She was also called to other life roles including wife, mother, home-maker, and volunteer in the community. But her life wasn't only work.

She also engaged in leisure pursuits and remained physically fit; she worked with her hands in "delight" (v. 13), did strength training (v. 17), and delighted in fashion (v. 22).

Duty

The virtuous woman reminds us that doing mundane and ordinary work well is also part of a calling. She was industrious and arose early to tend to her home (v. 15, 27); she generously cared for the household staff and managed them (v. 15, 21); and she insured that there were adequate reserves for difficult seasons (v. 21). These weren't particularly enjoyable or fitting tasks, but they were necessary. People who are called "are diligent in their work and in the private side of their work precisely because they are committed first and foremost to good work."[8] As an example, Smith described Chesley "Sully" Sullenberger's heroic airplane landing on the Hudson River—the crash landing without fatalities! Sully faithfully completed routine aspects of his job with care for decades and was therefore able to rise to the occasion when circumstances required it. According to Smith, "The quality of our work depends, in large measure, on the integrity of the work we do when others are not watching."[9]

Disposition

The Proverbs narrative focuses on the woman's many character strengths. She has faith and is focused on something beyond herself (v. 10), and she is a trustworthy and noble wife with good intentions (v. 11, 12). Even though she is a working woman with varied leisure and community interests, she has not neglected the needs of her children, who praise her (v. 28). She showed wisdom and good judgment in business and life affairs (v. 16, 18, 26); courage and prudence regarding life challenges (v. 15, 21); and kindness (v. 26), optimism (v. 25), empathy, and generosity (v. 20). There is no direct indication that she exercised coping skills. However, the notion that her husband was a public servant (v. 23) suggests that she may have coped with public scrutiny and a husband who earned less income than she did.

Cosmology

The virtuous woman embodies vocational integrity. There is no apparent tension between her roles; she demonstrates commitment to an ethical and excellent life, including her business and family. Her life illustrates how the system of duty, destiny, and disposition interrelate and are embedded in a unifying cosmology that defines one's life. Thus, the issue isn't one of balancing core dimensions of calling, but of integrating them, which David Whyte alludes to in *The Three Marriages*.[10] He suggests that ideally there are three different marriages in one's life that are unified by a deep commitment: the first marriage is a commitment to one's highest self; the next is a commitment to relationships, regardless of marital status; and the third marriage is to work. I contend that those deep commitments can be expressed as a calling. The virtuous woman narrative shows that one can have multiple callings to ethical and excellent work, across different life domains, that are unified by a guiding cosmology. This phenomenon is best understood as an ecology of calling.

An Ecological Model of Calling

In Chapter 6, I illustrated the core dimensions of calling (see Figure 6.1) and how they are anchored in foundational cosmologies. Here, I show how that system is inseparable from and integrates life roles into one's calling that is composed of many elements. The ecological model of calling depicted in Figure 8.1 is composed of asymmetric concentric circles. The darkly shaded circle denotes the foundational cosmology of early life experiences, while additional cosmologies from subsequent life experiences are illustrated in the surrounding circles. As the concentric circles in the model illustrate, additional cosmologies may be acquired through leisure activities, relationships with peers, involvement in the larger community, and work. In this way, all life experiences have the potential to become part of a calling. Each circle is also influenced by diverse cosmologies that may reinforce or conflict with one another. Hence, cosmologies are not static; they are amenable

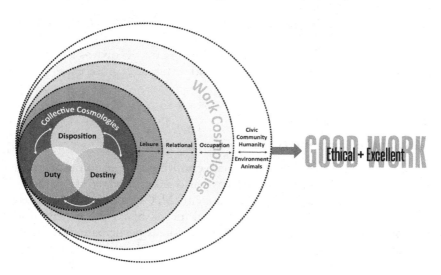

Figure 8.1 An ecological model of calling across the life roles.

to change as one is exposed to, adopts, or rejects various ideologies that expand or challenge their worldview.

Herein lies the problem or the opportunity: absent a strong cosmological foundational from one's home community (e.g., family, cultural group, or religious institutions), any number of influences can and will fill the vacuum of a coherent worldview, including the media, peers, professional groups, colleges and universities, and work organizations. The lack of a foundation can be psychologically and existentially precarious, as Parker Palmer noted. Although he achieved career success, it was unsustainable due to "a distorted work ethic that led me to live by images of who I ought to be or what I ought to do rather than by insight into my own reality, into what was true and possible and life-giving for me."[11]

Further, misaligned belief systems can create a cosmological crisis. For example, being told that one is destined for failure in a role that one is, in fact, equipped to perform, or being asked to engage in questionable activities as one's duty can lead to dissonance that is not easily resolved. What if one's professional or peer group condones white-collar or no-collar crime as their behavioral standard? Without an alternative schema to provide coherence, standards, and coping strategies, a person may feel compelled to accept inaccurate beliefs or acquiesce to unseemly behaviors. Ideally, people *bring* calling cosmologies to work that elevate and enrich the organization, rather than rely on their organization to *provide* a cosmology to guide one's calling. Relying on work organizations to cultivate a calling can be risky, as I have shown; it is not part of their core business or core competency, and as the next section shows, the corporate calling itself has been diminished.

In sum, the ecological model of calling shows how collective cosmologies influence core attributes of one's calling, how that core calling influences various life roles, and how the core may evolve as a result of engagement in and exposure to new and different cosmologies.

The Call of Business

Serving the Common Good

Business is a noble profession that can contribute to the common good in myriad ways, but practitioners have also acknowledged its shadowy side. Management scholars and consultants McGee and Delbecq stated it thusly: "Business is also the principal means of wealth distribution in modern economies, because most individuals participate in the economic order through salaries and wages rather than inherited wealth. And it is the private sector that creates the 'surplus' wealth through which government, education, churches and temples, parks, the arts, environmental causes, and other essential good works are supported."[12] Hence, business can help make the world a better place and, according to some, can be called. Indeed, this is how American corporations were intended to function—in service of the common good.[13]

Initially, businesses were chartered to align their goods and services with social needs. Kise and Stark noted in their historical analysis:

> To incorporate, a business had to demonstrate some contribution to the common good. Until 1800, of the little over three hundred corporations in this country, only thirteen were chartered for manufacturing or commerce purposes. The rest provided some kind of public service ranging from building docks or canals to providing banking or insurance services. But then states started competing for business. In 1811, New York changed its laws so that businesses only provided a description of their intended enterprise to receive their charter. Other states followed suit over the next decades. Real power, though, came in 1886, when the Supreme Court ruled that a corporation was entitled to the same rights as a person under the Fourteenth Amendment of the Constitution: "nor shall any State deprive any person of life, liberty, or property, without due process of law." Companies used that ruling as leverage to overturn state laws covering working conditions and wage controls, and to declare any labor union activity as unconstitutional because it infringed on the rights of the corporation.[14]

In a sense, legislative changes of 1811 absolved corporations of the social responsibilities of a calling; in 1886, corporations gained the rights of individuals but were absolved of moral duties and responsibilities of a calling. I am not suggesting that all commerce was conducted ethically prior to 1811. For example, Weber cited General Cromwell's letter to Parliament in 1650: "Be pleased to reform the abuses of all professions: and if there be any one that makes many poor to make a few rich, that suits not a Commonwealth."[15] Instead, I am highlighting the dilution of social responsibility and ethics through formal legislative actions—this is where the problem lies.

People who behave badly generally experience negative consequences—they are fired, incarcerated, or otherwise institutionalized. In contrast, the psychopathy of a corporation is rewarded; corporations face few consequences for immoral and socially harmful actions that money and power cannot satisfy so that "business as usual" can continue. Law professor Joel Bakan wrote about the legally supported moral descent of corporations, which was depicted in the documentary film *The Corporation*.[16] In the film, a clinical psychologist, Dr. Robert Hare, used the *Diagnostic and Statistical Manual of Mental Disorders* to identify psychopathic behaviors of corporations.[17] The behaviors are technically legal but socially and environmentally unethical and harmful. One example involves Stewart Parnell, another man who worked with peanuts.

Parnell, the CEO of the Peanut Company of America (PCA), was implicated in a massive salmonella outbreak in 2009. Physical tests revealed salmonella in his plant as early as 2006 and on at least 12 different occasions.[18] Employees e-mailed Parnell to notify him of risks, as did the external testing agency, indicating that the peanut shipments should be withheld. Parnell, concerned about lost revenue, shrinking profits, and the cost of delays, ordered employees to ship the peanut products anyway. He then fired the testing lab that found evidence of salmonella.[19] As a result, PCA contaminated 2,000 food items that used its products. Nine people died, and 700 people across the country were made ill. When Parnell testified at a congressional hearing, he pled the Fifth Amendment and remained silent. Ultimately, a congressional committee member challenged him to eat his own peanut butter—Parnell refused. He never apologized to the victims or their families. He is someone who needs to take the mirror test[20] and ask himself: "What would the world be like if everyone behaved the way that I do?"

PCA went bankrupt, and employees lost their jobs. But Parnell retained all of his personal wealth and property, including the factory that he "leased" to the company.[21] What Parnell did was technically legal. He simply failed to comply with FDA guidelines to destroy tainted products. Eventually, the federal government filed felony charges against Parnell. The 76-count indictment includes charges of "conspiracy, wire fraud, obstruction of justice and introducing adulterated food into the market."[22] If Novak's assertion is true, that the moral health of business and its leaders is inextricably linked a nation's moral health, then what do organizations like PCA, and those still in business, portend for society and individual callings?

The Moral Duty of Business

Practitioners contend that businesses must live up to a calling in order to support individuals who follow their callings. Kise and Stark recommended a corporate calling—a guiding ideology that transcends, yet includes, interests of the firm and that is "an appropriate comparison for when it runs amuck that guide."[23] To counter moral malaise, practitioners recommend that corporations fulfill explicit moral duties relative to (1) aligning corporate and societal interests; (2) legal, political, and regulatory systems; (3) employees; (4) the environment; and (5) profits, growth, rewards, and new businesses. Novak offered rather general guidelines and broad principles; Kise and Stark were more prescriptive, with specific top-down and bottom-up solutions.

Practitioners agreed that first, a corporate calling should be a commitment to contribute to their surrounding community, consider its impact on the community, and produce goods and services that add real value. They believe that a corporate calling must recognize the interconnectedness of business and human needs. On this point, Gardner and his colleagues said that "genetics appears to be a beautifully aligned enterprise: the aspirations of the practitioners, the values of the domain, the practices of the field, and the desires of the shareholders and the stakeholders blend together harmoniously."[24] This is a very different way of thinking about alignment and calling—aligning corporate destiny and human destiny. Misalignment, however, can leave one side of the equation lacking.

Second, Novak suggested that the call of business is to exemplify respect for the law and social justice and to "protect the political soil of liberty."[25] He also noted that corporations should be watchful of the political society and encourage civic engagement of employees. This is tricky territory indeed; during the 2012 elections, employers tried to coerce their employees to vote for a particular candidate and threatened them with job loss if they didn't. Needless to say, this is not encouragement. Alternatively, Kise and Stark suggested that the call of business is to preserve human rights with the appropriate regulation of business.

Third, McGee and Delbecq noted that "Calvin also saw the role of institutions to be facilitators of the individual's skills. Consequently, he also believed that any social structure that impeded the development and use of those gifts must be reformed."[26] Novak agreed that businesses should respect human dignity and consider growing one's employees as important as growing the business. But Kise and Stark went further to say that cultivating employees should focus on the whole person—mind, body, spirit, and economic well-being. Furthermore, a called business doesn't treat people as dispensable instruments. They believe that the language used to describe employees should change—they are people with potential and not talent to be developed.

Novak also advocated for helping employees to be entrepreneurial—even if they end up leaving to go into business for themselves. Thus, both practitioner conversations agree that an individual's calling might also entail leaving an organization; it is not only about being committed. As Smith noted, "Something is askew when we cannot imagine being anywhere else and when our whole lives are consequently wrapped up in a particular organization. We set ourselves up for vocational crisis when we identify ourselves too closely with either an organization or a purpose, such that we are lost and at sea when inevitable changes come."[27] This may be one reason that professors Pratt and Ashforth contended that a sense of calling may undermine organizational commitment.[28] Thus, when work commitment wanes, it may be appropriate for that person to leave the organization—it is no longer part of his or her calling.

In addition to relationships between the firm and employees, (e.g., cultivating entrepreneurs) practitioners also expressed ideas about relationship dynamics among employees at different levels. For example, Novak was concerned about how wage disparities might erode the sense of community and inflame animus among employees at different levels in organizations. Therefore, the business calling is "to defeat envy through generating upward mobility and putting empirical ground under the conviction that hard work and talent are fairly rewarded. Conspicuous privilege, ostentation, and other forms of behavior, even when not necessarily wrong, typically provoke envy. Unusually large salaries or bonuses, even if justified by competition in a free and open market (since high talent of certain kinds is extremely rare) may offer demagogues fertile ground on which to scatter the seeds of envy."[29]

Jim Sinegal, former cofounder and CEO of Costco, put this relationship principle into practice. Sinegal voluntarily capped his annual salary at $350,000, plus bonuses and stock,[30] which was 48 times the average employee's annual salary of $45,800. Based on the company's performance, he earned $2.2 million in total compensation. In contrast, Wal-Mart CEO Michael Duke's salary was $1.3 million, plus bonuses and stock, representing 796 times the average employee's annual salary of $22,100. Duke earned $17.6 million in total compensation.[31] The stark difference between how these organizations treat their employees and suppliers is legendary in terms of wages, benefits, and pricing demands. Under Sinegal, Costco behaved more like a called corporation.

Fourth, a called corporation is responsive to the environment. For Novak, that means communicating fully and often with investors, shareholders, customers, and employees and protecting the "moral ecology of freedom." He criticized television executives for not doing more in this regard, because of their power to shape culture. For Kise and Stark, this means taking a long-term view of corporate actions, considering the natural limits of the planet, purchasing and producing fair-trade goods, and stopping environmental abuse and pursuit of profits at any expense. Either way, called businesses have obligations to positively cultivate the social and material environment.

Fifth, a called business seeks to make a reasonable return on the investor funds entrusted to it.[32] Kise and Stark suggest that there should be an "appropriate" return on investment, not just pursuing larger and larger profits. Furthermore, there should be consequences for how profits are earned. For example, selling tainted peanut products should have negative legal and financial consequences. Stark noted, "We could make directors legally responsible to make profits, but not by hurting employees or by increasing costs to the public, or by stomping on human rights, the environment, or other areas that are matters of public interest."[33] They also believe that nationally, success should not be measured by gross domestic product, which only measures goods and services sold. Instead, they believe nations and corporations should shift to a "genuine progress indicator"[34] (GPI), for which some economists advocate as well. The GPI includes invisible productivity such as uncompensated work at home and subtracts invisible costs such as commute time.

Finally, Novak says that the calling of business is to create new jobs and new wealth. Kise and Stark called for changing the culture and indicated that we should "stop thinking of ourselves as mere consumers—who have no obligations or responsibilities—but as citizens who do."[35] Furthermore, business should "stop fueling the global pie-eating contest,"[36] which is the fierce competition for and consumption of scarce resources, without regard for those who lack and are literally hungry. In order to fulfill such a calling, organizations must reexamine and redefine what they hold sacred.

What Is Sacred?

As I indicated in Chapter 4, what is sacred is highly subjective; it is a matter of what an individual or an organization imbues with divine significance and for which they strive, even at great cost. At one time, serving the common good was considered sacred in business; for the PCA, profits were sacred, even above human life. Among the many things that may be sacred in business, I focus here on several: consumption, profits, and hierarchy.

Consumption and Profits

The authors of *Good Work* asserted that "market forces have assumed overwhelming importance in contemporary professional life, and that increased emphasis on profitability has caused tension for employees."[37] To me, this is most apparent in retailing, as I write this chapter on Black Friday—the day after the Thanksgiving holiday. Thanksgiving is a symbolic U.S. holiday, not a sacred one, at least in religious terms.

Traditionally, Thanksgiving is spent celebrating the country's bounty by consuming turkey and the fruits of the fall harvest. In today's commercial view, however Thanksgiving officially begins the "holy season" of binge consumption of retail goods. It marks the day when U.S. retailers and customers metaphorically plan to worship at the altar of bargain shopping. Retailers incite shopping frenzies with the promise of unparalleled prices for desired goods in limited quantities. Consumers' Pavlovian response to Black Friday marketing has now escalated to a level of combative competitive shopping; people have been trampled by crowds, assaulted with pepper spray, and endured bodily injury in pursuit of trendy deals.[38] Meanwhile, low paid retail employees must forego their own holiday for the sake of consumers and profits. Weber described it best: This "nullity imagines that it has attained a level of civilization never before achieved."[39] Could marketing consultant Victor Lebow have predicted this outcome when he wrote "Price Competition in 1955"?

> Our enormously productive economy demands that we make consumption our way of life, that we convert the buying and use of goods into *rituals,* that we seek our *spiritual satisfactions,* our ego satisfactions, in consumption. The measure of social status, of social acceptance, of prestige, is now to be found in our consumptive patterns. *The very meaning and significance of our lives* today expressed in consumptive terms. The greater the pressures upon the individual to *conform* to safe and accepted social standards, the more does he tend to express his aspirations and his individuality in terms of what he wears, drives, eats- his home, his car, his pattern of food serving, his hobbies.
>
> These commodities and services must be offered to the consumer with a *special urgency.* We require not only "forced draft" consumption, but "expensive" consumption as well. We need things consumed, burned up, worn out, replaced, and discarded at an ever increasing pace. We need to have people eat, drink, dress, ride, live, with *ever more complicated and, therefore, constantly more expensive consumption.* The home power tools and the whole "do-it-yourself" movement are excellent examples of "expensive" consumption.[40]

Harvard Business School historian Nancy Koehn traced the origins of the term *Black Friday* to the 1950s,[41] when managers described high employee absenteeism the day after Thanksgiving. Later, it denoted large shopping crowds the same day, much to the chagrin of local police. By 1980, Black Friday had a more positive connotation—the beginning of the holiday shopping season. Black Friday is now a retailer's holiday, as it marks the day when they "historically came out of the red and went into the black by beginning to turn a profit."[42] In recent years, it has expanded to include Cyber Monday, Small Business Saturday, and in 2011, sales began on Thanksgiving night! Koehn noted that "at this rate, Thanksgiving might disappear altogether or the month of November will be called 'Black November.'"[43] The evolution of Black Friday raises numerous questions regarding the intersection of business and individual callings.

Studies show that people in business are more "thinking" oriented (80%) compared to only 50% of the general population, which is guided by feelings. This renders the general population susceptible to emotional manipulation and exploitation.[44] If the call of business is profits, what does the call to consumption mean for the collective soul of a nation that is emotionally malleable? What happens when and if shopping somnambulants wake up? What effects would the real spiritual awakening of a calling mean for business and economic stability in a country where economic strength is based on consumption? Moreover, because business has a vested interest in somnambulance, can we truly expect corporations that exclusively hold profits sacred to cultivate employees' transcendent callings to work? Currently, this is not a core competency of business. But, should it be?

Individual callings can fuel business and capitalism in many ways including through innovation and commitments to ethical and excellent work; as such, corporations have an interest in individual callings as well. But, if an individual calling is only in service of a vapid corporate calling that has corrosive social consequences, what is the point? As somnambulant and semiconscious employees and consumers wake up, this is a tension that they must reconcile with noneconomic cosmologies and then take responsibility for following the right actions. It may be easier to remain asleep.

Hierarchy

In work settings, certain occupations can be deemed sacred. To illustrate this point, George Smith described sacred hierarchies in academia: "[T]here is a remarkable inclination to celebrate the research scholar and not recognize the sacredness of every role that is critical to what makes a college or university effective."[45] To address this issue at the University of Michigan, where the slogan is "Go Blue," human resources and facilities staff have collaborated to counter the norm and honor the contributions of facilities workers. Their uniforms and vehicles carry the slogan, "We Make Blue Go!"

The problem is not sacred occupational hierarchies per se, but the real potential for abusing power and privilege that is associated with those occupying the higher ranks. Robert Fuller coined the term *rankism* to define the problem.[46] According to Fuller, rankism is the mother of all "isms" (sexism, racism, classism, homophobism, able-ism, etc.); all have a common underlying mechanism—indignification of others based on social identity or status. Rankism runs the gamut of subtle to extreme forms of interpersonal aggression, including dismissiveness, sabotage, and overt threats. Rankism is perpetrated by "somebodies" against "nobodies" that they attempt to demean, dismiss, put in their place, or deny access. Meanwhile, somebodies assume privileges and perks while remaining oblivious to the human toll of their actions. Hence, rankism is a character problem, in fact, multiple character problems, which I described in Chapter 6 (e.g., lack of empathy and open-mindedness or selfishness, self-deception, and grandiosity).

Any industry or organization with rigid hierarchy is subject to rank abuse, including health care, where doctors are esteemed and sometimes deified, which might adversely affect patient care. I developed the *Rankism and Regard Organizational Climate Assessment*[47] to test hypotheses about rankism in 24 hospitals in the Midwest and 1,172 employees within them. Respondents included chief nursing officers and nurse managers (12%), nurses (55%), nurse assistants, allied health professionals (e.g., pharmacy technicians and respiratory technicians) (18%), clerical staff (8%), and others—almost everyone except physicians. The sample was somewhat racially diverse, with 81% Caucasian and 19% people of color (e.g., African American, Latino, and Asian). Results showed the following:

- Forty-seven percent of respondents experienced rankism by their team members; 45% from their managers. Managers were largely oblivious to high levels of rankism among their staff.
- The targets of rankism varied by hospital. In some hospitals, only low-status staff experienced rankism, much as we might expect. In other hospitals, people at every level of the hierarchy experienced rankism, which indicates that it pervades the culture.
- Where there is a culture of rankism across departments and occupations, senior leader ethics (or lack thereof) are significant predictors of the problem.
- Most important, relative to hospital climate and quality, higher levels of rankism predicted undesirable handling of medical mistakes.

The bottom line is that in extreme hierarchies, when somebodies treat others as nobodies, everybody suffers! So-called nobodies have limited opportunities to live their calling and must cope with assaults to their dignity and humanity. At the same time, the organization has not created conditions for them to do their best work, which puts patients at risk and threatens the hospital's stability and survival in the long run.

Results from the hospital study beg the question: Who is a somebody and why? Who is presumably destined to nobody status? How sacred is the hierarchy? What are the implications for the quality of goods and services that businesses produce?

In *Common Sense*, Thomas Paine wrote about the risks of people who hold hierarchy sacred and feel entitled to positions at the top of it: "Men who look upon themselves as born to reign, and others to obey, soon grow insolent; selected from the rest of mankind their minds are early poisoned by importance; and the world they act in differs so materially from the world at large, that they have but little opportunity of knowing its true interests, and when they succeed to the government are frequently the most ignorant and unfit of any throughout the dominions." In such instances, real leaders are needed to challenge prevailing norms about the sacred hierarchy so that everybody benefits—individuals, the organization and society.

The goals that businesses pursue, whether transcendent or pecuniary, what becomes sacred, what constitutes good work, and how hierarchy is managed are all the product of leadership. Fulfilling the call to business is determined by whether leaders feel entitled to reign versus leaders who are called.

The Call to Leadership

According to Kise and Stark, there once was a time when business leaders were personally and publicly accountable, not just to shareholders but directly to the community. They recounted the fate of businessman Robert Keaynes, who was on trial for usury because he earned 33% to 50% profit from selling sewing notions. Stark explained, "He was convicted of greed and corrupt business practices. First the civil courts fined him. Then the Church declared he had to publicly acknowledge his sins or be excommunicated."[48] Keaynes violated the sacred trust of his community. In contrast, today's failed business leaders get golden parachutes, move to another firm or become consultants.

McGee and Delbecq offered an outline of what the call to leadership might encompass. For them, it is not just a matter of principles, but spiritual maturity. Foremost, called leaders create the conditions for "good work" and bring their own goodness and gifts to the organizational tasks that they confront. According to McGee and Delbecq, "For spiritually aware leaders the primary challenge is the transformation of their own organization into an 'oasis of goodness,' modeling not only the best practices of contemporary management but also going beyond these practices so that the just and loving presence of the Transcendent is transparent."[49] In doing so, they act as agents of called businesses that develop: high quality/low cost performance, models of sustainable development and environmental support, decision and governance processes that are inclusive and just, and processes that facilitate management change. To create the conditions for called employees to do "good work," called leaders ensure just and inclusive gain-reward systems, erect empowering structures in which all employees reach toward their potential, and encourage entrepreneurship that allows for creative expression. These actions are congruent with those mentioned by Novak, as well as Kise and Stark. In sum, called leaders are the agents of called businesses that both meet their societal obligations and support called employees in their pursuit of good work.

A problem arises however, when called leaders find that they are not employed by called businesses. In this case, they can choose to act decisively against individuals and institutions that violate their norms or values. "On the other hand, if leading figures succumb to pressures—for example, from corporate stakeholders bent on short term-profits—others are likely to become confused or disillusioned."[50] Ideally, one who is called to leadership finds the moral courage to be an agent for system change against the status quo. Debra Meyerson refers to people with this kind of courage as being "tempered radicals."[51] Even in the midst of corporate corruption or simply less-than-ideal conditions, a called leader asks him- or herself: "How can I carry out my calling where I'm currently employed?"[52] More specifically, with regard to our model of calling thus far, what resources can I draw on to cope with this situation and how can I draw on my gifts, virtues, and vices to fulfill my duty and do my best today?

Kise and Stark noted that "your job may be a conduit to something far more significant than you ever imagined."[53] For poet and professor Melvin Tolson, doing his duty and fulfilling his destiny meant cultivating a great debater and future leader that helped change the course of history. (You're not always the central figure in your calling.) For Oskar Schlinder, it was supplying the Nazis vices to save lives.

Kise and Stark described Oskar Schindler as an example of a leader who was apparently not called to business, but an awakening enabled him to draw on his vices and virtues and step up to his calling. Schindler was a failed German businessman who became a salesman during World War II; his life is captured in the film *Schindler's List*.[54] His vices and carousing (e.g., drinking, womanizing, and gambling) enabled him to profit from peddling to the tastes of gestapo elites. In return for his favors, the Nazis helped Schindler acquire an enamelware factory where he employed cheap labor provided by Jews. When Schindler realized that Nazis were killing other Jews, but not those on his payroll, he hired more and more of them. Schindler traded his wealth to bribe officials and saved 1,100 lives! And yet, he never ran another successful business—it wasn't his occupational destiny. Business served as a conduit to something much higher, a moral duty and higher purpose that he fulfilled. As Schindler's life illustrates, having a calling doesn't mean that all dimensions are or should be equal, or that one needs to be perfect. Nor does it mean that you are consistent in your calling throughout your life—Schindler wasn't.

Calling across the Life Span

The model presented in Figure 8.2 builds upon the notion of interdependent core dimensions and a cosmological ecology to suggest that calling is a recursive system of relationships among them that evolves throughout one's lifespan. This interplay ideally results in a generative effect that simultaneously elevates and advances a person on the trajectory of his or her calling. My idea of recursive generativity is derivative of Hall and Chandler's short learning cycles of psychological success;[55]

the difference is that the interaction of duty, destiny, and disposition produce transformation and growth. With each interaction in the life span or across life roles, the dimensions of calling dynamically realign and expand to meet situational demands and opportunities; each incremental step up refines and strengthens one's destiny, disposition, and duty, and therefore one's calling.

As a life trait, calling has tonic, phasic, and fluid properties that vary across individuals. Destiny may be fluid as interests, opportunities, and life roles change over the life span. Alternatively, some aspects of destiny may be singularly focused from youth through adulthood, such as C.S. Lewis' boyhood love of literature and literary career. Aspects of one's sense of duty and their disposition are by necessity tonic and phasic; some tonic or stable attributes are the product of early socialization and education. Yet situational demands may elicit or mute one's sense of moral duty, character strengths, or coping skills, making them

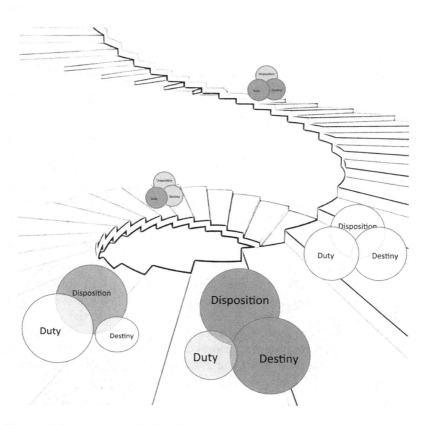

Figure 8.2 Dynamic model of calling throughout the life span.

more phasic. For example, a demoralizing work environment might cause uncharacteristic hopelessness and carelessness at work, yet foster new coping skills to manage the situation. In addition, leaders who ascend to positions of power because of their sense of duty and disposition may find that more power and less accountability makes them vulnerable to ethical missteps. Conversely, seizing a career opportunity might mean abandoning familiar coping skills and developing new competencies and character strengths. Thus, the prominence or salience of each dimension will change throughout different life stages, as illustrated by different size circles in Figure 8.2.

Practitioners note that awakenings to one's calling can occur at any life stage relative to any life role. Oprah Winfrey, for example, said that she knew her life calling at six years old. C. S. Lewis's awakening occurred at age 30. One's central calling may be to the unpaid work of parenting or volunteer service. Therefore, it would be a mistake to dismiss such roles as inconsequential because they are not classified as occupations. This is why Smith asserted that a vocational view of calling is liberating;[56] no two are the same, so there is no need for comparison. Therefore, a strict interpretation of the following examples is unwise; they are simply illustrative ideal types. My goal is to identify common elements of a calling that vary from person to person.

Youth may be the time when cultivating a sense of duty and disposition are most salient. Although life goals and dreams might be forming at this age, a sense of destiny has not yet crystalized. In adolescence, however, destiny can become clearer. In early adulthood, destiny is central but its fulfillment will be contingent upon character strengths, various competencies and coping skills. In midadulthood, life roles typically expand, yet are sustained by all three dimensions of a calling. During early and middle years, the goal is to develop core dimensions in order to ascend; in later years, the goal is to maintain, ascend, and fully integrate duty, destiny, and disposition. This pattern is evident in Barbara Walters's memoir, in which she acknowledged and was puzzled by her own character flaws. She explained how duty and a little fear were the catalysts for her career ascent; how her courage and temperance equipped her to deal with rampant sexism and excel; and how looking back, she was be proud of her legacy, despite her failings. We needn't wait to assess legacy until the end; at every step along the climb, we can look back to see what we have contributed and how we've grown because of our commitment to moral duty, character strengths, ability to cope, and perhaps the fit of our skills for the task. As Levoy noted, we should spill both tears and champagne in pursuit of our callings.[57] Indeed, the personal satisfaction and enrichment that arise from a calling are the fruit of "good work."

But perpetual progress is not guaranteed. There will obviously be plateaus during learning cycles and transitions. Furthermore, we can regress if there is a distortion in any dimension or due to life circumstances; dimensions of calling can be generative or degenerative. I've already mentioned how an overdeveloped sense of duty can derail a calling. And, an overdeveloped sense of destiny can be myopic. And how many people have had the gifts, talents, and drive to pursue a role, and the character and sense of duty to fulfill it for years, only to falter as humans do? Such lapses create a crisis in one's calling that ripples across life's roles. President Bill Clinton and General David Petraeus, former director of the U.S. Central Intelligence Agency, come to mind. Both men were faithful to their country and work obligations but were unfaithful to their wives while on duty. The height of each man's ascent magnified his failings in the public eye and became a source of derision (by some). As Matthew Crawford notes, "not only do things tend to go to hell, but your own actions contribute inevitably to that process."[58]

At this point, we don't yet know what will become of General Petraeus, but we do know that President Clinton did not shrink into oblivion or allow his missteps to define him. President Clinton remains a political force and leader of his party; he has a thriving charitable foundation whose mission is to advance "global health, strengthen economies, promote healthier childhoods, and protect the environment."[59] After all of the upheaval, including a heart attack and potential impeachment, he is still married to his wife and has another career aspiration. We fall down; what is in us, the cosmologies that guide us, and the people around us determine whether or not we get back up. I am optimistic that there are few distortions in one's calling that are truly, utterly irredeemable—although there may be premature plateaus.

In sum, calling is a series of daily choices that are made in response to life's rhythms. There will be steps back and setbacks because we are human; we have personal limits and confront externally imposed limits. From a positive organizing perspective, however, a calling offers the possibility that even setbacks and limits can be transformed into new opportunities to do good work. Furthermore, the recursive relationship of core dimensions across life roles and the life span offers infinite ways to live up to one's calling; some ways are more fitting, enjoyable, and enriching than others.

Advancing the Discourse

Practitioner insights about the calling to entrepreneurship, business and leadership show how leaders, through their guiding cosmologies and the regulatory environment, influence society and shape the context in which others live their callings by defining what is sacred (e.g., excellence and virtue, stewardship of the environment, equitable rewards, or consumption, profits and hierarchy). Organizational notions of the sacred, whether implicit or explicit, signal which goals that organization deems worth striving for and how it will pursue them.

The calls to entrepreneurship, business, and leadership are inherently noble but can go awry. The virtuous woman exemplifies a calling because of *what* she produced, *how* she worked, and the value that she added to society, not for what she consumed, the wealth that she amassed, or even her physical appearance. Her guiding cosmology is explicit and influenced her calling across life roles. She stands in stark contrast to the profit-only, competitive, consumptive, individualistic norms that pervade our society today. Examples throughout the chapter highlight the fact that, even though individual workers may have a calling, they may be employed by organizations and managers that have very different ideas about what is sacred and worthwhile. Research is needed to examine that tension and to understand the relationship between individual, administrative and organizational callings.

In addition, research is needed to understand which cosmologies have influenced people's sense of destiny, duty, and disposition, and to what degree—positively or negatively. Some cosmologies cultivate a calling, while others corrupt it. Insights into cosmological influences and gaps relative to destiny, duty, and disposition can elucidate points for educational intervention. In addition, research is needed to understand which cosmologies are complementary or competing at any given point, as well as the consequences of different types of cosmological dissonance.

Weber was concerned that the calling cosmology would no longer be taught by traditional institutions and, as a result, would be secularized and left to the caprices of work organizations. Lessons that were once learned at home, in schools, communities, and religious organizations are now increasingly learned in work organizations and diffused via corporate culture. Given practitioners' perspectives about shifts in the calling to business and leadership, do we really want organizations to play that role? Should employee callings be nurtured in corporations that, due to lax legislation, have diluted callings or no calling at all?

The two-dimensional ecological model in Figure 8.1 shows calling across life roles; the three-dimensional model in Figure 8.2 helps us comprehend the dynamic nature of calling across the life span. The ecological model highlights why cultivating a person's calling at work is both quite late in the life course and is potentially risky. It can be subject to influences of an "administrative theology" or corporate culture without noneconomic ideologies to moderate it, resulting in a hypercompetitive orientation toward "winning," with little regard for nonprofit-oriented goals. This practitioner conversation about calling brings the role of organizations and leaders into vivid and much-needed light, while alerting us to the shadowy side and negative implications for employees and society. In Chapter 11, I present a case study that illustrates the confluence of organizational, leader, and individual callings that benefit society. The case affirms what practitioners have stated here: whether you represent a business, are a leader, or are functioning as a worker, your calling is a community affair.

We have now examined practitioner perspectives about the essence and enactment of calling and compared them with diverse management perspectives. The only way to objectively determine whether the management literature should be modified is to compare these perspectives with historic theological notions of calling, which I do in the next chapter.

NOTES

1. Howard Gardner, Mihaly Csikszentmihalyi, and William Damon, *Good Work: When Excellence and Ethics Meet* (New York: Basic Books, 2001).
2. Jane Kise and David Stark, *Working with Purpose: Finding a Corporate Calling for You and Your Business* (Minneapolis, MN: Ausberg Fortress, 2004).
3. Michael Novak, *Business as a Calling: Work and the Examined Life* (New York: Free Press, 1996).
4. J. J. McGee and A. L. Delbecq, "Vocation as a Critical Factor in Spirituality for Executive Leadership in Business," in *Business, Religion and Spirituality: A New Synthesis,* ed. Oliver F. Williams, 94–110 (Notre Dame, IN: University of Notre Dame Press, 2003).
5. Gordon T. Smith, *Courage and Calling: Embracing Your God-Given Potential* (Downers Grove, IL: InterVarsity Press, 2011).
6. Lake Lambert III, *Spirituality Inc.: Religion in the American Workplace* (New York: New York University Press, 2009).
7. Ibid., 150.
8. Ibid., 40.
9. Ibid., 39.
10. F. Parsons, *Choosing a Vocation* (Boston: Houghton Mifflin, 1909).
11. P. J. Palmer, *Let Your Life Speak: Listening to the Voice of Vocation* (San Francisco: Jossey-Bass, 2000), 67.
12. McGee and Delbecq, "Vocation as a Critical Factor."
13. Novak, *Business as a Calling.*
14. Kise and Stark, *Working with Purpose,* 20.
15. Max Weber, *The Protestant Ethic and the Spirit of Capitalism* (London: Routledge, 1904/1992), 82.
16. Jennifer Abbott and Mark Achbar, dir., *The Corporation* (New York: Zeitgeist Films, 2003).
17. See http://www.youtube.com/watch?v=ui9C6xVpVf0.

18. Julie Schmit, "Peanut Boss Refuses to Testify at Salmonella Hearing," *USA Today* (2009), http://usatoday30.usatoday.com/news/washington/2009–02–11-house-salmonella_N.htm#.
19. Ross McLaughlin, "Tracking Down Stewart Parnell, Owner of the Peanut Corporation of America," *11 Alive News,* March 25, 2010, http://www.11alive.com/news/local/story.aspx?storyid = 142129.
20. Gardner, Csikszentmihalyi, and Damon, *Good Work.*
21. McLaughlin, "Tracking Down Stewart Parnell."
22. Brent Kendall and Delvin Barrett, "Four Accused of Salmonella Coverup," *Wall Street Journal,* February 22, 2013, A2.
23. Kise and Stark, *Working with Purpose.*
24. Gardner, Csikszentmihalyi, and Damon, *Good Work,* 90.
25. Novak, *Business as a Calling.*
26. McGee and Delbecq, "Vocation as a Critical Factor in Spirituality," 103.
27. Smith, *Courage and Calling,* 134ff.
28. M. G. Pratt and B. E. Ashforth, "Fostering Meaningfulness in Working and at Work," in *Positive Organizational Scholarship: Foundations of a New Discipline,* ed. J. E. Dutton, K. S. Cameron, and R. E. Quinn, 309–27 (San Francisco: Berrett-Koehler, 2003).
29. Novak, *Business as a Calling,* 144.
30.. Melissa Allison, "Costco Sets Pay for Incoming CEO," *Seattle Times,* http://seattletimes.com/html/businesstechnology/2016881535_costco29.html.
31. "Fortune 50 CEO Pay vs. Our Salaries," http://money.cnn.com/magazines/fortune/fortune500/2012/ceo-pay-ratios/.
32. Novak, *Business as a Calling.*
33. Kise and Stark, *Working with Purpose,* 74.
34. Ibid.
35. Ibid.
36. Ibid.
37. Gardner, Csikszentmihalyi, and Damon, *Good Work,* 254; See Gary Strauss, "Black Friday Arrests, Injuries Irk Shoppers at Walmart," *USA Today,* http://usatoday30.usatoday.com/money/industries/retail/story/2011–11–25/black-friday-walmart/51399030/1.
38. "Twenty Injured after Woman Uses Pepper Spray on Black Friday Crowd," FoxNews.com, November 25, 2011, http://www.foxnews.com/us/2011/11/25/ten-injured-after-woman-uses-pepper-spray-on-black-friday-crowd/.
39. Weber, *The Protestant Ethic,* 182.
40. Victor Lebow, "Price Competition in 1955," *Journal of Retailing* (Spring 1955), http://ablemesh.co.uk/PDFs/journal-of-retailing1955.pdf (emphasis added).
41. Nancy Koehn, "The History of Black Friday," *Marketplace Commentary* November 25, 2011, http://www.marketplace.org/topics/life/commentary/history-black-friday.
42. Ibid.
43. Ibid.
44. Kise and Stark, *Working with Purpose,* 162.
45. Smith, *Courage and Calling,* 133.
46. Robert W. Fuller, *Somebodies and Nobodies: Overcoming the Abuse of Rank* (Gabriola Island, British Columbia, Canada: New Society Publishers, 2004).

47. Analysis of these data was funded by the Blue Cross Blue Shield of Michigan Foundation, Grant #1854.11, Rankism and Behavioral Competencies in Hospitals.

48. Kise and Stark, *Working with Purpose*, 92.

49. McGee and Delbecq, "Vocation as a Critical Factor in Spirituality," 108.

50. Gardner, Csikszentmihalyi, and Damon, *Good Work*, 217.

51. D. E. Meyerson, *Tempered Radicals: How People Use Difference to Inspire Change at Work* (Cambridge, MA: Harvard Business School Press, 2001).

52. Kise and Stark, *Working with Purpose*, 55.

53. Ibid., 57.

54. Steven Spielberg, dir., *Schindler's List* (Hollywood, CA: Universal Studios, 1993).

55. Douglas T. Hall and Dawn E. Chandler, "Psychological Success: When the Career Is a Calling," *Journal of Organizational Behavior* 26, no. 2 (2005): 155–76.

56. Smith, *Courage and Calling*.

57. Gregg Michael Levoy, *Callings: Finding and Following an Authentic Life* (New York: Three Rivers Press, 1997), 325.

58. Matthew B. Crawford, *Shop Class as Soulcraft: An Inquiry into the Value of Work* (New York: Penguin Press, 2009), 203.

59. See the Clinton Foundation at http://www.clintonfoundation.org/.

9

Ideologies and Industrialism: 16th through 21st Centuries

That which has been is that which will be, and that which has been done is that which will be done. So there is nothing new under the sun.

—Ecclesiastes 1:9

Historically, traditional institutions in Europe and the United States such as family, churches, community organizations, professional guilds, and schools provided the cosmologies that cultivated and reinforced the core dimensions of calling. Across geography and demography, the calling ethic[1] endured for centuries, benefitting workers, work organizations, and society. Workers benefitted from transcendent meaning and significance that infused their daily activities. Work organizations benefitted from workers' clear standards for ethics and excellent performance, and transcendent motivation to pursue them. And society benefitted because a sense of calling motivated workers to produce high-quality goods and services that met real societal needs. As industrialism gained momentum, however, it produced major cultural shifts and uncertainty. Such changes caused traditional institutions to enter into new and different conversations about calling, to become much less vocal, or to disengage from the conversation completely. During the past 100 years, religious institutions have joined the latter groups.

In a 1997 survey, sociologist Robert Wuthnow found that Protestant and Catholic churches, which once monopolized religious and spiritual life in Europe and the United States, were viewed with skepticism by their members when and if they sought to address workplace issues.[2] Wuthnow's findings punctuated results from Lori Fox's study which showed a steady decline in published studies about church-based vocational programs from 1960–2000.[3] In addition, as noted, clergy and religious institutions did not lead the spirituality at work movement.[4] So, how did Protestant institutions, once the authoritative voice on calling, become so detached from work-related issues? This chapter explores answers to this question.

Despite management scholars' references to Luther, Calvin, and then Weber, a vast body of philosophical thought about calling exists in between. In fact, the idea was refined and advanced by cultural carriers across the centuries, including the 20th century, prior to the revival of calling in management scholarship.

Conversations about calling from a Protestant perspective have ensued since the Middle Ages. To understand how religious institutions' once-upon-a-time influence on calling changed so drastically, I conduct a brief review of sociological and theological shifts. I begin with conversations about calling from the 16th-century Reformation and progress through the birth and maturation of the Industrial Revolution in the 19th and early 20th centuries. Each era provides insights into religious and other institutional influences on the meaning and enactment of calling, as well as historic publications that assisted individuals in quest of their calling. Within these eras, I describe cultural shifts that provide insights into institutional alliances and influences on the social construction of calling, as well as cautionary lessons. I conclude by suggesting promising pathways to reinvigorate calling in practice.

Given the time span involved, it is impossible to present detailed accounts of how all traditional institutions changed their perspectives over the centuries or to survey the entire religious literature. My approach to this literature is cursory by necessity. Instead, I highlight inflection points throughout history that were associated with evolutionary shifts in capitalism, spawned new institutional partnerships, and resulted in profound changes in how various institutions framed, reinforced, or diluted the idea of calling.

To advance this discourse toward a theory, I provide historic theological references that verify, refute, or expand theoretical claims about calling that I presented in Chapters 2 through 8. Toward this end, I liberally insert direct quotes from Christian theologians to introduce readers to relevant voices about calling that are never cited by modern management scholars but that offer important theoretical insights. These theologians are the cultural carriers of calling who have understood its importance in spiritual and economic life and have helped it to endure. To place authors in historical context and orient readers when I compare perspectives, I have inserted publication dates within the text. Notice as well that I have preserved the original spelling from archived documents; archival text does not conform to modern spelling or punctuation standards. Finally, to provide a sense of philosophical continuity across centuries, this chapter is much longer than others. Many of the historical writings in this chapter can be found in William Placher's anthology *Callings: Twenty Centuries of Christian Wisdom on Vocation*,[5] or they have been archived in the Hathi Trust digital library.[6]

In bridging this vast literature that spans disciplines, I hope to inspire similar and more in-depth analysis of how this and other theological and philosophical traditions can yield comparable and different theoretical insights about calling in the future. The themes expressed in archived theological writings about calling are closely aligned with modern practitioner perspectives discussed in the preceding chapters. I draw on all of these insights to construct a comprehensive theory of calling that is presented in the next chapter.

The 16th Century: The Protestant Reformation

In the 1520s, German Protestant reformer Martin Luther (1483–1546) posed the revolutionary idea that calling was a sacred approach to ordinary work, not just monastic work. He believed that a person was called to work in ways that glorified God in a particular role, but with no opportunities for mobility. This was a grim prospect indeed for those whose aspirations exceeded their current station in life.[7] But Luther lived in a place and time when such simple divisions of labor made sense.[8] In his writings about *"Trade and Usury,"* Luther also espoused views about the calling to business (see Chapter 8).

> The rule ought to be, not, "I may sell my wares as dear I can or will," but, "I may sell my wares as dear as I ought, or, as is right and fair." For your selling ought not to be an act that is entirely within your own power and discretion, without law or limit, as though you were a god and beholden to no one. Because your selling is an act performed toward your neighbor, it should rather be so governed by law and conscience that you do it without harm and injury to him, your concern being directed more toward doing him no injury than toward gaining profit for yourself. But where are there such merchants?[9]

As Weber noted, Luther's ideas would have faded into irrelevance if John Calvin (1509–1564), a French theologian, hadn't adapted them to address societal shifts. According to theology professor Lee Hardy (1990): "Shortly after Luther's time, however, European civilization underwent a dramatic transformation under the combined influence of a rapidly expanding market economy, accelerated urbanization, technological innovation, and vast political reorganization."[10]

Calvin extended Luther's ideas in the *Institute of the Christian Religion* in 1536, in which he described calling as way of life that included using one's gifts, helping neighbors, enduring and enjoying work. "[E]ach man will bear and swallow the discomforts, vexations, weariness, and anxieties in his way of life, when he has been persuaded that the burden was laid upon him by God."[11] In contrast to Luther, Calvin's idea of calling included social mobility and social action; he encouraged taking stands against tyrannical interests, fallen institutions, and unjust social arrangements.[12] After all, it was a movement that advocated "reform." Calvin's activist sentiments were echoed in the writings of Gardner and his colleagues'[13] about good work and McGee and Delbecq's[14] notion of calling to leadership. Calvin affirmed leaders' responsibility to remove barriers and create the conditions for people to flourish in their callings.

The power of Luther's and Calvin's ideas is apparent in philosophies about calling that ensued across the centuries. Moreover, as their ideas gained popularity, they were refined by theologians and academics that succeeded them. Professor William Perkins was highly instrumental in this regard. In the late 1500s, Perkins wrote about "rules" that govern calling in his *A Treatise of the Vocations.*[15] Here, he described two callings: one to a general way of life that demonstrates Christian character and a second to a particular calling to certain roles. In addition, Perkins provided more elaborate definitions and also opined about theoretical aspects of calling. I have included direct quotes from Perkins in the section that follows; these quotes verify scholars' and practitioners' claims about calling from previous chapters.

Calling and Integration across Life Roles

Every person, of every degree, state, sex, or condition without exception, must have some personal and particular calling to walk in.[16]

Every particular calling must be practiced in and with the general calling of a Christian . . . And thus may we reap marvelous content in any kind of calling, though it be but to sweep the house or keep sheep, if we can thus in practice unite our callings.[17]

Criteria for Leadership

Such as bear public callings, must first reform themselves in private . . . How shall he order public matters for the common good, that cannot order his own private estate?[18]

Alignment, Destiny, and Community

[E]very man must examine himself of two things: first, touching his affection, secondly, touching his gifts. For his affection, he must search what mind he has to any calling, and in what calling he desires most of all to glorify God . . . . Yet, because many men are partial in judging of their inclination and gifts, the best way for them is to use the advice and help of others that are able to give direction herein, and to discern better than themselves.[19]

Parental Duty and Childhood Experiences

Now touching children, it is the duty of parents to make choice of fit callings for them before they apply them to any particular condition of life . . . Athenians, who before they placed their children in any calling, did first bring them into a public place, where instruments of all sorts were laid, and they observed with what kind of instrument they took delight, and to the like art did they afterwards apply them with good success. And it will not be amiss for Christians to be followers of the Heathen in this, or any other commendable practice.[20]

And here all parents must be warned, that the neglect of this duty is a great and common sin.[21]

Changing Callings

A change of calling is a lawful going from one calling to another . . . Nevertheless, a change may not be made, but upon urgent and weighty causes, and they are two especially: Private necessity and the common good. Private necessity is when men cannot maintain themselves and theirs by the callings in which they are; for then they may betake themselves to other callings . . . And it must be remembered, that as often as we change, it must be to better and more excellent callings, in which we may glorify God more, and bring greater benefit to the Church and Commonwealth.[22]

Protestant reformers' original ideas variously conveyed the concepts of duty, destiny, disposition, as well as calling as a way of life that spanned multiple roles. Their ideas were greatly reinforced and elaborated on during the next century.

The 17th Century: Establishing Calling across the Institutional Landscape

The idea of calling swept Europe and the colonies that later became the United States, thanks to a proliferation of influential writings and sermons by clergy in various contexts. Often, clergy were also professors, which gave their writings additional weight, reach and perhaps made them more accessible to the masses. Philosophers who addressed calling during this era include Reverend Thomas Case, Thomas Shephard, Reverend Richard Baxter, John Bunyan, and Richard Steele.

In 1641, Reverend Thomas Case carried the mantle of Calvinism and social reform into the new century with his address to the English House of Commons when he said: "Reformation must be universal. Reform all places, all persons, and callings; reform the benches of judgement, the inferior magistrates . . . Reform the universities, reform the cities, reform the countries, reform the inferior schools of learning, reform the Sabbath, reform the ordinances, the worship of God . . . you have more to do than I can speak."[23]

In 1655, Thomas Shephard—"Sometimes of Emanuel College in Cambridge, Now Preacher of God's Word in New England"[24]—wrote *Certain Select Cases Resolved, Specially, Tending to the Right Ordering of the Heart That We May Comfortably Walk with God in Our Generall and Particular Callings*. In it, he clarified questions about the ontology of calling by distinguishing between the general calling to Christian faith that ideally resulted in certain character traits and particular callings to different life roles. He also spoke of ethical duty, excellent work, distractions, character weaknesses, and prayer.

In the mid to late 1600s, British minister Richard Baxter wrote the classic *Directions about Our Labors and Callings*.[25] Here, Baxter answered lingering questions about calling in a common-sense way that enabled people to practice the concept in their daily lives. Baxter's work subsequently influenced Max Weber. Some of Baxter's ideas are reflected in the subsequent quotes that follow.

Status, Wealth, and Calling

"Is Labor necessary to all? Or to whom if not to all?" Answer: It is necessary (as a duty) to all that are able to perform it, but to the unable it is not necessary: as to infants and sick persons, or distracted persons that cannot do it.[26]

"Will not riches excuse one from laboring in a calling?" Answer: No, but rather bind them to it the more, for he that has most wages from God should do him most work. *Though they have no outward want to urge them, they have as great a necessity of obeying God and doing good to others as any other men have that are poor.*[27]

Sacred Meaning of Work

"Why is labor thus necessary to all that are able?" Answer: God hath strictly commanded it to all, and his command is reason enough to us.[28]

Job is a Calling

Lastly, it is God's appointed means for the getting of our daily bread, and as it is a more real honor to get our bread ourselves than to receive it by the gift of our friends or parents, so is it more comfortable to a well-informed mind. We may best believe that we have our food and provisions in mercy, and that they shall be blest to us, when we have them in God's appointed way, who hath said, "If any man will not work, neither should he eat."[29]

If thou be called to the poorest laborious calling, do not carnally complain of it because it is wearisome to the flesh, nor imagine that God accepts the less of thy work and thee; but cheerfully follow it, and make it the matter of thy pleasure and joy that thou art still in thy heavenly Master's service, though it be about the lowest things.[30]

Multiple Callings

May a man have diverse trades or callings at once? Answer: Yes, no doubt, if it be for the common good or for his own and no injury to any other; nor so inconsistent, as that one shall make him unfaithful in the other: then God forbids it not.[31]

Social Influences on Calling

Choose no calling (especially if it be of public consequence) without the advice of some judicious, faithful persons of that calling.[32]

Ethics, Choice, and Soul Care

It is not enough that the work of your calling be lawful, nor that it be necessary, but you must take special care also that it be safe, and not very dangerous to your souls.[33]

When two callings equally conduce to the public good, and one of them hath the advantage of riches, and the other is more advantageous to your souls, the latter must be preferred, and next to the public good, *the soul's advantage must guide your choice*.[34]

Calling, Work, and Health Consequences

Labor is needful to our health and life: the body itself will quickly fall into mortal diseases without it (except in some very few persons of extraordinary soundness). Next to abstinence, labor is the chief preserver of health. It stirs up the natural heat and spirits, which perform the chief offices for the life of man; it is the proper bellows for this vital fire; it helps all the concoctions of nature .... *For want of bodily labor a multitude of the idle gentry, and rich people, and young people that are slothful, do heap up in the secret receptacles of the body a dunghill of unconcocted, excrementitious filth,* and vitiate all the mass of humors which should be the fuel and oil of life, and *die by thousands of untimely deaths* (of fevers, palsies, convulsions, apoplexies, dropsies, consumptions, gout, &c.) more miserably than if thieves had murdered them by the highway, because it is their own doing, and by their sloth they kill themselves. For want of bodily exercise and labor interposed, abundance of students and *sedentary persons fill themselves with diseases, and hasten their death,* and causelessly blame their hard studies for that which was caused by their bodily sloth.[35]

More than 300 years ago, Baxter wrote about soul crafting and volunteering, and he foreshadowed the negative health consequences of sedentary lives that require minimal physical effort! He wrote a great deal about the mind, body and soul connection as it relates to work, and he lectured to merchants on these topics.

While clergy and scholars clarified the meaning of calling overall, different traditional institutions focused on select dimensions and sometimes multiple dimensions. With regard to destiny, increased interaction between economic and ecumenical communities led clergy and laity to make explicit connections between calling, commerce, and specific occupations. One example is Gervaese Markham and his colleagues. In 1676, they wrote *A Way to Get Wealth: Containing Six Principal Vocations, or Callings, in Which Every Good Husband or House-Wife May Lawfully Imploy Themselves.*[36] In this work, they exhaustively described (more than 600 pages) the requisite skills and "inward virtues" to excel in agriculture, gardening, home economics, and wholesome recreational activities for husbands "after the toil of more serious business."[37] Clearly, the calling ethic was not antiwealth, profits, or extrinsic rewards. Moreover, calling was understood as a trait that applied to all of life's roles—employment, marriage, and recreation.

In 1684, Minister Richard Steele's *The Trades-Man's Calling*[38] dealt with issues of a general calling, the "right ends" of which are God's glory, the common good, and one's own good. He also praised business as a worthwhile "particular" calling for which to educate children, not unlike McGee and Delbecq[39] or Kise and Stark[40] (see Chapter 8). With regard to other particular callings, Steele advocated for trade-specific virtues (e.g., ingenuity) and personal conduct such as prudence, discretion, diligence, justice, truth, contentedness, and wisdom. He also noted that calling was the result of an awakening: "upon a serious Reflection you will find, that ye have been all this while asleep, in a pleasant foolish Dream, and that it is high time to awake to action and employment."[41] Another important philosophical contribution Steele made was that wealth did not absolve a person from the dictates of calling: "Let no Man therefore plead his Birth, Estate, his Parts or Graces, to justify an idle Life."[42] Numerous times, he admonished against self-interest and selfish behavior, which are antithetical to calling. Steele's ideas were so influential that his book was published again 63 years later—in 1747—with a new introduction. Other clergy followed his example and addressed different occupational groups about normative skills and conduct. For example, in 1610, Thomas Wilson delivered a sermon to blacksmiths about their calling.[43]

With regard to destiny and moral duty to a profession, the idea of calling was powerfully reinforced through the guild system, which established standards of membership, training, and workmanship for various crafts—in other words, the standards for good work (e.g., ethics and excellence). Guilds gave workers control over their work and their industry. According to theology professor Lake Lambert (2009), "The guilds also included a religious-ethical dimension, with the organization providing support for needy members, widows, and orphans. Rules stipulating the quality of goods and the limits of competition were also developed."[44] Guild members worshipped together and some types of work even became associated with certain saints. Occupational standards were also reinforced in the home, which at that time was the center of economic life.

The calling disposition was also cultivated through leisurely pursuits such as literature and song. John Bunyan's *The Pilgrim's Progress*[45] (originally published in 1678) was an allegory of spiritual qualities and character traits needed for one's life journey and beyond. Songs were used to convey messages about occupation, virtue, and skill, including anonymous ditties such as *A True Character of Sundry Trades and Callings* (1670),[46] *The Devil's Oak* (1685),[47] and *True Blew the Plowman* (1685).[48] The use of literature and song to reinforce the cosmologies of calling parallel African Americans' activities in pursuing and responding to delayed and denied callings (see Chapter 7). Moreover, the cosmologies of calling were similarly diffused and reinforced through symbiotic relationships between traditional institutions: the family home was the workplace; the guild was composed of family and community members; families and guild members worshiped together; and leisure activities throughout the culture included character building (see Chapter 6).

The end of the 17th century also seeded the Industrial Revolution, as agricultural work became mechanized. Industrialism had not yet radically changed the nature of most work or the culture. As mechanization and calling became established, both flourished and changed as the Industrial Revolution gained momentum in the next century.

The 18th Century: Emerging Industrialism and Distorted Callings

Archived writings about calling during the 1700s are few, in part because this was a tumultuous era in which the colonies revolted against Britain and declared independence to form the United States of America. Mechanized labor spread rapidly to other industries including energy, transportation, and textiles. Technological and economic shifts began to change the culture drastically, in ways no one could have ever imagined. Calling was increasingly at risk of being distorted, particularly among business and civic leaders. Some sought to amplify and exploit those distortions, whereas others sought to prevent distortions and preserve the original ideas of calling.

In 1735, Robert Warren, a British minister, delivered a sermon titled *Industry and Diligence in Our Callings Earnestly Recommended* that highlighted regional differences in the evolution of calling, particularly in the South. More specifically, Warren used the idea of calling to perpetuate social injustices by keeping certain people "in their place." Warren spoke this way about the establishment of the colony of Georgia and its economy: "The Usefulness and Advantageousness of these Settlements in Plantations does not only visibly appear, at this Day, in the immense effects they send us, *but the Profits of them are like to descend to future Times, to the Children that are yet unborn*."[49] Equality index statistics presented in Chapter 7 validate his claim about the advantages that accrued to plantation owners and the perpetuation of multigenerational wealth.

Warren went on to say that: "The Employment of our Poor, the Improvement of our Manufacturers, the Increase of our Revenues, and the Enrichment of our Merchants are all of them the glorious Consequences of these Establishments. Blessings that are like to last, as long as the Plantations themselves."[50] Economic imperatives to preserve the status quo with this version of calling are obvious. Warren advocated for the existing social arrangement (e.g., exploiting poor whites and slaves) under the guise of the common good. He further proclaimed that "certain people" should be trusted as honorable simply because of their social status: "Nor is it possible to conceive that this Scheme can be carry'd on with any view to private Interest. For those most eminent and honorable Persons who have undertaken the Trust and Direction of this Establishment, have entirely disclaimed all prospects of selfish advantage . . . The nobleness of their Birth, and the Dignity of those Stations so eminently fill, exempt them from all suspicion of Fraud or collusion, as not only contributing to the Design in a bountiful manner themselves, but as promoting the encouragement of it in others."[51] How dare anyone accuse them of being self-interested business men!

Because these men profited so greatly from this arrangement, Warren also explained the moral imperative of "honorable persons" to demonstrate charity: "To you therefore, whom our good and gracious God has abled by your Wealth and Opulence to be liberal and beneficent to those below you and whom he has therefore distinguish'd from the inferiour Part of Mankind."[52] Warren's idea of calling was aligned with Martin Luther's static, class-based idea. In addition, Warren favored a highly instrumental notion of calling that preserved a tyrannical and inequitable social order, which Calvinism opposed.[53] Warren embraced the older idea of calling because it served his economic and cultural goals.

In contrast, William Law (1729), a would-be British professor and preacher who stood on principle and was consequently denied his occupational destiny, spoke of calling as sacred work. In *A Serious Call to a Devout and Holy Life*, Law said, "Men may, and must differ in their employments, but yet they must all act for the same ends, as dutiful servants of God, in the right and pious performance of their several callings."[54]

Law was most concerned with how callings could be distorted as the pursuit of personal glory and wealth became idealized emblems of capitalist's success. Law cautioned against making profits sacred and amassing wealth just for the sake of becoming wealthier: "The husbandman that tills the ground is employed in an honest business that is necessary in life and very capable of being made an acceptable service unto God. But *if he labors and toils, not to serve any reasonable ends* of life, but in order to have his *plough made of silver,* and to have his *horses harnessed in gold,* then honesty of his employment is lost as to him, and *his labor becomes folly.*"[55]

To illustrate his points, Law went on to describe a fictional character named Calidus, whose calling to business was diminished by the very pursuit of it:

> Every hour of the day is with him an hour of business; and though he eats and drinks very heartily, yet every meal seems to be in a hurry, and he would say grace if he had time. Calidus ends every day at the tavern, but has not leisure to be there till near nine o'clock. He is always forced to drink a good hearty glass, to drive thoughts of business out of his head, and make his spirits drowsy enough for sleep. He does business all the time that he is rising, and has settled several matters before he can get to his counting-room. His prayers are a short ejaculation or two, which he never misses in stormy, tempestuous weather, because he has always something or other at sea. It must also be owned, that the generality of trading people, especially in great towns, are too much like Calidus. *You see them all the week buried in business, unable to think of anything else;* and then spending the Sunday in idleness and refreshment, in wandering into the country, in such visits and jovial meetings, as make it often the worst day of the week.[56]

Law's views are congruent with those of the practitioners described in Chapter 8 in several ways. He set guidelines for the calling to leadership. He also advocated for a holistic calling to business that does not make profits and work sacred, while considering the spiritual and social consequences of doing so. Law critiqued not only the race for wealth but also how its unbridled pursuit would negatively impact individual and social life—as did Weber.

The writings of Warren and Law suggest that central tensions about calling in the 18th century were not about the sacred or secular nature of calling or whether calling subsumed one's whole life versus occupation. Indeed, these were settled matters. Instead, the central controversies were about how business and government leaders should pursue their callings; the appropriate guidelines for acquiring wealth; issues of social justice reflected in assumptions about owners who were "somebody" and workers who were "nobody"; and how pursuing a calling in commerce might morph into the sheer pursuit of profits and negatively impact one's soul. These ideological differences persisted and were amplified in the 19th century, as industrialism reached its zenith, and the wealth gap between the owning and working classes erupted into major social conflicts—including the Civil War.

The 19th Century: Diluted Calling and the Promise of Industrial Betterment

The idea of calling persisted into the new century, with various institutions continuing to reinforce the notion. As a cultural ideal, however, the idea changed yet again due to economic, technical, and social shifts. History professor Daniel Rodgers (1974) wrote exhaustively about these shifts in *The Work Ethic in Industrial America 1850–1920*.[57] Rodgers noted that "the work ethic radiated not only from the secular pulpits of journalism but from all the institutional fortresses of the middle class. Campaigns to inculcate the values of industriousness in schoolchildren, and to impose it upon employees and social dependents, gathered and spent their force over and over again in nineteenth-century America, leaving behind a crust of middle-class morality of uncertain but perceptible depth."[58] According to Rodgers, "Endless repetition—in conduct guides, boys' storybooks, handbooks of business advice, and magazine fillers—ingrained the idea as one of the century's most firmly held commonplaces."[59]

The influence of traditional institutions on calling waned, however, as life became more uncertain. The home, once the center of economic activity, was displaced as factory work increased. Guild-defined standards of ethics and excellence (duty) became irrelevant, much to the consternation of craftsmen, as they relinquished control of their work to managers and machines. This shift not only demoralized workers but also became a source of conflict between management and labor that ultimately resulted in strikes near the end of the century and the advent of labor unions and labor laws. The trade or work of one's family and community were no longer the dominant predictors of one's occupational destiny—a whole new world of work in factories and life in urban centers was now possible.

Toward that end, the new discipline of "vocophy" was established, a precursor to today's career counselors. In 1881, Lysander Salmon Richards wrote *Vocophy: The New Profession. A System Enabling a Person to Name the Calling or Vocation One Is Best Suited to Follow*.[60] Through this work,

Richards offered help to a new breed of professionals that assisted people as they navigated occupational possibilities in the new economy. Richards's immodest goal was to "benefit every inhabitant on the face of our planet, not so much those who have passed the meridian of life, as the young and middle aged, whose success depends upon the choice of the most *fitting* pursuit . . . in which he can reap the greatest success that is possible for him individually to gain."[61] He believed that a *fitting* occupation was synonymous with calling.

In Richards's book, we begin to see three important shifts in the conversation about calling. First, the focus on calling shifts from one's whole life to employment only, and that "fit" was of paramount importance. Second, sacred meaning and glorifying God through work disappeared from his conversation. Third, this philosopher/consultant "scientized" calling and made grandiose yet unsubstantiated claims about his own work as a vocopher: "To every nation on the earth it is of equal value."[62] Furthermore, Richards equated material consumption with civilization and maturation; having a fitting occupation was a means to achieve those ends. Among the many things that Richards said, he explicitly connected career with calling, and both to consumptive habits and capitalism. A teenaged Max Weber may have been paying attention.

Richards wrote:

> Wherever on the face of the globe a class of beings is found whose desires are small, there is seen the savage and barbarian. Instill into the Indian, part of the desire for luxuries which some of our fast Americans have in excess, and progress is stamped on the future of the red man. Let him yearn to build a well-finished house instead of a hut, and gain a farm with all the accessories for successful cultivation, and he is no longer a savage, but a full-grown man. Better want too much than too little. Civilization is the outgrowth of want . . . but in our eagerness we must not lose sight of the fact that our wants should not exceed the absolute impossibility of successful attainment.[63]

According to Richards, lack of fit was the source of poverty. His perspective reveals how "calling" had become an instrument for the working class, not just 17th-century capitalists. Given people's myriad opportunities to be exposed to new information and experiences in urban centers, Richards counseled vocophers and encouraged readers to be open to pursuing unfamiliar pathways that might reveal "hidden powers"[64] and latent "geniuses"[65] that were previously unimaginable. Like the practitioners reviewed in Chapter 6, he extolled the need for broad exposure before foreclosing on a life path and mustering the courage to pursue it.

"Let a factory start in any town with facilities to employ a thousand men, the majority of the young men in town would seek employment therein, because it is close at hand, easy to get at, and the first thing that presents itself to enable them to earn a living and take care of themselves; they did not stop to consider whether there is some other pursuit in which they will find greater success," wrote Richards.[66]

Notably, Richards may have created the first interest/occupational inventory, which he called "examination charts."[67] Among all of the examinations (e.g., physiognomy, heredity, ingenuity, home ties, and language), no trace of religion or the sacred meaning of calling was mentioned. Instead, Richards devoted one-fifth of his book to introduce his new professional tool (e.g., examination charts) and to describe essential character traits of different occupations including apothecary, elocutionist, political statesman, and tinman. His goal was to help people align their character strengths with a fitting occupation. His novel way of framing calling not only offered help to eager young people in an uncertain economy but also ingeniously accelerated his own new profession. Meanwhile, ministers such as J. Llewelyn Davies[68] persisted in the view that calling was a sacred approach to work and life and that the focus on consumption without concern for justice was an increasing problem.

Davies addressed the disposition and character strengths of calling on a macrolevel. He opined about the deification of consumption, the need for social justice rather than an elitist sense of entitlement, and the transcendent value of sanctity in the mundane, including character strengths in ordinary work. The following quotes illustrate his views.

What Is Sacred?

Now, it would be a very bad thing for us if no one could call what he had his own, if life had no stability, and industry no secure reward. All that is patent. It would be a downfall, indeed, if we were to lose the protection of a settled law of rights and ownership. But what I am noting, from the Christian point of view, is this, that *we have given ourselves up to a kind of worship of property and vested interests and bequests.* Our regard for these things, instead of being cool and moderate and conditional, has been touched with the imaginative emotion which turns it into a religion. *The very phrase, "the sacredness of property," discloses the feeling with which we regard it. We are inclined to exalt possessions, as objects of worship, above the irreverent discussions of reason.*[69]

Rankism and Justice

With regard to the relationship between secular justice and theology, Davies said:

It teaches us to throw our sympathies on the side of the poor when their interests seem to come into competition with those of the rich, on the side of the weak more willingly than on that of the strong. To do this is not mere condescending benevolence; it is justice, the justice that renders to all their dues . . . *What is due to the weak and defenceless?* Protection. What is due to the ignorant? Enlightenment. What is due to the misunderstood? Endeavours to enter into their thoughts and feelings. What is due to those that are down? Efforts to lift them up. Your Christian hearts, I hope, brethren, have given these answers freely. Once more, *What is due to the rich and great? An answer does not, I imagine, rise so readily to the lips.* Shall we say, Honour, flattery, gaping admiration, sedulous anxiety to take out of their way any hindrance that would restrain them from doing what they like with their own, not only while they live but down to the twentieth generation after them?[70]

Transcendent Meaning of Calling

Be not persuaded to take a worldly view of life and to make respectability your standard. *We cannot afford to lose the elevating influence of the consciousness of sanctity.* You know what the sense of honour has done for the privileged classes of society, how it has made men regard it as an intolerable insult to be charged with lying, cowardice, or meanness, and has thus been in some degree a real safeguard to them against the faults deemed unworthy of a gentleman.[71]

Disposition and Duty

The way to serve your Christian profession is to shew how *considerate,* how delicately *just,* how *courageous,* how *devoted to the common good,* Christians can be.[72]

To cope with new opportunities and leverage economic shifts, workers presumably needed a different disposition—new virtues and character strengths and, consequently, new stories. Children's stories are perhaps most illustrative of the uncertain climate, shifting adult morals, and the increased focus on individuals as opposed to community.[73] Narratives changed as children aspired to life beyond the farm. However, because no precedent had been established for work in a mechanized and urbanized economy, writers had no referent for the type of disposition that would fare best in the new economy. So they invented it. (Notably, the unintended negative consequences of what writers "invented" at the time have not been fully examined, to my knowledge, in any research studies.) Rodgers noted that "as they moved from metaphors of diligence and self-control to those of heroism, boys' story writers did not mean to denigrate work. A fervent faith in duty endured. But the new stories no longer praised the character-building reward of effort; rather they made a romance of victory."[74] Character strengths, such as those identified by Peterson and Seligman[75] and described in Chapter 6, receded in importance. The focus on adventure, rugged individualism, and athletic prowess were firmly established in the late 1800s, thereby grooming young men who would become elite industrialists or dutiful laborers in the Gilded Age (1865–1890). The term 'Gilded Age' is a metaphor for an economic era that glitters on the surface but is substantively corrupt.

During the latter part of the 19th century, messages about calling became increasingly bifurcated by class as sermons and novels were broadcast, such as those by Henry Ward Beecher (1867). Beecher encouraged workers to be diligent and disciplined, while he encouraged the elite to find leisurely and creative escapes from their economic endeavors.[76] Wealthy industrialist families, enriched by child laborers and workers who endured dangerous and demeaning working conditions, felt a moral obligation to provide for their workers; many others industrialists did not. The authors of *Habits* wrote: "In the predatory capitalists the age dubbed robber barons, some of the worst fears of earlier republican moralists seemed confirmed: that by releasing the untrammeled pursuit of wealth without regard to the demands of social justice, industrial capitalism was destroying the fabric of democratic society, threatening social chaos by pitting class against class."[77] Unfortunately, traditional institutions were instrumental in deepening this cleavage, as they simultaneously gave less attention to calling. According to *Habits*, "Particularly powerful in molding our contemporary sense of things has been the division between the various 'tracks' to achievement laid out in schools, corporation, government, and the professions on the one hand, and the balancing life-sectors of home, personal ties, and 'leisure,' on the other."[78]

Regional differences also emerged in accepting (or rejecting) the new calling or "work ethic." Northern middle-class factory workers and elites embraced the idea; Southern workers rejected it, rightly believing that it was a manipulative ideology from which they had little to gain.[79]

After the Civil War, capitalists' attention turned to minimizing conflict during Reconstruction, which began the industrial betterment movement of 1870 to 1900. Sociologists Stephen Barley and Gideon Kunda (1992) identified the ideological underpinnings of industrial betterment, a means of managerial control.[80] "The movement consisted of a loose coalition of clergy, journalists, novelists, academics, and capitalists. Prominent among the early spokespersons was Washington Gladden, a Congregationalist minister who linked religious visions of morality to a 'new stage of industrial evolution' premised on the 'principle of co-operation' and characterized by 'industrial partnerships' that would improve 'the mental and moral qualities of the working-people.'"[81]

Guiding themes of the movement were mixed. The goals were to ameliorate the growing conflict between elites and laborers, ensure profitability, heighten elite leaders' awareness of their moral responsibility for employee well-being, and ultimately change the worker through various social influences of the community. Although it could be argued that this movement was a calling to business leaders to "make the world a better place," the entanglement between their economic self-interests with philanthropic endeavors was undeniable.

Railroad magnate Cornelius Vanderbilt funded the construction of Young Men's Christian Associations (YMCAs) in industrial centers during the 1870s and beyond. He hoped to build on the YMCA's historic success in England of cultivating men who were reliable workers and who avoided vices that might undermine their performance (e.g., drunkenness and gambling). As a community organization that reinforced dimensions of the calling ethic (duty, disposition, and destiny), the YMCA was ideal because it reached broad swaths of the population. According to archived historical information,[82] it was founded in Boston in 1851; established for blacks in Washington, D.C., in 1853; and established to serve Asians in 1875. The YMCA, in addition to Bible study, helped socialize, house, and ease the transition of European immigrants to the United States, Southern migrants to the Northern factory towns, and rural migrants to urban centers. Thus, the cosmologies of calling that were once primarily defined by religious institutions and diffused through multiple traditional institutions (e.g., guilds, family, schools, and media) were defined and diffused by fewer organizations, like the YMCA. Some of these organizations depended heavily on the largess of a few corporate donors to which they became beholden.

Alternatively, some industrialists built entire communities for their workers; the industrialists' work ideologies were diffused through multiple institutions that they owned or influenced. George Pullman, who developed the Pullman luxury railcar, was among the first to adopt such holistic business practices in 1885. Pullman noticed the social unrest that industrialism created in his hometown of Chicago. In response, he built a new factory in Chicago and a surrounding community of shops, hotels, parks, and a single church. Lake Lambert (2009) noted that "by building a model town where his workers resided, Pullman hoped to foster an improved moral ethos. Pullman was also able to maintain absolute control over the continued use and upkeep of the property by retaining full ownership and allowing only renters."[83] It was a way to reconcile capitalism and the Social Gospel—to a degree.

Numerous other industrialists followed suit and established holistic communities for their employees, which partially fulfilled their moral obligation to the workers whose labor contributed to their wealth. The problem, though, was this: industrialists didn't seek to change working conditions; rather, they aimed to change the interior conditions of workers with an "administrative theology" that advanced their business interests. Consequently, journalists, academics, and trade unionists began to challenge these social arrangements. Economics professor Richard T. Ely (1885) criticized Pullman's efforts in *Harpers New Monthly Magazine*. Barley and Kunda described Ely's analysis: "Ely warned that Pullman was a 'gilded cage' for the workingman, 'a benevolent, well-wishing feudalism which desires the happiness of the people but in such a way as shall please the authorities.'"[84] As a result, violent strikes ensued despite corporate benevolence, notably against the Pullman Palace Car Company in 1894.

The strike against Pullman and other corporations, despite their largess, called into question whether industrial betterment was effective to achieve desired organizational goals. The techniques of scientific management seemed to offer a more promising form of managerial control. Britain, having traveled the path of betterment and strikes, offered lessons about what techniques did and did not work.

The preceding analysis suggests that the 19th century, perhaps more than any other, resulted in diluted institutional messaging about calling from family, community, schools, professional organizations, congregations, and the media. Mixed messages of industrial betterment distorted the focus of calling from glorifying God to glorify industrialists and advancing their economic interests, rather than mere parochial commercial interests as it was positioned in past centuries.

New institutional partnerships that were forged in the new economy had potentially positive social benefits. However, attempts to transform workers' "dispositions," exploit their sense of duty, and limit their destinies, while failing to change dismal working conditions backfired as a managerial tool. Labor strikes ensued and cleared the way for greater efficiency through scientific management. This is the context within which Max Weber wrote *The Protestant Ethic and the Spirit of Capitalism*. Throughout the century, calling had indeed become a ghost of its former self in popular and managerial culture; the trend continued during the 20th century.

The 20th Century: Calling and Human Relations

After World War I, fascination with scientific management waned as it became a "taken for granted" way of improving performance. Although the 20th century brought a flurry of social, technological, and economic changes, I focus here on several events that help explain the waning influence of religious institutions on calling and commerce—the mill strikes in Gastonia, North Carolina (1929), World War II (1939–1945), and the civil rights movement (1950s–1960s).

Gastonia Mill Strikes

Across the country, industrialists replicated the all-encompassing corporate communities built by George Pullman, Henry Ford, and others—including textile towns in the southern United States. Liston Pope, a clergyman, Yale theologian, and native of North Carolina, conducted an in-depth study of relationships between clergy, industrialists, managers, and workers in his book *Millhands and Preachers: A Study of Gastonia.*[85] The story gives new meaning to the terms *company town* and *getting religion.*

Mill owners and corporations built towns around their factories; towns included housing, schools, recreational facilities, and churches. Mill owners strategically built churches of different denominations so that all of their workers would be served. Mill owners also gifted land for churches, made large cash contributions to construct churches, and in some cases, ministers were even on the mill payrolls, just like other employees. But ministers had the added benefit of free housing in a corporate-sponsored parsonage.

Mill owners themselves didn't join these churches; they sent their wives instead (much to their wives' dismay). But mill managers were expected to become members and to assume leadership roles. These arrangements were considered essential to 'make Gastonia a better place' (in the modern language of calling). But the arrangement between mills and preachers wasn't a collaboration; it was a coup. From the pulpit to Sunday school to church socials, corporations controlled the message that helped to cultivate millhands' disposition to be compliant workers, despite their horrific working conditions.

Eventually, millhands took a stand against their subpar wages, working conditions, and the influx of Northern industrialists who bought Southern mills. Mill workers initially garnered some community support for their cause. Then, pastors staged religious revivals to divert the community's attention from the workers' protests. When that failed, clergy and the press colluded with mill owners in a propaganda campaign that incited community violence against the strikers.

According to Richard Peterson and N. J. Demerath (1942), who wrote the introduction to *Millhands and Preachers,* "The most striking of Pope's findings is the extent to which the millhands were deserted by their preachers. The churches were inextricably bound to mill management by their finances if not by their ideology. Organized religion was a key instrument in creating a manipulatable labor force and in resisting the union's efforts to break with the exploitative status quo. Ministers not only justified management practices; they were mute in reaction to the violent recriminations exerted by the community against union organizers."[86] Peterson and Demerath noted that Gastonia was not an anomaly; it illustrated how relationships between some clergy and capitalists evolved across the country. Rather than challenge tyranny as Calvin had urged, clergy stayed silent to preserve their own and their church's economic survival. In the process, some lost their prophetic voice about work—and calling.

World War II

Annoyed by the church's inordinate focus on cultivating workers' disposition, Dorothy Sayers used World War II as an opportunity to ignite imaginations and conversations about the need to change the relationships between ecumenical and business communities. Sayers, a British mystery writer, Christian philosopher, and daughter of an Anglican minister, wrote incisive essays about economics, work, and faith. In 1942 Sayers, along with other British leaders, contemplated *A Christian Basis for the Post-War World*.[87] In an essay titled *Vocation in Work*,[88] she said that "the sense of Divine vocation must be restored to a man's daily work."[89] She was especially concerned with how capitalism had adversely impacted the meaning and quality of work. Sayers viewed the post-war recovery period as an opportunity to rethink and reconfigure existing arrangements. Her piercing insights still challenge us today.

Like theologians that preceded her, Sayers wrote about occupational destiny, disposition, and duty with regard to calling. Her primary focus, however, was on the outcomes of calling and the duty to do good work. She believed that the church, to a degree, had colluded with industrialists in the demise of calling thanks to benign neglect and sentimentality. Although it is difficult to pinpoint exactly when the church's prophetic voice about work became less audible, Sayers unambiguously yearned to hear it again. Her unrestrained critique of the church for its engagement with and failure to address issues of vocation and commerce was published in an essay titled "*Why Work?*"[90] Sayers chastised the church for its growing timidity and ineffectiveness related to work and vocation and, by extension, the synthetic ideologies that emerged from collaborations between industrialists and the ecumenical community to cultivate 'good workers' rather than "good work." She wrote, "The Church's approach to an intelligent carpenter is usually confined to exhorting him not to be drunk and disorderly in his leisure hours, and to come to church on Sundays. What the Church should be telling him is this: that the very first demand that his religion makes upon him is that he should make good tables . . . No crooked table legs or ill-fitting drawers ever, I dare swear, came out of the carpenter's shop at Nazareth. Nor, if they did, could anyone believe that they were made by the same hand that made Heaven and earth."[91] Sayers soundly critiqued sentimental and self-interested behaviors that undermined calling and work quality, by clergy and business people, respectively. Through her writings, she sought to vivify calling at every level of society—individuals, leaders, and organizations, not unlike the practitioners discussed in Chapters 6 and 8. The following selected quotes from Sayers' work convey her ideas, while echoing Calvin, Baxter, Law, and other theologians in prior centuries.

Institutional Influences on Calling

In nothing has the Church so lost Her hold on reality as in Her failure to understand and respect the secular vocation. She has allowed work and religion to become separate departments, and is astonished to find that, as a result, the secular work of the world is turned to purely selfish and destructive ends, and that the greater part of the world's intelligent workers have become irreligious, or at least, uninterested in religion.[92]

How can anyone remain interested in a religion which seems to have no concern with nine-tenths of his life? [93]

Sacred Meaning of Work

It is the business of the Church to recognize that the secular vocation, as such, is sacred . . . . The Church must concern Herself not only with such questions as the just price and proper working conditions: She must concern Herself with seeing that work itself is such as a human being can perform without degradation—that no one is required by economic or any other considerations to devote himself to work that is contemptible, soul destroying, or harmful. It is not right for Her to acquiesce in the notion that a man's life is divided into the time he spends on his work and the time he spends in serving God. He must be able to serve God in his work, and *the work itself must be accepted and respected as the medium of divine creation.*[94]

What Is Sacred to Business and Society?

A society in which consumption has to be artificially stimulated in order to keep production going is a society founded on trash and waste, and such a society is a house built upon sand.[95]

What is going to happen when the factories stop turning out armaments? No nation has yet found a way to keep the machines running and whole nations employed under modern industrial conditions without *wasteful consumption*. For a time, a few nations could contrive to keep going by securing a monopoly of production and forcing their waste products on to new and untapped markets. When there are no new markets and all nations are industrial producers, the only choice we have been able to envisage so far has been that between armaments and unemployment. *This is*

the problem that some time or other will stare us in the face again, and this time
we must have our minds ready to tackle it.[96]

When war ceases, then the problem of employing labor at the
machines begins again. The relentless pressure of hungry labor is
behind the drive toward wasteful consumption . . . If we do not deal
with this question now, while we have time to think about it, then the
whirligig of wasteful production and wasteful consumption will start
again and will again end in war. And the driving power of labor will
be thrusting to turn the wheels, because it is to the financial interest
of labor to keep the whirligig going faster and faster till the inevitable
catastrophe comes.[97]

Unless we change our attitude—or rather unless we keep hold
of the new attitude forced upon us by the logic of war—we shall
again be bamboozled by our vanity, indolence, and greed into keeping the squirrel cage of wasteful economy turning.[98]

The habit of thinking about work as something one does to
make money is so ingrained in us that we can scarcely imagine
what a revolutionary change it would be to think about it instead in
terms of the work done. To do so would mean taking the attitude
of mind we reserve for our unpaid work—our hobbies, our leisure
interests, the things we make and do for pleasure—and making
that the standard of all our judgments about things and people. *We*
should ask of an enterprise, not "will it pay?" but "is it good?"; of a man,
not "what does he make?" but "what is his work worth?"; of goods, not "Can
we induce people to buy them?" but "are they useful things well made?"; of
employment, not "how much a week?" but "will it exercise my faculties to the
utmost?"[99]

Good Work

That, in practice, there is this satisfaction, is shown by the mere
fact that a man will put loving labor into some hobby which can
never bring him any economically adequate return. His satisfaction comes, in the godlike manner, from looking upon what he has
made and finding it very good.[100]

In war, production for wasteful consumption still goes on: but
there is one great difference in the good produced. None of them
is valued for what it will fetch, but only for what it is worth in itself.
The gun and the tank, the airplane and the warship have to be the
best of their kind. A war consumer does not buy shoddy. He does
not buy to sell again. He buys the thing that is good for its purpose,
asking nothing of it but that it shall do the job it has to do. Once
again, war forces the consumer into a right attitude to the work.[101]

We should fight tooth and nail, not for mere employment, but for the quality of the work that we had to do. We should clamor to be engaged in work that was worth doing, and in which we could take pride. The worker would demand that the stuff he helped to turn out should be good stuff—he would no longer be content to take the cash and let the credit go. Like the shareholders in the brewery, he would feel a sense of personal responsibility, and clamor to know, and to control, what went into the beer he brewed. *There would be protests and strikes—not only about pay and conditions, but about the quality of the work demanded and the honesty, beauty, and usefulness of the goods produced.* The greatest insult which a commercial age has offered to the worker has been to rob him of all interest in the end product of the work and to force him to dedicate his life to making badly things which were not worth making.[102]

The only Christian work is good work well done.[103]

Despite Sayers's common sense pleas to rethink calling and revive the prophetic voice about vocation and work, much like numerous theologians after her, the church went in a different direction. According to Lambert, who traced the evolution of the faith at work movement in his book *Spirituality Inc.*,[104] "By the 1960s, the World Council of Churches (WCC) and its members were changing their social witness away from the idea of vocation and toward the critique of economic, political, and social structures."[105] This shift coincided with the emerging civil rights movement and helps explain Lori Fox's finding about the continual decline in research about church-based vocational programs from 1960 to 2000.[106]

To fill the void left by religious institutions, business people, clergy, psychologists, theologians, and management scholars continued to write and speak about vocation and transcendent callings. They also created new institutions, which have supported the faith at work movement in which calling has historically resided (e.g., centers of faith, ethics, and work). So, religious ideas about calling did not die, as some management scholars have claimed; since the 1960s, calling has lacked the broad institutional support that it had in previous eras. As a result, individuals' attachment to and understanding of the idea has changed some—and not for the better.

Baby boomers' mistrust of "the establishment" and "institutions" in the 1960s caused some to abandon the church as young adults. But many returned to faith as they reached their middle years and are leading the faith at work movement. Their spiritual quest for deeper meaning at work is now facilitated by books, workplace prayer groups, and the like, rather than institutions exogenous to work. Although Lambert contended that "while some would argue that religion and spirituality in American have been de-centered from traditional religious institutions, they are not totally free floating and have found other institutional homes. The corporate office, the local bookstore, the family business, and the university's business department provide the setting for the new religious movement of workplace spirituality."[107] Based on history, we know that these institutions can be highly influential in cultivating and reinforcing calling—or diluting it. The question that we face today is which institutional influences and partnerships are most effective and beneficial for individuals, organizations, and society given the information and insights at our disposal? I use evidence to offer some suggestions in Chapter 12.

Advancing the Discourse

This brief survey of archival documents about calling shows that indeed, there is nothing new under the sun. Calling has endured as a worthy idea despite time, wars, slavery, economic upheaval, economic depressions, new technologies, social revolutions, and managerial manipulation. It has survived because of its practical and spiritual value in the lives of ordinary people and its residual benefits to organizations and society. The evolution of calling is curious indeed. The revolutionary new idea of a sacred calling to secular work of the 1520s was made *more* robust to respond to major societal shifts and continually elaborated on through the 18th century. In contrast, major societal shifts in the 19th century resulted in calling's dilution, deinstitutionalization, and instrumentality. Even so, as Rodgers noted, the idea has been engrained in the collective psyche.

Different dimensions of calling have captivated the imagination and energy of cultural carriers in different eras. In the 16th century, the focus was on good work that glorified God; 17th century philosophers elaborated the specifics of disposition, duty, and destiny to achieve good work; the 18th century revealed distortions regarding the ends and means of calling (whether profits are sacred and whether people are mere instruments in the quest for profit or are all worthy of dignity); 19th-century mechanization began the erosion of institutional supports of calling, a focus on cultivating the correct disposition of calling (even through coercion and manipulation), the loss of focus on "good work," and calling as a tool to achieve material success with advice from vocophers; and the 20th century showed a steady decline in institutional support for calling as well as a revival in sacred meaning as individual interest increased. Most notably, however, the core idea endures, which is evident in contemporary books.

At the end of the 20th century and the beginning of the 21st, theological scholars still contemplate calling in ways that parallel thinking in bygone eras. Miroslav Volf, in his book *Work in the Spirit*, contends that calling is sacred meaning of ordinary activities; calling encompasses one's whole life; it's moral universe is not individually determined; it is a quality of life that is reflected in one's character, in this case Christian character; Luther was indifferent to alienating labor and exploitation relative to calling and the need for what I call soul-crafting, as well as transforming systems, so that people can live their callings with dignity; and that reducing vocation to mere employment "contributed to the modern fateful elevation of work to the status of religion."[108]

Other 21st century theologians similarly echo the ages. John Haughey wrote about the cognitive, behavioral, and affective dimensions of calling as awakening to reality, knowledge and truth, behaving ethically, and acting lovingly toward for others.[109] He also considers the impediments to discernment, particularly inner barriers. Marcia Hermansen analyzed parallel notions of calling in Islam such as the sacred meaning of jobs; awakenings that recalibrate one's trajectory; the need to prevent buying and selling from distracting one's focus from God, moral duty, destiny, and the community's role as a guide.[110] Finally, Mark McIntosh wrote about the importance of story and allegory as tools to cultivate character strengths for the journey of one's calling.[111] But where are those stories today?

Most themes that practitioners identified in Chapters 6 and 8, and that were embedded in the case example in Chapter 7, or that are emerging among management scholars as described in Chapters 3 and 4 have preserved original ideas about calling. The concept has endured despite diminished institutional support for it in practice. Moreover, I have shown that recent "discoveries" by contemporary management scholars are not discoveries at all but have been embedded in historical documents just waiting to be uncovered again. By avoiding religious literature about calling, management scholars have missed a plethora of theoretical insights that can advance serious, rigorous scholarship about this vital concept. Some key insights from this chapter relate to the ontology of calling, the social construction of calling, the importance of social and cultural contexts and what becomes sacred, and the perils and promise of institutional partnerships that seek to cultivate calling.

The Ontology of Calling

Calling relates to all productive activities, including jobs, careers, volunteering, ordinary duties, and leisure activities. Thus, the job-career-calling distinction often made in management scholarship is meaningless in a conversation about calling. Ideologies across the ages have elucidated how these concepts interrelate, yet these relationships remain murky in mainstream management scholarship. Furthermore, material or extrinsic rewards are not antithetical to calling; theologians throughout the ages have been explicit about this point, as well as the calling to do more profitable work that edifies one's soul and does not harm society. It is of paramount importance, however, that extrinsic rewards not be made "sacred" and that pursuing them does not compromise spiritual well-being. Weber could have elaborated on those points—but didn't.

The unifying element among all productive activities is the triple thread composed of duty, disposition, and destiny, which may be delight or fit. It is important to note that duty and disposition relate to all productive activities; destiny is related to career, leisure pursuits, and other desired roles. Thus, destiny deserves no more prominence in theorizing than the other two core dimensions.

The Social Construction of Calling

Calling was such a worthy idea that many different institutions have embraced and reinforced its transcendent dimensions—destiny, duty, and disposition. Family, schools, professional groups, churches, community organizations, the media, arts, and national culture have all been instrumental in strengthening calling or enfeebling it. Weber claimed that calling was the product of education in one's "home community." The review in this chapter shows that it indeed took a village to cultivate one's calling. Management research that has examined only religious institutions as an antecedent of calling overlooks and underestimates how various institutions have provided congruent, reinforcing messages that made calling robust in practice. If calling is a good idea that has endured, it is worth examining what value different village voices added to calling and are worth preserving. This is particularly important in the midst of shifting from an industrial age to a technological age and as capitalism becomes entrenched in emerging markets such as Brazil, Russia, India, China, and South Africa (BRICS). Rather than examining only religious influences on calling, we need to ask ourselves an important question: What, if anything, do today's village voices say about calling—about duty, disposition, and destiny? Or is work now seen as a mere tool to acquire social symbols of "civilization" and "maturity," as Richards suggested? How does the village positively or negatively influence dimensions of the calling ethic? What are the implications for organizations and society? How can the voices of calling be vivified? These are questions that must and should be answered before measuring the presence or absence of calling and its effects on work outcomes.

Clearly, the village's voice has been diluted and distorted with time and for myriad reasons. Chief among them is uncertainty about how to help people successfully navigate the transition from one economic base to another—from an agrarian to an industrial society—and opportunistic or well-intended attempts to facilitate the transition. One example of well-intended actions is authors' shifts in the themes of children's stories, from character-building metaphors to heroic and athletic conquests that later gave business the character of "sport," which Weber cautioned against. The shift to industrialism caused some traditional institutions to drop their tools relative to calling. However, with the shift from industrialism to the technology age, which coincided with the faith at work movement, uncertainty caused some to attempt to reclaim those tools, but with some difficulty.

Lessons about calling and sacred meanings of work that were readily accessible in the village are now primarily found in books. Although clergy and professors historically used books and pamphlets to disseminate information about calling, this approach wasn't the only mechanism. Messages about calling were widely disseminated and reinforced throughout the culture via traditional institutions, the media and public gatherings. But there are few, if any, parallel institutional and cultural supports today. This shift has resulted in individually organized self-directed searches for calling. But Holland[112] contended that a self-directed search is a poor substitute for social interactions—it takes a village.

It will take a village of scholars and practitioners working across disciplines to preserve and refurbish useful old tools regarding calling, and to use evidence to develop appropriate new ones. In recent years, scholars and practitioners have intuitively done this by turning their attention to disparate elements of calling vis-à-vis ethics education, career planning, corporate social responsibility, spirituality and professions, and so forth. By drawing on and integrating information across the "village," rather than our own "hamlets," actors can collaborate to reconstitute calling in new, more robust and relevant ways.

Cultural Context and What Is Sacred

I've clearly shown how management conversations about calling have been divorced from considerations of work and social contexts. This chapter shows the importance of understanding context, at a macro-level, before interpreting results about the secularization of calling. Furthermore, it reveals the perils of analyzing calling apart from serious consideration of how society, organizations' callings, and leaders' callings influence individual workers' callings.

As this chapter has shown, work context, regional context, leadership, organizational culture, and social responsibility are considered vital elements of the conversation about calling. William Law and Dorothy

Sayers have written brilliantly about the perils of elevating profits to sacred status and the negative consequences for individual workers, leaders, the quality of work, and society. These contextual elements deserve far more attention than they have received in management conversations about calling. And, if calling is truly about making the world a better place, we cannot ignore Sayers's indictment against an economic system that thrives on mindless consumption and war. Indeed, 70 years later, we confront the same challenges of sustaining an economy based on consumption, with fewer emerging markets to buy goods of variable value.

Sayers is one of few women who thought critically and deeply about calling at every level of analysis and about the interdependence of factors at different levels. Most importantly, her insights about calling, vocation, and work have implications for institutional, organizational, social, and economic policies. Her writings are a model for making similar connections in interdisciplinary conversations about the psychology, sociology, economics, theology, and politics of calling, and how the sacred purposes of business impact society. Indeed, her conceptualization of calling has policy implications for education, economics, social issues, human resources, and program planning of various organizations. It is hardly an individualistic concept.

Perils and Promise of Institutional Partnerships

Given that the Protestant calling originally meant bringing sacred meaning to secular work, the most obvious partnerships to cultivate are between religious and business leaders. This was certainly true in the 16th and 17th centuries, and it continues today in workplace ministries. But no evidence suggests that this partnership is the only or the most effective one. It has also met with a healthy skepticism by workers and church members who question the clergy's understanding of work and management's credibility with issues of faith.

Millhands and Preachers is an extreme but real example of the inherent risks of workplace spirituality and created theologies—or as Schorr[113] called them, administrative theologies. The goal of these arrangements was to cultivate workers' dispositions for capitalistic ends, not to cultivate the generative, transformative disposition of a calling. Perverse arrangements that result in ministers and managers as "chief ideology officers" of a corporate calling are not inherently altruistic, nor do they serve individual callings or society well. The result depends on what is considered "sacred" and the extent to which workers are truly free to accept or reject that ideology. In fact, these partnerships can lead to a great deal of individual and social harm if the message is not created independent of corporate interests, but is instead used to further them.

On a more hopeful note, this chapter reminds us of the vast array for potential partnerships that may be forged among institutions to cultivate calling—partnerships that are beyond managerial control—namely, community, academic, professional, cultural, media, and religious institutions. Furthermore, these institutions can and did cultivate calling long before a person went to work, which reduced the burden on managers and human resource departments. Historically, many people who wrote about calling stood at the interstices of such institutions, much the same as practitioners do today. Their examples show us that academics, professors, and theologians have important roles to play—if we can find a common language and collaborate with effective methods. The possibilities for engaging diverse institutions in new conversations about calling are only limited by our imaginations; I discuss some possibilities in Chapter 12.

In summary, the seeds of theory and seeds of distortion about calling were sown and flourished together throughout history and across the institutional landscape. With each chapter of this book, I've attempted to sift through those seeds to sort out myths and find germs of promising ideas that can be collected into a comprehensive theory—one that turns historic tales of calling into a better reality.

NOTES

1. Max Weber, *The Protestant Ethic and the Spirit of Capitalism* (London: Routledge, 1904/1992).
2. Robert Wuthnow, *The Crisis in the Churches: Spiritual Malaise, Fiscal Woe* (New York: Oxford Press, 1997).
3. Lori A. Fox, "The Role of the Church in Career Guidance and Development: A Review of the Literature 1960–Early 2000s," *Journal of Career Development* 29, no. 3 (2003): 167–82.
4. David W. Miller, *God at Work: The History and Promise of the Faith at Work Movement* (New York: Oxford University Press, 2007).
5. William C. Placher, *Callings: Twenty Centuries of Christian Wisdom on Vocation* (Grand Rapids, MI: Eerdsman, 2005).
6. See the Haithi Trust's website, www.hathitrust.org/.
7. Placher, *Callings*.
8. Lee Hardy, *The Fabric of This World: Inquiries into Calling, Career Choice, and the Design of Human Work* (Grand Rapids, MI: Eerdsman, 1990).
9. Placher, *Callings*, 216.
10. Ibid., 65.
11. Placher, *Callings*, 237.
12. See Hardy, *The Fabric of This World*.
13. Howard Gardner, Mihaly Csikszentmihalyi, and William Damon, *Good Work: When Excellence and Ethics Meet* (New York: Basic Books, 2001).

14. J. J. McGee and A. L. Delbecq "Vocation as a Critical Factor in Spirituality for Executive Leadership in Business," in *Business, Religion and Spirituality: A New Synthesis*, ed. Oliver F. Williams, 94–110 (Notre Dame, IN: University of Notre Dame Press, 2003).

15. William Perkins, "A Treatise of the Vocations," in *Callings: Twenty Centuries of Christian Wisdom on Vocation*, ed. William Placher, 262–73 (Grand Rapids: Erdsman, 2005).

16. Ibid., 266.

17. Ibid., 269.

18. Ibid., 270.

19. Ibid., 271.

20. Ibid., 271.

21. Ibid., 272.

22. Ibid., 272.

23. Thomas Case, *Two Sermons Lately Preached Ii* (London, 1642), 13, 16.

24. Thomas Shephard, *Certain Select Cases Resolved, Specially, Tending to the Right Ordering of the Heart That We May Comfortably Walk with God in Our Generall and Particular Callings* (London: Printed for John Rothwel, 1655).

25. Richard Baxter, "Directions about Our Labor and Callings," in *Callings: Twenty Centuries of Christian Wisdom on Vocation*, ed. William Placher, 278–85 (Grand Rapids, MI: Erdsman, 2005).

26. Ibid., 279.

27. Ibid., 279–80 (emphasis added).

28. Ibid., 280.

29. Ibid., 281.

30. Ibid., 285.

31. Ibid., 282.

32. Ibid., 285.

33. Ibid., 282.

34. Ibid., 283 (emphasis added).

35. Ibid., 281 (emphasis added).

36. Gervase Markham, Simon Harward, William Lawson, and George Sawbridge, *A Way to Get Wealth: Containing Six Principal Vocations, or Callings, in Which Every Good Husband or House-Wife May Lawfully Imploy Themselves* (London: Printed by E. H. for George Sawbridge . . . 1676).

37. Ibid.

38. Richard Steele, *The Trades-Man's Calling. Being a Discourse Concerning the Nature, Necessity, Choice, & C. Of a Calling in General: And Directions for the Right* (London, 1684), 8 of the 1804 edition.

39. McGee and Delbecq, "Vocation as a Critical Factor in Spirituality."

40. Jane Kise and David Stark, *Working with Purpose: Finding a Corporate Calling for You and Your Business* (Minneapolis, MN: Ausberg Fortress, 2004).

41. Steele, *The Trades-Man's Calling*, 8.

42. Richard Steele, *The Religious Tradesman; or, Plain and Serious Hints of Advice for the Tradesman's Prudent and Pious Conduct . . . of Religion; of Leaving Our Callings* (Charlestown [MA]: Printed by Samuel Etheridge, and sold by him at the Washington head bookstore, 1804), 14.

43. Thomas Wilson, *A Sermon Preached in August the 13. 1610. In Canterbury to the Corporation of Black-Smiths . . . By Thomas Wilson Preacher, Sermon*

Preached before the Corporation of Black-Smiths (London: Printed [by N. Okes] for Simon Waterson, dwelling in Pauls Church-yard at the sign of the Crowne, 1610).

44. Lake Lambert III, *Spirituality Inc.: Religion in the American Workplace* (New York: New York University Press, 2009), 23.

45. John Bunyan, *The Pilgrim's Progress* (New York: Signet, 1964).

46. *A True Character of Sundry Trades and Callings . . . Licensed According to Order, New Ditty of Innocent Mirth* (London: Printed for P[hilip]. Brooksby, at the Golden-Ball in Pye-corner, 1670).

47. *The Devil's Oak . . . To a Very Pleasant New Tune, Devil's Oak* (London: printed for C. Bates, at the Sun and Bible in Pye-corner, 1685).

48. *True Blew the Plowman, . . . Character of Several Callings Which He Could Not Freely Fancy, When He Found Their Grand Deceit* ([London]: Printed for P. Brooksby, 1685).

49. Robert Warren, *Industry and Diligence in Our Callings Earnestly Recommended in a Sermon Preached . . . March 17, 1736–7. At the Parish-Church of St. Bride, . . . London. By Robert Warren, D.D . . . . Published at the Unanimous Request of the Trustees* (London: printed for W. Meadows, 1737), 11 (emphasis added).

50. Ibid., 12.

51. Ibid.

52. Ibid., 13.

53. See the previous quote from Case, *Two Sermons Lately Preached Ii.*

54. In Placher, *Callings*, 305.

55. Ibid., 308 (emphasis added).

56. Ibid., 308–9.

57. Daniel T. Rodgers, *The Work Ethic in Industrial America, 1850–1920* (Chicago: University of Chicago Press, 1978).

58. Ibid., 16.

59. Ibid., 12.

60. Lysander Salmon Richards, *Vocophy: The New Profession. A System Enabling a Person to Name the Calling or Vocation One Is Best Suited to Follow* (East Marsh-field, MA: Pratt Brothers, Steam Job Printers, 1881).

61. Ibid., Preface (emphasis added).

62. Ibid.

63. Ibid., 9–10.

64. Ibid., 26.

65. Ibid., 28.

66. Ibid., 13.

67. Ibid., 76.

68. J. Llewelyn Davies, *The Christian Calling* (London: Macmillan and Co., 1875).

69. Ibid., 81 (emphasis added).

70. Ibid., 85.

71. Ibid., 115–16 (emphasis added).

72. Ibid., 86 (emphasis added).

73. Joanne B. Ciulla, *The Working Life: The Promise and Betrayal of Modern Work* (New York: Times Books, 2000); Rodgers, *The Work Ethic in Industrial America.*

74. Rodgers, *The Work Ethic in Industrial America*, 144.

75. Christopher Peterson and Martin E. P. Seligman, *Character Strengths and Virtues: A Handbook and Classification* (New York: Oxford University Press, 2004).
76. Rodgers, *The Work Ethic in Industrial America*.
77. Robert N. Bellah, Richard Madsen, William M. Sullivan, Ann Swidler, and Steven M. Tipton, *Habits of the Heart: Individualism and Commitment in American Life: Updated Edition with a New Introduction* (Berkeley: University of California Press, 1996), 43.
78. Ibid., 43.
79. Ciulla, *The Working Life*; Rodgers, *The Work Ethic in Industrial America*.
80. Stephen R. Barley and Gideon Kunda, "Design and Devotion: Surges of Rational and Normative Ideologies of Control in Managerial Discourse," *Administrative Science Quarterly* 37, no. 3 (1992): 363–99.
81. Washington Gladden, *Working People and Their Employers* (Boston: Lockwood, Brooks, 1876), 44–50.
82. See the YMCA's webpage, http://www.ymca.net/history/.
83. Lambert, *Spirituality Inc.*, 28.
84. Barley and Kunda, "Design and Devotion," 368.
85. Liston Pope, *Millhands and Preachers: A Study of Gastonia* (New Haven, CT: Yale University Press, 1942).
86. Ibid., xx.
87. A.E. Baker, ed., *A Christian Basis for the Post-War World: A Commentary on the Ten Peace Points Preface by The Bishop of Carlisle* (New York: Morehouse-Gorham, 1942).
88. Dorothy L. Sayers, "Vocation in Work," in *A Christian Basis for the Post-War World: A Commentary on the Ten Peace Points by The Bishop of Carlisle*, ed. A.E. Baker, 89–105 (New York: Morehouse-Gorham, 1942).
89. Ibid., 89.
90. Dorothy L. Sayers, "Why Work?" in *Creed or Chaos? And Other Essays in Popular Theology*, 63–84 (Manchester: Sophia Institute Press, 1948/1999).
91. Ibid., 77. In the quote, "Nazareth" refers to Jesus Christ, a carpenter of Nazareth.
92. Ibid., 76.
93. Ibid., 77.
94. Ibid., 76.
95. Ibid., 64.
96. Ibid., 67–68 (emphasis added).
97. Ibid., 69.
98. Ibid., 70.
99. Ibid., 70–71.
100. Ibid., 73.
101. Ibid., 71.
102. Ibid., 75.
103. Ibid., 78.
104. Lambert, *Spirituality Inc.*
105. Ibid., 14.
106. Fox, "The Role of the Church in Career Guidance and Development."
107. Lambert, *Spirituality Inc.*, 20.

108. Miroslav Volf, *Work in the Spirit: Toward a Theology of Work* (Eugene, OR: P Wipf & Stock Publishers, 2001), 109.

109. John C. Haughey, "The Three Conversions Embedded in Personal Calling," in *Revisiting the Idea of Vocation: Theological Explorations*, ed. John C. Haughey (Washington, D.C.: Catholic University of America Press, 2004), 1–23.

110. Marcia Hermansen, "Islamic Concepts of Vocation," in *Revisiting the Idea of Vocation: Theological Explorations*, ed. John C. Haughey (Washington, D.C.: Catholic University of America Press, 2004), 77–96.

111. Mark A. McIntosh, "Trying to Follow a Call: Vocations and Discernment in Bunyan's Pilgrim's Progress," in *Revisiting the Idea of Vocation: Theological Explorations*, ed. John C. Haughey (Washington, D.C.: Catholic University of America Press, 2004), 119–40.

112. J. L. Holland, *Professional Manual for the Self-Directed Search* (Palo Alto, CA: Consulting Psychologists Press, 1979).

113. Philip Schorr, "Public Service as a Calling: An Exploration of a Concept," *International Journal of Public Administration* 10, no. 5 (1987): 465–93.

Part III

Connecting Conversations in Theory and Practice

10

A Cross-Cultural Theory of Calling

Management scholars routinely acknowledge that there is no theory of calling to guide research. Hence, research has commenced by analyzing the presence or absence of variables. Such an approach is appropriate for a nascent field that seeks to develop a new idea. Calling, however, is not a new idea, and the field of management scholarship is maturing. To advance research and practice, we need a theory.

What Is Theory?

I have used the preceding chapters to examine ontological theories of calling and to engage in disciplined theory construction. Ontologies describe the nature of being or existence, as well as processes and relationships.[1] As such, ontological theories may be *referential, ideational, verifiable,* and *relational.*[2]

Referential theories explain what people were or are referring to when they use a particular term. In this case, I have used the term *conversations* to illustrate how management scholars, practitioners, the general public, and theologians have referred to calling and how the meaning varies across groups. *Ideational* theories explore "ideal types" that provide a way to classify, categorize, and compare elements; they are foundational for theory building.[3] In the management literature, three ideal types of calling have emerged: (1) the dominant secular individualistic person-environment (P-E) fit ideal type; and (2) emerging transcendent and (3) sacred ideal types that focus on moral duty and calling across life roles. Because ideal types are inherently overgeneralized, oversimplified, and fraught with omissions, and because they accentuate certain points of view,[4] they demand further *verification.*

Calling is an idea that has endured for centuries, beyond the boundaries of management; therefore, many ways exist to *verify* management scholars' claims and assertions. To verify whether the idea that religious notions of calling are irrelevant in the modern era and that people no longer think of calling in religious or spiritual terms, I analyzed the perspectives of practitioners who wrote during the same decades as management scholars (1980s–2012) and I found no basis for the claim. Practitioners offered numerous insights about calling that differed from management scholars. Since there was no consensus between the dominant management perspective, emerging management perspectives, and practitioners, I verified all of their claims with historic theological perspectives and found management ideal types lacking.

To verify and compare historic and contemporary ideas about calling, I deployed a disciplined approach to constructing theory derived from articles in a special issue of the *Academy of Management Review* (vol. 14, no. 4 [1989]). For our purposes, we want to know: What are the antecedents and origins of calling? Who gets a calling? How does it evolve and change? What conditions enable or undermine a calling? And, what are the predicted outcomes of a calling? In addition, a theory should explain *how* something operates by delineating causal mechanisms that are often implicit.[5] Mechanisms help us understand processes, causality, and links across micro- and macrolevels; connections across disciplinary boundaries; and testable relationships among variables.[6] I have used the preceding chapters to progress toward a theory of calling. In the process, I have analyzed, identified, illustrated, and empirically supported core elements of calling, as well as its antecedents, outcomes, and enabling conditions. Ultimately, this process results in a *relational* theory that reveals intersubjective understandings among all the relevant actors;[7] in this case, all relevant perspectives culminate in a comprehensive, cross-cultural theory of calling. Let's recap before moving forward.

In Chapter 2, I reviewed research related to the dominant management view of calling, which advances a secular individualistic perspective. I showed data that refute the idea that calling is no longer thought of in religious or spiritual terms. In addition, I discussed the unexamined perils of an individualistic calling, which Weber foreshadowed and *Habits* lamented. In fact, the dominant management conceptualization of calling is not a calling but is instead an intense form of P-E fit. Although fit, destiny, and occupational *specialization* are part of a calling, *specialization* also refers to careful methods, which have been ignored in the dominant conversation. Careful methods result from a *spirit* that animates the work; spirit can be defined in religious or nonreligious terms.

In Chapter 3, in the emerging conversation about transcendent callings, moral duty was brought to the forefront, thereby linking calling to the Protestant work ethic, much as it was 100 years ago. This conversation also expanded the boundaries of calling to include all life roles, not just occupational work. More importantly, empirical results showed that transcendence is more central to calling than P-E fit; one may be called *by the transcendent, to transcendent purposes,* and *to behave in accordance with transcendent standards* that communities define collectively. Scholars have described how communities define objective (quality) and subjective (ethics) standards; achieving those standards is the ultimate goal of calling, that is—"good work." Good work is the common feature and goal of calling across life roles, but management has been largely mute about morals and quality. Because callings are sometimes denied, management scholars have offered job crafting as a remedy. However, communities may also provide cosmologies that provide coherence and enable soul-crafting, which helps people cope with delayed, denied, and difficult callings.

Chapter 4 linked management scholarship to the original idea of calling as a sacred construct. Evidence suggests that a minority group of scholars still considers calling sacred. Overall, however, empirical connections between faith and religiosity are weak, which is likely due to inadequate measurement. To make any compelling claims about faith and calling in either direction, more rigorous research is needed that uses new measures of spirituality and religious involvement from other disciplines. In addition, I showed that calling is not merely meaningful and meaningfulness. It is possible to impute work with *sacred* meaning by drawing on religious and nonreligious cosmologies.

In Chapter 5, to conclude the management conversations, I described the ways that academic norms of constructing knowledge have impeded our understanding of calling. I suggested widening the scope of the literature reviewed to include knowledge from others who are involved in the common enterprise of contemplating calling—practitioners, historians and theologians. I did so in Chapters 6 through 9.

Practitioners' insights greatly accelerated the path toward constructing theory by giving texture and substance to existing variables and adding important new ones. In Chapter 6, practitioners noted that the source of one's calling may be spiritual, situational, social, internal, or existential. I also showed that a vital dimension of theorizing is missing—disposition. Disposition consists of character and coping skills. I illustrated the recursive, generative, and interdependent core dimensions of calling as disposition, destiny, and duty. The essential core of one's calling is formed in youth, with education and socialization in the collective cosmologies of traditional institutions (e.g., family, schools, and religious and community organizations), which ideally are mutually reinforcing. The core is somewhat malleable based on exposure to new cosmologies and ideologies throughout life in society, the workplace, and other organizations. Initial and additive cosmologies may be reinforcing or competing.

Practitioners elaborated on intrapersonal and contextual barriers to calling. Intrapersonal barriers include fear, resistance, low self-esteem, conformity, worry, distractions, busyness, and internally imposed "oughts." Contextual barriers may be situational, social, or structural. Situational barriers include disruptive or excessively demanding life events (e.g., sudden disability, crisis, or caring for an aging parent). Social barriers include lack of support, low social status, inadequate mentoring, dysfunctional teams, and negative influences from the community or media. Structural barriers include inadequate resources, education, or training; lack of exposure; limited opportunity structures; poor fit; discriminatory policies; rankism; neglect; unethical leaders; and an organizational culture that focuses myopically on profits, "winning" and quantitative bigness (e.g., size, rank, units produced, etc.). Situational, social, or structural barriers can delay or deny a calling; hence, the need for character strengths and coping skills to persist and rise above them. However, the quantum nature of calling means any number of spiritual, structural, developmental, social, or situational factors might enable calling to emerge or evolve at any time in one's life.

In Chapter 7, I provided a case example, *unthinkable*, to show how mutually reinforcing cosmologies can cultivate a sense of destiny, duty, and disposition in ways that can lead to unthinkably positive performance outcomes despite monumental obstacles. Those unthinkable outcomes were achieved through job crafting, soul crafting, and innovative institutional partnerships. Nevertheless, some barriers require structural and organizational changes in order for people to live their callings.

In Chapter 8, I discussed how practitioners shifted the focus away from individuals to discuss the context of calling, which is seldom considered, and how the calling to entrepreneurship, business, and leadership can profoundly influenced individuals and society. Using an example of entrepreneurship, I illustrated the ecology of calling and how disposition, duty, destiny, and cosmology interrelate to influence multiple life roles in ways that produce "good work"—ethical and excellent results. That is not always the case in business.

Practitioners indicated that businesses once had a calling to serve the common good, but this requirement was abolished by regulatory and legislative changes; the business calling to serve the common good is now completely voluntary. The idea of a corporate calling entails a commitment to social responsibility, cultivating human potential, producing high-quality and necessary goods and services, and adhering to moral standards, not just the letter of the law. As profits, hierarchy, and consumption became sacred, often eclipsing a corporate calling, the lapse has adversely affected national and business cultures, leaders, and employees. Leaders, as corporate agents, have an opportunity to influence the corporation's calling. It is up to the called, rather than the entitled leaders, to elevate and expand the goals of business beyond mere profits to create the conditions for "good work." I used the lives of several leaders and a three-dimensional model to illustrate the quantum way that calling evolves across the life span, as well as the tonic and phasic properties of disposition, duty, and destiny.

Many of the insights from Chapters 2 through 8 were confirmed (or refuted) by the theological perspectives about calling that were presented in Chapter 9. In addition, theologians have offered insights about the context of calling and transitions throughout life, which are the final elements of a complete theory. Although the dominant theological reference has been Christianity, my analysis reveals that calling is not only a Christian concept. Constituent elements are, in fact, multicultural, as I have explained and will continue to explain in this chapter.

My approach has been both deductive and inductive. Deductively, insights from the preceding chapters led me to the definition of calling that follows, as well as elements of theory. Inductively, I have exhaustively analyzed a case study example of calling, which I present in Chapter 11, to identify and illustrate the elements of my theory. My intent is that this initial theory will provide a foundation for empirical testing and refinement and will be expanded and applied across cultures.

A Cross-Cultural Theory of Calling

To date, there has been no consensus about the definition of calling or a comprehensive theory to guide research. Based on my analyses in preceding chapters, I am offering both—a definition of calling and a theory of calling. Although the definition indicates that individuals and organizations can have a calling, based on practitioner and theological insights, for the purposes of this discussion, I focus my theory on the individual calling. In sections that follow, I offer theoretical propositions that elucidate ideas that are embedded in the definition of calling. The propositions suggest testable hypotheses that offer innumerable new trajectories for research.

Definition of Calling

Calling is a transcendent and generative ethical system that seeks to produce "good work"—ethical and increasingly excellent results. The beneficiaries of these results are individuals, organizations, and society. The source of the call is subjective and may be spiritual, intrapersonal, interpersonal, situational, social, or existential. Individuals and organizations can have a calling.

An individual's calling spans life roles, including employment. It is composed of the interdependent, recursive dimensions of duty, disposition, and a sense of destiny, which vary in strength and salience throughout one's life span. Ideally, the core dimensions of calling are influenced positively and sustained by reinforcing cosmologies that are acquired in youth through education and socialization in one's "home community" and society; in adulthood, one is exposed to and may acquire additional cosmologies from their involvement in various organizations, including employers and society. Certain individuals are predisposed to perceive and pursue a calling, due in part to their personality (e.g., openness, conscientiousness, and an orientation toward learning) and environment. Due to the quantum nature of calling, infinite structural, social, situational, developmental, and spiritual factors may provide the impetus to set its mechanisms in motion and to enhance outcomes. Although structural, social, and situation barriers may directly impede one from enacting their calling or diminish its outcomes, those impediments indirectly influence the spirit that animates core dimensions of a person's calling.

An organizational calling spans the contingent's guiding mission and operational functions. It, too, is composed of interdependent dimensions of duty, disposition, and destiny; its destiny or mission, and moral duty to align their offerings with societal needs and the common good, and culture are ideally tonic, whereas disposition or its character may be somewhat phasic. Ideally, the dimensions of an organizational calling are positively influenced by the institutional landscape, industry norms, the regulatory environment, as well as what the organization itself holds sacred—beyond profits. The individual traits and callings of the founders and senior leaders predispose organizations to possess and enact a calling; organizational culture reinforces it. However, an organizational calling may be subject to the caprices of inevitable changes in leadership.

Theoretical Propositions

1 *The primary goal of calling is good work; more specifically, ethical and increasingly excellent results.* The benefits of good work accrue to organizations, society, communities, and individuals. Good work includes all productive activities, including leisure pursuits, relationships, occupation, citizenship, and volunteering.

2 *Individual factors that predispose a person to have a calling include personality traits, spiritual well-being, and intrapersonal awareness.* With regard to the "big five" personality traits,[8] moderate introversion, openness, and conscientiousness will positively predict calling. Extreme extroversion, neuroticism, and risk aversion will negatively predict

the enactment of a calling because of the inherent need for introspection and courage.

3 *Individual barriers to a calling include fear, resistance, low self-esteem, conformity, busyness, and distraction.*

4 *The core dimensions of calling include (moral) duty, disposition, destiny, and transcendence, all of which are cross-cultural and can be understood in secular, psychological terms.* As such, existing psychological measures can provide a basis for measuring the absence or presence of a person's calling by examining the constellation of dimensions and their relative strength at any particular point in time.

   a. There is a recursive relationship between the dimensions that promote growth.

   b. Weakness in duty or disposition dimensions will weaken the entire system.

   c. Strength in all dimensions will result in generativity and advancement.

   d. Courage, conscientiousness, introspection, and adaptive coping are minimally required for system effectiveness.

5 *From an ecological perspective, diverse cosmologies influence how core dimensions of calling develop in youth and throughout adulthood. Multiple reinforcing cosmologies enhance calling, whereas contradictory cosmologies will dilute calling.* Internalizing specific messages, as opposed to merely being exposed to general messages, is the quality that interests us. In youth and young adulthood, traditional institutions such as family, community, religious organizations, and schools/universities provide cosmologies about calling that are most enduring. That is because these institutions provide emotional ties to and physical proximity of family and friends; religious organizations offer rich narratives about ethics and work; and youth are immersed in educational systems for years. In adulthood, additional cosmologies are acquired from socialization in formal networks of professional associations and work organizations, as well as informal networks. Cosmologies can be reinforced or undermined by messages from the media, arts, and popular culture.

   a. All major world religions and philosophical traditions espouse standards related to destiny, moral duty, and character strengths. Different religious and philosophical traditions also impute sacred meaning to work and other life roles. When they exist, specific religious cosmologies about calling will be equal to or more potent than other cosmologies.

   b. Absent a dominant religious cosmology, a person may still derive coherence, transcendent meaning, moral standards, standards of excellence, a sense of destiny, and strategies for coping from other cosmologies. Hence, from an academic perspective, calling can be, but is not exclusively, secular.

    c.   The point at which one adopts a guiding cosmology about calling may vary, particularly if a foundational set of cosmologies is not provided during one's youth.

6 *Calling is enabled by myriad spiritual, developmental, social, structural, or situational factors. Enabling factors might directly enhance a core dimension of calling, stimulate the recursive relationship between core dimensions, or provide material or psychosocial resources that foster "good work."* These factors encompass the following:

    a.   Spiritual: insight or awakening
    b.   Developmental: training and education
    c.   Social: mentoring, support, and actual or virtual role models
    d.   Structural: leadership, access to opportunities, just culture, and organizational calling
    e.   Situational: exposure, experience, experimentation, opportunity, crisis, serendipity, ennui, dissatisfaction, and challenge

7 *Given sufficient enabling conditions, a person's calling will be integrated across his or her life roles.*

8 *Calling may be delayed or denied due to social, situational, or structural barriers.* This includes the following:

    a.   Social barriers: lack of support/undermining, inadequate mentoring, interpersonal or group dysfunction, negative community influences, negative media influences, hyperconnectivity, discrimination, rankism, neglect, or exploitation
    b.   Situational barriers: excessive demands, crisis, disability, or other temporary impediments
    c.   Structural barriers: lack of exposure, poor fit, inadequate training, inadequate resources, limited opportunity structures, unethical leaders, unethical culture, or exclusionary laws and policies

9 *Effective tactics to manage delayed and denied callings include job crafting, soul crafting, taking a stand, leaving a job (or other situation), and creating institutional changes. These are also enabling conditions.*

The cross-cultural theory that results from the preceding theoretical propositions is illustrated in Figure 10.1.

How This Theory Can Be Applied

This cross-cultural theory offers numerous interesting pathways for intervention, research, and practice. The following suggestions are illustrative, not exhaustive. Comparison studies might be conducted to examine core dimensions of calling within different age cohorts as a way to understand how core dimensions of calling develop and subsequently wax and wane over the life span. Regarding the development of calling,

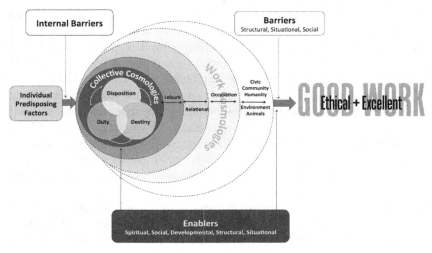

Figure 10.1 Myers's cross-cultural theory of calling.

controlled experiments could be conducted within and across cohorts in diverse institutional settings to understand which educational methods are most effective with each cohort. Furthermore, analysis might involve comparing educational interventions that use different cosmologies (e.g., secular, spiritual, or religious education) to present content about calling. It would be particularly interesting to analyze differences in the core calling of people who are engaged in solo reading of books about calling versus those whose quest involves education within social settings. Longitudinally, studies might examine the effects of reinforcing cosmologies on ethical behavior and performance outcomes, as well as how callings develop over time.

This theory might also be used to analyze subgroup differences in the personalities of people who consider their calling transcendent, religious, or completely secular. Understanding personality differences might provide insights into enabling tactics that might be used, avoided, or prescribed in the face of delayed and denied callings. Similarly, insight into personality and individual barriers might be instructive in jump-starting stalled callings. The amount of time that people spend using social media or consuming popular media and the relationship to calling might be of particular interest as a way to analyze cultural effects on calling.

Throughout this book, I have used narratives to illustrate seminal moments in individual callings such as awakening, changing course, coping, producing extraordinary outcomes, and sense making about legacy. Narrative methods might be used to understand inflection points along the long, winding trajectory of a calling as well as instances of short recursive cycles that fostered generativity or growth. For example, how do additional character strengths or undesired duties foster progress toward a desired destiny at work or in life? Or, in what ways does social support or a virtual role model (e.g., narratives or biographies) provide inspiration and courage? How have people drawn on their cosmologies in times of uncertainty (e.g., George Washington Carver) or crisis to persist?

When considering the intersection of individual and organizational callings, how did a change in leadership, from an entitled to a called leader, enable an entire team, department, or organization to deliver "good work"? What were the implications for the organization and society more broadly? These are but a few suggestions for future research.

In the next chapter, I provide a case study to which the cross-cultural theory can be applied. The case study illustrates calling across life roles, as different dimensions are strengthened, and how calling is manifest throughout the life span. In addition, it reveals insights and answers to some of the preceding questions and indeed shows how individual, leader, and organizational callings intersected to improve society.

NOTES

1. Willis F. Overton and Michelle D. Ennis, "Relationism, Ontology, and Other Concerns," *Human Development* 49, no. 3 (2006): 180–83.
2. M. Ruef, "Social Ontology and the Dynamics of Organizational Forms: Creating Market Actors in the Healthcare Field, 1966–1994," *Social Forces* 77, no. 4 (1999): 1403–33.
3. Max Weber, *The Protestant Ethic and the Spirit of Capitalism* (London: Routledge, 1904/1992); Max Weber and Edward Shils, *Max Weber on the Methodology of the Social Sciences* (Glencoe, IL: Free Press, 1949).
4. Weber and Shils, *Max Weber.*
5. Klaus Weber, "From Nuts and Bolts to Toolkits: Theorizing with Mechanisms," *Journal of Management Inquiry* 15, no. 2 (2006): 119; Peter J. J. Anderson, Ruth Blatt, Marlys K. Christianson, Adam M. Grant, Eric J. Neuman, Scott Sonenshein, and Kathleen M. Sutcliffe, "Understanding Mechanisms in Organizational Research: Reflections from a Collective Journey," *Journal of Management Inquiry* 15, no. 2 (2006): 102–13.
6. Gerald F. Davis, "Mechanisms and the Theory of Organizations," *Journal of Management Inquiry* 15, no. 2 (2006): 114–18; Weber, "From Nuts and Bolts to Toolkits"; Anderson et al., "Understanding Mechanisms in Organizational Research."
7. Ruef, "Social Ontology and the Dynamics of Organizational Forms"; Weber and Shils, *Max Weber.*
8. Warren T. Norman, "Toward an Adequate Taxonomy of Personality Attributes: Replicated Factor Structure in Peer Nomination Personality Ratings," *Journal of Abnormal Psychology* 66 (1963): 574–83.

11

Case Study: Not Your Average Working Joe

At the height of his career, with a wife, two children, and material symbols of success, Joseph could hardly believe his life—and neither could his siblings. While working abroad, separated from his family for 22 years, Joseph's accomplishments catapulted him into a position of political and economic leadership. Years of dirty work, gang violence, and the fragmentation of his family after his mother died were all a distant memory. Joseph was no longer just the big-mouthed little brother. He was a highly capable, respected, and internationally renowned leader with real power. His countercyclical economic policies steered a nation through economic surplus, crisis, and recovery. So much had changed since he and his brothers were young—or had it?

When the family reunited, past hurts and deceptions seemed to disappear. In reality, the siblings just never mentioned old offenses for the sake of peace and harmony. But family secrets, schisms, and drama are often amplified in the midst of crisis. This is exactly what happened when their elderly father fell ill. As Joseph's father uttered his last words, he stoked smoldering sibling rivalries that had lain dormant for years. After the funeral, Joseph's siblings started conspiring.

In the prime of his career, it seemed that Joseph had it all—except authentic relationships with his family of origin. His extraordinary power and wealth widened the gap even further between them. How could people from the same family have such different lives? When Joseph's siblings looked at him with awe and incredulity, they saw an impossible childhood dream being fulfilled. When his nieces and nephews looked at him, they saw a hero. When his children looked at him, they saw a dad, whose success they took for granted. But when Joseph looked at his siblings, their children, and his own, he, like his father, saw people with great potential that had not yet been realized. "If only they knew what it took to get here," he thought. "How can I help them understand that fulfilling my calling and becoming the transformational leader that they esteem (or envy) is no great mystery?" Nor was it easy.

Joseph feared that without their father, the family would devolve into factions and feuds rather than moving forward. But Joseph had come too far to go backward, and he certainly did not want family drama to cascade into his new life. So, he reached out to them. He desperately wanted a better relationship with them and to share the lessons he had learned. He wanted all of them to flourish. Joseph pondered how to use this moment as an opportunity to launch conversations that would simultaneously heal past rifts and inspire his family to live their own callings.

Case History

Joseph's compelling story transcends time and place. He could be from Detroit, Durban, or Delhi. His seemingly contemporary story about how to live your calling is nearly 4,000 years old; it is common to the Abrahamic faiths of Judaism, Christianity, and Islam, all of which have adherents worldwide. Thus, Joseph's story is directly relevant for people in established and emerging economies—and indirectly relevant for people of other faiths and philosophies.

Although the Torah (Genesis 37–50), Qur'an (Surah 12), and Bible (Genesis 37–50) focus on different details of the story, all agree that Joseph (or Yusuf) was not an "average working Joe." As such, the details from all three religious texts are integrated here to provide an interfaith perspective of Joseph's calling. Additional archaeological information provides historical context and details about his work. The confluence of information from all sources conveys practical lessons about Joseph's calling, leadership, and talent development in organizations.

Joseph, a Hebrew shepherd from Canaan, left home and lived up to his Hebrew name, which means "to increase or may God add." He was ultimately appointed Pharaoh's vizier and second in command over Egypt during the 12th dynastic era under the Pharaoh Amenemhat III.[1] At that time, Joseph was given an Egyptian name, Zaphenath-pa'aneah, which means "who is called to life."[2] As Egypt's top administrator, Joseph developed and implemented revolutionary economic policies that led the nation through a famine to fecundity.[3] How did he do it? Between each line of Joseph's résumé are clues about how he lived and fulfilled his calling (Figure 11.1).

Joseph's story elegantly illustrates the dynamic relationship between destiny, duty, and disposition, guided by a collective cosmology that resulted in extraordinarily "good work" across life roles and throughout the life span. His story provides insights into discovering, developing, and fulfilling one's calling as well as attendant risks and challenges. It also illuminates the role that leaders, organizational policies, and colleagues play in developing talent and

Joseph, Son of Jacob
Birth date: 1700 B.C.E.   **Previous Address:** Canaan
Birth Place: Padan Aram   **Current Address:** Egypt
Employment History:

1671 - 1643 (and beyond) **B.C.E. Ruler over Egypt** – 2nd in command after Pharaoh.
Administrator responsible for infrastructure development and maintenance, agricultural
policies, economic policies, human services, and foreign relations during Egypt's 12th and 13th
dynastic era.

- Accomplishments:
    - o   Major reorganization of government administration.
    - o   Established counter cyclical economic policies to manage national resources during
      times of economic prosperity, recession and recovery.
    - o   Established and implemented the first national tax system
    - o   Supervised infrastructure projects (e.g., construction of pyramids and hydraulic water
      system)
    - o   Developed and managed international relief programs
    - o   Mentored immigrant workers
- Other responsibilities: material resource acquisition, management and distribution, accounting,
  social service provision, talent development, livestock management, land/real estate
  management and secretary of agriculture.

1682-1670 B.C.E.   Prison overseer – 2nd in command of Egyptian prison. Monitored all inmate
activities; promoted from prison worker.

1682 B.C.E.   Steward in the home of the Egyptian captain of the guard; responsible for
monitoring all household property, inventory maintenance and land management.

1683 -1682 B.C.E.   Servant in the Egyptian captain of the guard's home; responsible for
preparing and serving food and beverages. Promoted to steward.

1688 - 1683 B.C.E.   Shepherd in the family business. Cared for livestock (e.g. cattle, sheep) in
Shechem, responsible for inventory and reporting quality issues to the owner (dad).

Service: Prison ministry, mentor, cross-cultural/interfaith ambassador
Hobby: Dream Interpretation
*B.C.E. = Before the Common Era, dates are approximate

Figure 11.1   Joseph's résumé. Valerie Myers "Calling and Talent Development: Not
Your Average Working Joe." Published by GlobaLens.com, Business
Case #1-429-200. Copyright © 2011 by Valerie L. Myers.

cultivating workers' callings, as well as the implications of fulfilled callings for individuals, organizations, and society.

Early Work Experience: Family Business

Everyone worked in the family business shepherding livestock, including Joseph. Their primary responsibilities included feeding, watering,
mating, and counting the flock. But Joseph was different.

First, he was his father's (Jacob's) favorite child, the firstborn of his
cherished favorite wife. Consequently, Joseph enjoyed special attention
and affection, special privileges, and a special multicolored coat made
just for him. Joseph evoked Jacob's favor; his siblings evoked Jacob's fury.
Reuben had sex with his father's concubine. Dinah disgraced the family
by wandering into territory that made her vulnerable to rape. Her rapist
fell in love with her and tried to do the right thing by marrying her. But
her brothers, Levi and Simeon, according to custom, wanted to defend
her honor and avenge the wrong by killing the rapist. When they did, they

went overboard and massacred all of the men of his town. Judah had a penchant for prostitutes and was caught in a sex scandal. By comparison, Joseph was faultless.

Second, Joseph was entrusted with different tasks. Sometimes he stayed at home with his father when his brothers went into the fields. Joseph also supervised his brothers' work and reported back to their father. His brothers hated him.

Third, despite the family's agricultural legacy, at 17 years old Joseph dreamed of doing something different. Trying to make sense of his dreams, he shared one with his family. In the dream, he and his brothers tied up bundles of grain. Suddenly, his bundle arose, while their bundles gathered around and bowed to his. "So you think you will be our king, do you? Do you actually think you will reign over us?"[4] They hated him all the more because of his dreams and the way he talked about them. Joseph, oblivious to the impact he had on his brothers, ignored his father's warning to be discrete and inflamed their anger even more by sharing another dream: "The sun, the moon, and 11 stars bowed down before me," he said. His brothers' hatred and jealousy grew even more. "Who has time to dream? There's work to do," they thought. Even Joseph's father was incredulous—the nerve of that kid! (But, he secretly considered the possibility.)

Such dreams made Joseph believe that he had discovered his calling—leadership! But Joseph led only livestock. The prospect of leading anything else seemed remote. His occupational vision seemed unattainable.

Joseph soon learned that vision and occupational passion are only part of a calling and not even the most important part. The way forward, however, was murky. Joseph didn't have a guidance counselor or mentor to help him plan or navigate his path. So, he just kept working. One day, Jacob/Israel asked Joseph, "Please go and see if it is well with your brothers and well with the flocks, and bring back word to me."[5] Joseph left the Valley of Hebron to search for his brothers in Shechem, but he did not see them. A stranger, noticing Joseph's perplexed look, said, "Your brothers are about 20 miles further north, in Dothan."

When the brothers saw Joseph in the distance, they started conspiring: "Here comes this dreamer! Now then, come and let us kill him and throw him into one of the pits; and we will say, 'A wild beast devoured him.' Then let us see what will become of his dreams!"[6] When Joseph approached, they wrestled him and stripped off his colorful coat. Joseph pleaded with them in anguish. Then, in a moment of conscience, his brother Reuben said, "Let us not take his life. Shed no blood."[7] Judah chimed in: "Instead of hurting him, let's sell him to those Ishmaelite traders. After all, he is our brother—our own flesh and blood!"[8] So, they tossed Joseph's coat aside and tossed him into a waterless pit.

Bruised, bewildered, and languishing in the dark pit, Joseph's thoughts wandered about: his mother's death . . . being "different" . . . his family's drama . . . and his dreams, which had suddenly turned into a nightmare. He was foolish not to recognize his brothers' growing envy, resentment, and animus. Meanwhile, the brothers dipped Joseph's coat in goat's blood, then presented it to their father as evidence that Joseph had been killed by wild animals. Jacob was inconsolable.

Later, Reuben secretly returned to the pit to rescue Joseph, but he was gone. Traders had lifted Joseph out of the pit and sold him into slavery in Egypt. That was his first step toward "leadership"!

The Core of Joseph's Calling

Several factors suggest that Joseph's personality predisposed him to experience a calling. First, he clung to his dream although he had no idea or models for how it might be fulfilled, which suggests that he had an open-minded personality. Joseph's willingness to go 20 extra miles for his father demonstrates conscientiousness. Further, Joseph's relationship with his father, connection to a higher being, intrapersonal awareness, and confidence in his dreams suggest that he had a modicum of spiritual well-being. Nevertheless, his destiny, duty, and disposition would need to be developed.

As a youth, Joseph had a clear sense of *destiny*, a dream that narrowly focused on a career with extraordinary prestige and power. It was a seemingly unattainable dream given his family background, limited life experiences, and lack of training. Nevertheless, he was *dutiful* in his role as a shepherd and son. With regard to Joseph's disposition, it was woefully underdeveloped. More specifically, the narrative suggests that Joseph was oblivious about his privilege as the favorite son, lacked empathy and awareness of his brothers' understandable jealousy, and lacked wisdom and discretion about sharing his dreams. Furthermore, because he was pampered and preferred over his brothers, he had limited experience coping with difficulty, except for his mother's death. This all changed once he was sold into Egypt.

As Joseph's résumé in Figure 11.1 shows, he had numerous jobs and life experiences between his work as a slave and leading the Egyptian government, including wrongful imprisonment. (The entire story is chronicled in the academic business case, which may be purchased at GlobaLens.com.) Each shift, step up, and setback realigned the core dimensions of Joseph's calling, acted as a catalyst for growth, and changed the dynamic recursive relationship between his duties, disposition, and sense of destiny. By necessity, Joseph became more self-aware and aware of others. As he adapted to and fulfilled his job duties, he grew in character and gained new skills; as he gained new skills, he was promoted to better low-status work, and his character was challenged. While waiting for his dream to materialize, he job crafted and soul crafted. Indeed, Joseph learned to master the mundane, deal with drudgery, and cope with *unthinkable* events.

Beginning with his mother's death and his brother's brutality, life for Joseph was no "crystal stair." But he didn't sit down. He kept climbing, stepping up to demands of the situation, doing good work, and experiencing the generative effects of his calling (e.g., posttraumatic growth). As he assumed new roles such as serving others, delighting in his hobby of interpreting dreams, and making new friends, core dimensions of his calling became more robust. Why was this the case?

The constants in Joseph's life, from Canaan to Egypt, were a well-developed work ethic and religious beliefs (cosmologies) that he learned from his father in his home community. Joseph retained and acted on his beliefs, even though they were not aligned with beliefs in the dominant culture; he was a monotheist in a polytheistic country. Nevertheless, Joseph acknowledged his faith, without being fanatical, as the spirit that animated his work. His employers didn't mind the ideological difference because Joseph was excellent and ethical in everything that he did. They benefitted in tangible ways and therefore provided Joseph with training and growth opportunities.

But he was still a minority—a "nobody" in the eyes of many, not "special" as he was at home with his father. Joseph worked and lived in Egypt throughout his early adulthood under dismal circumstances. Given his 13-year stay in Egypt, before ascending to power, it is conceivable that Joseph would have fully assimilated, or that his beliefs might have been diluted by the dominant national culture. Instead of waning, however, Joseph retained his beliefs and became bolder in them, perhaps buoyed by the foundational cosmologies from his father about work and faith. In fact, it was Joseph's beliefs, character, and continuous improvement in his leisure interests that positioned him for his meteoric rise to power.

Eventually, Joseph interpreted Pharaoh's dreams and told of coming prosperity, then warned of an impending famine. He added even more value by offering a countercyclical economic policy to manage the coming crisis. Joseph's advice was remarkable for several reasons. First, none of Pharaoh's Egyptian magicians were able to interpret the dream. Therefore, it was *unthinkable* that a "nobody" ex-prisoner like Joseph could interpret it. But Pharaoh ignored historic social barriers that excluded Hebrews and gave Joseph an opportunity, only to discover that Joseph's difference was an asset—a resource that provided novel tools to solve the problem.

Second, who wants to give leaders bad news? Joseph could have conveyed only the news of coming prosperity and withheld information about the famine. Instead, he acted with integrity and told the whole truth, even though he had a lot to lose—reimprisonment. Third, Joseph's plan was not only impromptu and innovative but it surpassed his previous skills and experience. When Pharaoh inquired about Joseph's ability to interpret dreams, Joseph replied: "It is not me; God gives me the interpretation."[9]

Promotion: You're Hired!

Despite their religious differences, Pharaoh said: "Can we find a man like this, in whom is the Spirit of God?" Then Pharaoh said to Joseph, "Since God has shown you all this, there is none so discerning and wise as you are. You shall be over my house, and all my people shall order themselves as you command. Only as regards the throne will I be greater than you."[10] Joseph replied with confident enthusiasm: "I'm a skilled steward."[11]

Pharaoh appointed 30-year-old Joseph steward and vizier—Pharaoh's representative and second in command over all of Egypt. He gave Joseph expensive garments, gold chains, a signet ring, a company vehicle (chariot), bodyguards, an Egyptian name, and a resounding public endorsement. In addition, Pharaoh commanded everyone, Egyptian and Hebrew alike, to respect and submit to Joseph's authority.

The good years were already underway, so Joseph's work began immediately. First, he reorganized the government to create a Department of People's Giving and a Department of Treasury. Early on, Joseph kept careful records of the grain reserve inventory; eventually there was more grain than he could count. He also ordered his staff to record Nile water levels in order to monitor shifting environmental conditions. Toward that end, Joseph's administration invested in massive infrastructure projects, including a complex water management system in Faiyum. (Egyptians had already used hydraulic engineering in the pyramids.) In the new system, hydraulics were used to channel excess water from the Nile River toward desert regions and other waterways, and away from farmlands. The system also served as a water reservoir that could be used during droughts. This canal, a sort of second Nile, became known as Bahr Yussef—the Waterway of Joseph.[12] Joseph excelled as a leader and administrator (see the summary in Figure 11.2).

Pharaoh subsequently invited Joseph into elite Egyptian society in the city of On. On was an intellectual and academic center in which physicians trained; it was also the location of a temple for sun worship. Here, Pharaoh honored Joseph with a choice bride, Asenath, the daughter of

Abundance: Joseph's First Seven Years as Vizier of Egypt
• Managed government infrastructure projects including constructing the pyramids and hydraulic systems.

• Created the Bahr Yussef Canal (Waterway of Joseph), a 24-kilometer (15-mile) channel that collected and disbursed water from the Nile River, resulting in abundant crops. Primary functions of the canal:
  – Control flooding from the Nile (to avert famine due to crop destruction)
  – Regulate Nile water levels during dry seasons (to avert famine due to crop failure)
  – Serve as a reservoir for surplus water
  – Irrigate surrounding desert regions

• Developed a system to collect and inventory surplus grain from all Egyptian cities.

• Reorganized the government to create:
  – The Department of the Head of the South, which supplied exotic produce from Nubia and Punt
  – Department of People's Giving to oversee farmers' agricultural labor for the state and grain given to the state, that was later distributed to the people by the state
  – Department of Treasury to manage revenue, land, and implement new tax policy

Figure 11.2 Joseph's countercyclical economic plan. Valerie Myers "Calling and Talent Development: Not Your Average Working Joe." Published by GlobaLens.com, Business Case #1-429-200. Copyright © 2011 by Valerie L. Myers.

an On priest. Soon, they had children, whom Joseph named Manasseh and Ephraim: Manasseh, because "God has made me forget all my trouble and all my father's household" and Ephraim because "God has made me fruitful in the land of my affliction."[13] After more than a decade of job-crafting and soul-crafting, life was good—but not perfect.

Despite Joseph's power, prestige, success, and high-society wife, he had daily reminders that he was still an outsider—a Hebrew in Egypt: "Egyptians could not eat bread with the Hebrews, for that is loathsome to the Egyptians."[14] Therefore, other Egyptian cabinet officials dined together while Joseph ate alone.

The Nile's water table rose 20% above normal levels, which devastated crops in Egypt and surrounding areas. The flood lasted so long that it took years for the water to abate, as Joseph predicted. His work became more demanding—agriculturally and administratively. When people came to him for grain and bread, he sold it to them from the national reserve and deposited money into the Department of Treasury. So far, his plan was working. Even people from neighboring cities came to Egypt in search of food. As vizier, it was Joseph's job to meet foreign emissaries entering Egypt. This is how he was unexpectedly reunited with his brothers; they came to Egypt in search of food.

Despite 22 years and 400 miles between them, Joseph immediately recognized his siblings, but they did not realize that the leader to whom they bowed was Joseph. Thirty-nine-year-old Joseph remembered his teenage dreams. Then, as he was jolted by the memory of his brothers' treachery, he devised an elaborate scheme to test their character and intent. They passed his test.

Eventually, the family relocated to Egypt, confronting the same institutionalized biases that Joseph did. They were "nobody" shepherds, but they were connected to "somebody," which made all the difference.

The Way Forward: Crossing Cultural Boundaries

Joseph knew that living in Egypt would be a big adjustment for his family. They did not understand the Egyptian ways, including its language, customs, and beliefs. They soon learned that Hebrew shepherds were considered an inferior minority. Nor did they know how to find work. So, Joseph helped them adapt to the new environment and exploit their talents. He gave them insider information about what to expect while living and working in Egypt, he coached them regarding what they should do, and then sponsored them in the organization:

> I will go up and tell the news to Pharaoh, and say to him, "My brothers and my father's household, who were in the land of Canaan, have come to me. The men are shepherds; they have always been breeders of livestock, and they have brought with them their flocks and herds and all that is theirs." So when Pharaoh summons you and asks, "What is your occupation?" you shall answer, "Your servants have been breeders of livestock from the start until now, both we and our fathers"—so that you may stay in the region of Goshen. For all shepherds are abhorrent to Egyptians.[15]
>
> Then Joseph came and reported to Pharaoh, saying, "My father and my brothers, with their flocks and herds and all that is theirs, have come from the land of Canaan and are now in the region of Goshen." And, selecting a few of his brothers, he presented them to Pharaoh. Pharaoh said to his brothers, "What is your occupation?" They answered Pharaoh, "We your servants are shepherds, as were also our fathers. We have come," they told Pharaoh, "to sojourn in this land, for there is no pasture for your servants' flocks, the famine being severe in the land of Canaan. Pray, then, let your servants stay in the region of Goshen." Then Pharaoh said to

Joseph, "As regards your father and your brothers who have come to you, the land of Egypt is open before you: settle your father and your brothers in the best part of the land; let them stay in the region of Goshen. And if you know any capable men among them, put them in charge of my livestock."[16]

Because they followed his advice, Joseph's brothers obtained government jobs as agricultural workers. Egyptians did not mind because they considered this menial work that was beneath them.

Leading and Legacy

Devastating effects of the famine tested Joseph's capabilities. Each year challenged him to adapt his crisis management strategy as the situation changed.[17]

During the first two years of the famine, people spent all of their money to purchase food from the government, which Joseph put in the treasury. During the third year, Joseph devised a new plan to provide food. "Give up your livestock, and I will give you food for your livestock, since your money is gone,"[18] he said. "So they brought their livestock to Joseph, and Joseph gave them food in exchange for the horses and the flocks and the herds and the donkeys; and he fed them with food in exchange for all their livestock that year."[19] Suddenly, Joseph's family had more work than they could have imagined—the "dirty work" of managing the Egyptian government's rapidly expanding livestock holdings. Shepherd's work proved vital to national security and sustainability. As the brothers' shepherding responsibilities increased, so did their wealth, their ability to acquire land, and their status in the community. The family prospered and grew.

Joseph's skilled and adaptable leadership, as well as collaborative work across ethnic boundaries, enabled him to lead the nation through a seven-year economic crisis. In addition to building water ways, he built bridges of understanding in the community. Eventually, Egyptians highly esteemed Joseph and his family.

Joseph's family, including his father, lived in Egypt for 17 years before Jacob fell ill. How Joseph must have grieved when his father died.

After the funeral, hearts sank, some spirits soared, and rivalries among the brothers reemerged. Without Jacob, there was no buffer between the brothers. Would the family collapse into conflict without him? Some brothers whispered among themselves, "What if Joseph bears a grudge against us and pays us back in full for all the wrong which we did to him!"[20] Joseph overheard them and wept, saying, "Do not be afraid, for am I in God's place?"[21] "As for you, you meant evil against me, but God meant it for good in order to bring about this present result, to preserve many people alive. So therefore, do not be afraid; I will provide for you and your little ones."[22]

At age 50, Joseph reflected on his life, work, family, and dear departed father. His guiding cosmology helped him to make sense of it all.

The Ecology and Evolution of Joseph's Calling

Young Joseph the braggadocio dreamed of a destiny that placed him at the center of the universe. At some point along his path, however, Joseph had an awakening, multiple awakenings in fact. His calling was not to individual success or a particular career, but to a much greater purpose that was revealed over decades. He didn't fully comprehended his ultimate destiny until he was 50 years old, when he proclaimed that he was *called by* God, *called to* a transcendent purpose, and realized that he was *called to* behave according to higher standards and not to sink to his brothers'(and others') level. Moreover, he was called to uphold the moral standards of his profession as a responsible steward and public servant who worked to benefit society. To get there, Joseph experienced several calls throughout his life. Each call was intermittently perceived, advanced, and fulfilled in the process of Joseph being awakened and making decisions in his day-to-day life—choices to be excellent and ethical in various roles. Joseph's repeated awakenings, and responsiveness to them, challenged him to climb ever higher toward his noblest self, his core beliefs and to mature in his calling.

The foundational cosmologies of Joseph's calling were derived from his home community, including negative family issues that he had to overcome. Additional cosmologies that he derived from new experiences in a different country and new work settings with different leadership added layers and texture to his world view and repeatedly enabled him to adapt to new situations. However, based on quotes in the narrative, his foundational cosmologies had the most profound influence on his quest to be ethical, excellent, and to cope with life's vicissitudes. The confluence of all of those multiple cosmologies and different life experiences formed the ecology in which his calling unfolded, barriers and all.

Abuse at the hands of his brothers, being exploited as a slave laborer, sexual harassment, and discrimination that led to wrongful and protracted imprisonment all seemed to threaten Joseph's destiny. Instead, those social, structural, and legal impediments were ironically instrumental in his posttraumatic growth and ascent. Other factors that enabled his climb include leaders along the way who provided employment and educational opportunities, recognized and cultivated Joseph's strengths, and created pathways for advancement. Most importantly, Pharaoh was willing to suspend cultural biases, expand the selection criteria, and risk hiring someone who was "different."

When Pharaoh hired Joseph, he acted as a called leader by providing equitable rewards and reinforcing Joseph's authority for the greater good of the community and its future well-being. Nevertheless, discriminatory practices and segregation persisted in the culture; Joseph ate alone. Still, the core cosmologies, ecology, and evolution of Joseph's calling show that it wasn't about finding "it" and fit. Instead, fulfillment of his calling was contingent on myriad individual, social, organizational, and, yes, spiritual factors.

A Specialist with Spirit

Evidence reveals that Joseph was a *specialist with spirit*; he did objectively and subjectively good work. This doesn't mean that he was perfect. Joseph was a *specialist* in the classic sense, behaving with integrity and taking care and pride in his work, even when he didn't feel destined to do it (although in several situations, he had no choice). Nevertheless, he continuously sought to and did improve. This was true not only at work but also in his leisure pursuits. Who knows what would have happened if Joseph had given up interpreting dreams because his own dream had not come true.

Regarding *specialization* in a career, being a servant was not remotely aligned with the youthful destiny that he envisioned to become a leader. Yet working as a slave, steward, and in a prison, combined with his dream interpretation skills, yielded precisely the experiences that groomed him for his ultimate leadership role. Through those experiences, he gained a refined sense of duty and willingness to do the mundane for someone other than his beloved father. He expanded his skill repertoire to include inventory control, logistics, and resource management, which were essential for the macro challenges that awaited him. Joseph's specialization literally saved thousands of lives (and more in the biblical sense), but that would not have happened if he had not done mundane work well.

With regard to subjectively good work, there was a positive *spirit* that animated Joseph's work. He openly acknowledged that faith guided his decisions, behaviors, and professional insights. In addition, he imputed *sacred* meaning, not more meaning, to his work.

In a secular sense, the spirit of Joseph's work was animated by character strengths and coping skills (disposition) that he cultivated with experience. Foremost, Joseph had the courage to believe that he could do something that no one in his family had done before him, and that none of the Egyptian magicians could do. He built on his core strengths of diligence, trustworthiness, self-control, and communicating with integrity.

For him, those tonic traits enabled him to be a fair and just steward of community resources during times of national prosperity and economic uncertainty. Throughout his story, flashes of phasic character strengths appear, rising and waning as the situation demands. For example, he showed compassion toward his fellow prisoners, agreeableness and cultural sensitivity when working with Egyptian colleagues and the community, and wisdom when approached by his less-than-honest brothers.

Despite undeniable successes, many things troubled Joseph. His brother's treachery and separation from his father weighed heavily on his heart. He desperately wanted to be released from prison, having been there for 10 years. He was not immune to being a "somebody" who was slighted, segregated, and still treated like a "nobody" because of his ethno-religious heritage. And after all, he was still in a strange land. His soul crafting is evident in the names of his children: Manasseh because "God has made me forget all my trouble and all my father's household"[23] and Ephraim because "God has made me fruitful in the land of my affliction."[24] When reconciled with his brothers, Joseph not only took the high road, but he was also welcoming, charitable, and forgiving. The combination of faith, character, and coping made his *spirit* indomitable; that spirit pervaded every aspect of his life—his leisure activities, family relationships, work relationships, career, volunteer work, and ultimately his work as an organizational leader.

The Calling to Leadership

Both Pharaoh and Joseph acted as called leaders. I have already described evidence of the Pharaoh's calling to leadership. In addition, Joseph behaved as a called leader in his role as vizier. First, he created the conditions for others to do their best work, including Egyptian citizens and his family. Egyptians had considerable experience constructing water systems for the pyramids long before Joseph arrived. He redirected their skills toward an innovative engineering project with which he had no prior experience. Under his leadership, yet lack of technical skills, they collaborated to create an infrastructure that sustained the nation. He also created the conditions for his family to do good work. He didn't promote them above their abilities, but he helped them find fitting work. As a result, they contributed to the organization and society, and they prospered too.

Second, Joseph sought and received buy-in for his economic policy decisions from those who would be most affected; he didn't abuse his power. With those policies, he promoted human and environmental sustainability. In his concern for the people and the land, he ensured that his policies would replenish the land for all rather than hoard resources for a privileged few, which was in the best interest of all. Hence, the government acted as a called organization.

Finally, Joseph fostered sustained positive relationships. The bridges of cross-cultural understanding that he built were apparent, not only in the Egyptian community's shared mourning of his father's death but also in the political good will that lingered between Hebrews and Egyptians for generations. Ultimately, Joseph worked to create an oasis of goodness wherever he was, even in literal and figurative deserts along the way.

Many attempt to plan a career trajectory and find "it," but Joseph's life illustrates that we cannot plan a calling, we respond to it. As we do, the calling strengthens our character, the quality and impact of our service, and the love in our relationships in surprisingly generative ways. Imagine what the world would be like if 80% of the population that are religious adherents similarly practiced what they professed with regard to their callings.

NOTES

Portions of this chapter were excerpted from Valerie Myers "Calling and Talent Development: Not Your Average Working Joe." Published by GlobaLens.com, Business Case #1-429-200. Copyright © 2011 by Valerie L. Myers.

1. Due to limited archaeological information from an Egyptian perspective, the timeline and historical details presented here are derived from D. M. Rohl, *Pharaohs and Kings: A Biblical Quest* (New York: Crown, 1995); Kitchen, http://www.biblearchaeology.org/post/2009/03/The-Joseph-Narrative-(Gen-372c-39e2809350).aspx; and C. Aling, "Joseph in Egypt (in 6 parts)," *Bible and Spade* 15, no. 1 (2002).
2. Kitchen, http://www.biblearchaeology.org/post/2009/03/The-Joseph-Narrative-(Gen-372c-39e2809350).aspx.
3. Buttonwood, "Spin and Substance: What the G20 Did and Did Not Achieve," *The Economist.com*, April 8, 2009, http://www.economist.com/node/13447131.
4. Genesis 37:8, New Living Bible Translation, hereafter NLT.
5. Genesis 37:14, New King James Version, hereafter NKJV.
6. Genesis 37:19–20 (NKJV).
7. Genesis 37:21 (NKJV).
8. Genesis 37:27 (NLT).
9. Based on Genesis 41:15–16.
10. Genesis 41:38–40 (ESV).
11. Based on Surah 100:55.
12. Rohl, *Pharaohs and Kings*.
13. Genesis 41:51–52, New American Standard Bible Updated, hereafter NASU.
14. Genesis 43:32 (NASU).
15. Genesis 46:31–34 from Tanakh.
16. Genesis 47:1–6 from Tanakh.
17. Ibid.
18. Genesis 47:16 (NASU).
19. Genesis 47:17 (NASU).
20. Genesis 50:15 (NASU).
21. Genesis 50:19 (NASU).
22. Genesis 50:20–21.
23. Genesis 41:51.
24. Genesis 41:52.

12

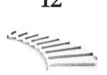

Cultivating Calling in Emerging and Established Adults

Joseph's calling was cultivated in community—not by reading a book. The process began in his home community. Although Joseph learned positive lessons from his father about the duty to use careful methods and be excellent at his craft, about his duty to himself, and to rely on his faith to cope, there were negative lessons as well. As a leader, his father failed to nurture the gifts of all of his children and his favoritism fomented vicious rivalries among them. Joseph's mother and brothers were also less than stellar examples of virtuous character, so he needed to unlearn or reject certain influences that could later threaten his performance, such as stealing, dishonesty, treachery, revenge, and sexual indiscretions. Moreover, Joseph was limited with regard to supports from his home community. They were not equipped to recognize or nurture his destiny; his dreams exceeded their grasp. That was up to his broader community. The Egyptian community continued the cultivation process directly and indirectly through new experiences, training, mentoring, developmental growth opportunities, relationships, and adversity. All of these community influences, positive and negative, helped to shift Joseph's youthful narcissistic gaze from his dreams, desires, and destiny toward a commitment to being ethical and doing excellent work that ultimately served others. It takes a village to cultivate calling.

Joseph's story highlights the fact that calling is a lifelong transcendent process of learning, growth, renewal, and responsiveness to situational demands that elevate performance. As Weber noted, it is a long arduous process of education, formal and informal. In this chapter, I explore different ways that today's village can facilitate that educational process. I draw on insights and examples that I presented in Chapters 6 and 9, and cite related research to suggest ways that various institutions might be instrumental in cultivating the callings of emerging and established adults.

Emerging Adulthood

In contemporary terms, emerging adulthood ranges from age 18 to the mid- to late 20s, but the range may vary across demographic and cultural groups.[1] Emerging adulthood is a life phase that is characterized by identity exploration that ideally results in identity resolution and integration, awareness of competencies, authenticity, and an occupational trajectory. The emergent process entails testing formative beliefs, making decisions independently, taking responsibility for actions, and becoming more reflective and self-aware.[2] According to psychologist Jeffrey Arnett, "a key feature of emerging adulthood is that it is the period of life that offers the most opportunity for identity explorations in the areas of love, work, and worldviews."[3] Since moral identity is part of one's overall identity, it may also be an ideal time to nurture the core dimensions of calling via the foundational collective cosmologies that animate them. For example, instead of narrowly focusing on career and what work one wants to pursue, questions to advance calling might be: What kind of worker and human being will I be? What character strengths will I bring to different life roles? What are my present and prospective obligations? Indeed, Barbara Walters recognized early in life that caring for her sister would eventually become her duty, moral obligation, and part of a responsible life whether she liked it or not. Throughout this book, I've shown that you don't have to have the perfect conditions to fulfill your calling—Joseph didn't.

Joseph

The narrative opens, introducing Joseph as a 17-year-old dreamer and concludes with his death as a 110-year-old esteemed statesman. The story reveals that he successfully navigated the transition from emerging adult to an established adult who fulfilled his calling. Despite serious challenges, he progressed through the typical milestones of physically and psychologically leaving home; exploring his identity and trying on different roles (e.g., pretending to be a slave); examining familial beliefs and forming a moral identity that guided his work behaviors. He made decisions independently and over time, becoming more reflective and self-aware. Most importantly, the religious cosmology that guided his calling was sustained in a context that did not support it (e.g., polytheistic Egypt).

Throughout his story, there is evidence of moral, identity, and vocational integration. For example, when he resisted the boss's wife's sexual advances on principle; when he interpreted positive and negative aspects of Pharaoh's dream and attributed his skills to God; and when he reconciled with his brothers who didn't recognize him by saying

"I am Joseph." It was a declaration not only of his identity but it was also an expression of his character and competencies as a forgiving, charitable, mature, and wise leader who saw them for who they were and was committed to fulfilling his familial obligation to them anyway.

Near the end of the narrative, 50-year-old Joseph has numerous responsibilities; he handles his relationships with skill and grace and he is concerned about posterity. His father's dying words convey pride for the adult that he has become. "Joseph is a fruitful bough, even a fruitful bough by a well; whose branches run over the wall."[4] More important, however, is Joseph's own assessment of the events of his life as part of a larger, transcendent story, when his brothers feared that he will seek revenge. "But Joseph said to them, 'Do not be afraid, for am I in God's place? As for you, you meant evil against me, but God meant it for good in order to bring about this present result, to preserve many people alive.'"[5] The same cosmology that awakened him to a leadership destiny, animated his work duties, sculpted his character, and taught him to cope with adversity now framed the real purpose of all of his jobs, hobbies, and his career trajectory—to save human lives. He, along with his vision of destiny, matured. He continued on his path until he was 110 years old, giving hope to seniors who seek to fulfill their callings.[6] He is a model for calling and vocation in the truest sense.

It is easy to understand how someone like Joseph successfully transitions from emerging adulthood, to established adult, to living their calling. His father doted on him, nurtured him, and lavished attention on him. Furthermore, he derived insights and comfort from his religious ideology. Those parental and spiritual supports compensated for the lack of other supports and helped Joseph overcome numerous situational impediments. But what about people who didn't have parental or community supports? Or those who, like Joseph, were subject to gang violence that they couldn't escape? Or who have had devastating life challenges that they have yet to overcome? Or who are well past emerging adulthood and feel uncertain and stuck? Or whose character weaknesses, circumstances, and lack of support has halted their climb—people like Joseph's brothers? How do they navigate the perils of emerging adulthood and go on to live their callings?

Risks of Emerging Adulthood: The Good, Bad, and Invisible Siblings

Emerging adulthood is also the peak age range for risky behaviors. Although some risky behaviors may be considered part of normal identity exploration that abate with time, activities such as unprotected sex, substance abuse, driving while intoxicated, or other unhealthy behaviors can have lasting negative consequences. However, religious involvement, negotiated parental relationships, and peer influences can be both protective factors against risky behaviors and facilitators of the transition to adulthood.[7] Empirical study of emerging adulthood is a relatively new field at just a decade old. However, it offers insights about the transition to adulthood and perhaps the inability to fulfill one's calling—like some of Joseph's siblings.

Joseph's siblings engaged in many typical risky behaviors of emerging adulthood such as sexual promiscuity, violence, and simply exploring unfamiliar territory. Rather than recognizing these behaviors for what they were, however, their father defined many of his children by outlandishly deviant behaviors; other children were seemingly invisible to him. Evidence of his persistent negative beliefs and biases is apparent in his dying words to them, and for some they were a self-fulfilling prophecy. In addition, he identified and affirmed the latent abilities of some offspring that he had previously disparaged.

In hindsight, Joseph may have recognized the role that their father, Jacob, played in his own development and failed to play in his siblings'.[8] Leaders' opinions and strong cosmologies can also become insular, oppressive, and arrogant notions of what is normative; they can be taken for granted as correct; and they can become irrationally and unquestioningly resistant to change. As management scholars Blake Ashforth and Deepa Vaidyanath note: "Individuals may lose their circumspection regarding cosmologies that may be 'wrong,' destructive, manipulated cynically, myopic, or resistant to needed change."[9]

Once their father died, there was an awakening. The narrative doesn't reveal the actual details of what happened to Joseph's brothers, who were by then, senior citizens. But we do know that many of the brothers and their offspring stepped up and into their callings. Succeeding books in the Old Testament reveal that many followed different work trajectories and/or more transcendent directions. With regard to occupational destiny, some remained shepherds, but others became administrators, merchants, warriors, a baker, and even a priest. One tribe even surpassed Joseph's legacy and accomplishments by becoming the first king and ultimate head of the family, despite earlier entanglements in a sex scandal. (Evidence of his incremental changes and emerging leadership abilities are also woven throughout the story.) To do so, it is likely that they developed new character strengths and different ways of coping. As with Joseph, perhaps influences from their new community, new leadership styles, additional resources, and exposure to new and different ideas were instrumental in them advancing in their respective callings.

The outcomes of Joseph and his brothers elucidate new directions for management scholarship, some of which I've described in previous chapters. For example, the vocational view of calling, in the traditional sense, is truly liberating. The quantum nature of calling means that awakenings and advancement can occur throughout the life span, even in advanced age. While emerging adulthood may be the opportune time to cultivate calling, the lives of C. S. Lewis and Joseph's brothers suggest that, given enabling conditions, change and progress are possible at any time throughout the life span. Progress is contingent, however, on personality traits, developmental opportunities, and an orientation toward continuous learning.[10]

Theories of adult development[11] indicate that, with appropriate content and supports, learning and growth continue into advanced age.[12] Therefore, it may be possible, to varying degrees, to cultivate core dimensions of calling well into late adulthood and senior years. In addition, research is mounting to show how existing cultural and religious cosmologies can be used to provide education that corrects and improves behaviors in adult populations, which I discuss later in this chapter.[13] Research is needed to examine the ways that formal and informal educational processes can be used to cultivate callings in emerging or established adults. In addition, research is needed to determine what types of educational supports are needed to complement gaps in foundational cosmologies of the "home community." It would be particularly interesting to examine the differential effects of secular, spiritual, and religious community influences on the core dimensions of calling. As I mentioned in Chapters 6, 7, and 9, we need to understand how the village, comprised of various traditional institutions, might support the cultivation of calling as it did in bygone eras.

Institutional Influences and the Ecology of Calling

Practitioner literature and historic documents suggest that the calling ethic was the product of multiple institutional influences—some secular and some religious or ideological. Secular institutions include the family, media, schools, higher education, professional organizations, and arts and cultural activities (including poetry, literature, and song). Religious and ideological institutions include congregations, community organizations (e.g., YMCA), and cultural organizations. The values and activities of these institutions were reinforced by the broader culture vis a vis values, norms, and the media. Uri Bronfenbrenner's notion of bioecological systems is useful for understanding how various institutions have and might influence the calling ethic.[14]

In his bioecological systems theory, Bronfenbrenner described the aforementioned institutions as the *microsystem* that directly influences human development through roles, relationships, and activities. The *mesosystem* consists of interactions among these microsystems or institutions—for example, the relationship between a person's workplace and community. The *exosystem* directly affects the microsystem, but one does not have direct involvement in it (e.g., a child's school and a community group). The *macrosystem* is composed of cultural values, laws, and mores. Finally, the *chronosystem* relates to the influence of time on a person's environment and development.[15]

I have indicated that various microsystems were instrumental in cultivating calling throughout history. Moreover, the mesosystems reinforced the cultivation process through interactions between congregations and other community institutions, as in the Unthinkable case example about African American organizations; clergy directly speaking to occupational groups as they did in the 17th century; and guilds, which served as surrogate family, educator, and ideological communities that also lived and worshiped together.[16] Because of the interdependent relationships within the mesosystem, the chronosystem of calling was supported throughout many phases of life (e.g., emerging and mature adulthood) and in multiple contexts, including the macrosystem of the regulatory environment (see Chapter 8) as well as national and regional cultures. If we want to understand how to cultivate calling today, we might consider a systems approach, beginning with the microsystem.

Very little research about calling has examined its microsystems— that is, the extent to which and how select institutions have deliberately attended to issues of vocation, calling, and its core dimensions or whether their activities have positively influenced the development of calling. Such research must precede any meaningful analysis of the presence or absence of calling. Indeed, a core argument in *Habits of the Heart*[17] was that waning institutional influences were eroding a sense of community, including the community in which calling is cultivated. Many institutions that previously nurtured dimensions of the calling ethic are still viable today and can reach diverse segments of the population, such as schools, colleges, and congregations.

Colleges and universities can play an important role in the formation of ethics and emerging adult development,[18] as can religious and ideological communities.[19] In recent years, the Association to Advance Collegiate Schools of Business established ethics standards and learning goals in hopes of improving the ethical behavior of organizational leaders and their impact on society. But little is known about the effects of those programs to date and whether they explicitly foster conversations about the calling ethic.

With regard to religious organizations, studies have shown that religion plays an important role in emerging adult development.[20] Religious involvement is also a protective factor against high-risk behaviors[21] that undermine the transition to adulthood and that might similarly impede progress in one's calling. Through education and socialization, religious organizations have the potential to nurture character strengths, coping skills, and spiritual well-being, which are essential to calling and offer sense-making cosmologies that provide coherence throughout life.

Religious organizations also reach large segments of the population[22]—including emerging, established and mature adults. As such, they are increasingly considered a local resource for providing culturally relevant regional programs that improve the health and health behaviors of youth, working adults, seniors, and different ethnic populations.[23] Indeed, because multigenerational involvement is normative, religious organizations may be ideal settings to facilitate coconstructivist approaches to cultivating calling that are enhanced by intergenerational interactions and information sharing. Furthermore, intergenerational interactions in this context that are specifically targeted at work issues (e.g., calling as a career) may help to both cultivate the calling ethic and promote more cross-generational understanding in the workplace, which is an increasing challenge for human resource professionals.[24] However, to date, little is known about how religious institutions cultivate the calling ethic. According to Lori Fox's research examining the decline of church-based programs,[25] I surmise the efforts are minimal.

Moreover, little is known about how other institutions within the microsystem (e.g., family, professional groups, etc.) influence calling. At minimum, we need research that examines how individual roles, activities, and relationships within the microsystem influence an individual's calling ethic today and how those institutions might partner.

Institutional Partnerships, Professional Practice, and the Mesosystem of Calling

In previous centuries, the mesosystem was vital to establish and sustain the calling ethic. The mesosystem was not comprised of purely secular or purely religious approaches to education. Instead, the calling literature suggests that hybrid approaches were frequently used (see Chapter 9)—some more effective or detrimental than others (e.g., guilds and the YMCA versus *Millhands and Preachers*). Indeed, the hybrid approach is consistent with Neil Brady and David Hart's recommendations for ethics education in general; pedagogical approaches should consist not only of standard professional ethics for the masses but also of a customized ethic that reinforces students' own cultural values.[26] This hybrid, customized approach is consistent with trends in other disciplines (e.g., health education) that integrate professional knowledge and local knowledge from religious organizations and cultural perspectives (e.g., beliefs among an age cohort or ethnic group) to provide education that fosters behavioral change. Guilds and workplace ministries were early hybrid approaches. More recently, business schools have developed hybrid models, but none as sophisticated as faith-based educational interventions in community settings, which have been empirically tested. Faith-based intervention research offers insights about how to improve both.

Workplace Ministries

Workplace ministries have taken various forms throughout history, beginning with clergy and church missions to address work, workplace chaplains, and chaplains on the corporate payroll.[27] As the spirituality and work movement progressed in the 1990s, more and more clergy/consultants started workplace ministries. These approaches are ideologically and professionally driven, but not evidence based. There is no research about the pedagogical approaches, content, processes, or outcomes of these initiatives. This is consequential because research shows that not all religious education and interventions are beneficial; extreme moralizing can have adverse effects. I contend that the most promising approach to cultivating calling within the mesosystem may be in higher education and through faith-based, evidence-based education that occurs in a variety of organizational settings.[28]

Business Schools

Recently, institutional partnerships have been forged between business schools and the faith community, and between the faith community and corporations. This is not unusual since, as Lake Lambert noted, most universities in the United States had religious origins and a guiding ethos until the 19th century; the synthesis of spirituality and management is, therefore, not new. But "market forces sometimes dictated the nonsectarian impulse as colleges competed for students from outside of their own sects."[29]

Lambert identified four types of business-school curricula that might be modified to support education about the calling ethic today: (1) maintaining Christian sectarianism, (2) fostering vocation, (3) being spiritual but not religious, and (4) emerging religious educators. Of these, he believes that the "being spiritual but not religious" model that McLellan, Delbecq, and others have used holds the most promise. Lambert said: "Since most collegiate and graduate education occurs in public institutions, it is also likely to be the model with most potential for growth and the most long-term influence."[30] For example, Joseph's story can be used to facilitate "spiritual but not religious" conversations about calling or it can be customized to promote sectarian conversations.

Since every discipline needs specialists with spirit who ethically and effectively practice their craft, more inclusive and interdisciplinary efforts are needed. In response to social trends, some universities have established new organizations—Yale's Center for Faith and Culture, devoted to ethics and spirituality in the workplace; the Tyson Center for Faith and Spirituality in the Workplace at the University of Arkansas; Princeton's Faith and Work Initiative; and the Coram Deo student organization at the University of Michigan.[31] The business school–based activities are still emerging. Research is needed to develop and test new models of targeted educational interventions that specifically relate to calling. Toward that end, business schools might draw on and transfer knowledge from other disciplines that have empirically tested hybrid educational models.

Faith-Based Educational Interventions

Faith-based behavioral education integrates theory and theology. The content is a synthesis of professional knowledge, participants' existing religious beliefs, local knowledge and practices that are combined to provide culturally and regionally relevant education about specific life domains.[32] Faith-based educational interventions have primarily been used to promote health behaviors, using various empirically tested models of change[33] and educational ecology.[34] Developments in religion and the social sciences research show that religious elements and activities such songs, symbols, stories, and community support can be combined in meaningful ways to produce cognitive, affective, and behavioral changes related to daily life[35]—the same tactics that were historically used to promote the calling ethic.

More than a decade of rigorous research now exists about effective faith-based educational designs, content, populations, organizational supports, and leadership, as well as iatrogenic effects.[36] Studies have shown that, compared to secular-only control groups, faith-based education resulted in significantly higher rates of engagement in health screening, smoking cessation, exercise, and positive changes in nutritional habits. Research has also shown that extreme moralizing associated with the breast cancer, smoking, weight loss, and nutrition interventions was a repeated factor in low participation, dropouts, and low follow-up rates.[37] Hence, these programs must be carefully designed.

Unlike hybrid models used during the industrial betterment movement, faith-based education may be a particularly effective way to cultivate the calling ethic because it (1) includes a third party, academics; (2) eliminates corporate influences on the message because it is based on evidence; and (3) minimizes the potential for clergy manipulation, by design. These interventions can potentially be used to promote individual cognitive changes that foster sacred meanings of work, behavioral changes and ethical behavior, and adaptive coping by using a culturally relevant cosmology.

In addition, during the past century, customized faith-based interventions have resulted in positive change at multiple levels. They have spawned social movements that positively changed the beliefs, behaviors, and outcomes of individuals, communities, organizations, and society.[38] Thus, it is an educational model that may be instrumental in bringing about the institutional changes about which Gardner and his colleagues wrote in *Good Work*,[39] the reformed mesosystem for which Calvin advocated,[40] the calling to business that practitioners urged,[41] and much needed improvements in the ethical climate and quality of work organizations and the culture at large.

The Culture and Exosystem

The review in Chapter 9 shows that national culture and cultural activities were also part of the system that educated people about the calling ethic. However, cultural messages changed during the 18th and 19th centuries, as industrialism became the engine of capitalism. Ultimately, sacred meanings of work and the importance of community were slowly displaced by sacred meanings of profits, consumption and the celebration of rugged individualism. That cultural shift has somewhat diminished the core of calling from disposition, duty, and destiny to a narrow focus on destiny. Yet modern practitioners, some management scholars, the religious community, and various authors have realized that society is not better because of it. Unending headlines about specialists without spirit—self-interested professionals who lie, cheat, and steal—are evidence.

Novak criticized the media for its negative influence and failure to positively contribute to a national conversation about calling. Other practitioners have noted the potentially negative effects of new technologies and hyperconnectivity. The questions now are how, given the ubiquitous nature of media and digital technology, do we use the new engines of capitalism to change the conversation? How can hyperconnectivity be used to create moral communities exogenous to the workplace that care about the character and quality work? To date, most research has focused on individual-level factors related to calling. However, advances in the social sciences combined with digital technology offer yet unimagined possibilities to revive and reinforce calling throughout the entire ecosystem. If we hope to cultivate, fortify, and sustain the calling ethic, we must begin with the community—the village and all of its voices.

NOTES

1. Jeffrey J. Arnett, "Emerging Adulthood: A Theory of Development from the Late Teens through the Twenties," *American Psychologist* 55, no. 5 (2000): 469–80; Larry J. Nelson and Carolyn McNamara Barry, "Distinguishing Features of Emerging Adulthood the Role of Self-Classification as an Adult," *Journal of Adolescent Research* 20, no. 2 (2005).

2. Shmuel Shulman, Benni Feldman, Sidney J. Blatt, Omri Cohen, and Amalya Mahler, "Emerging Adulthood: Age-Related Tasks and Underlying Self Processes," *Journal of Adolescent Research* 20, no. 5 (2005): 577–603; Arnett, "Emerging Adulthood."

3. Arnett, "Emerging Adulthood," 473.

4. Genesis 49:22.

5. Gen. 50:19–20.

6. Gordon T. Smith, *Courage and Calling: Embracing Your God-Given Potential* (Downers Grove, IL: InterVarsity Press, 2011).

7. John M. Wallace, Tony N. Brown, Jerald G. Bachman, and Thomas A. Laveist, "The Influence of Race and Religion on Abstinence from Alcohol, Cigarettes and Marijuana among Adolescents," *Journal of Studies on Alcohol* 64, no. 6 (2003): 843–48; J. W. Wallace, V. M. Myers, and E. Osai, *Faith Matters: Race/Ethnicity, Religion and Substance Use in America* (Baltimore: Annie E. Casey Foundation Press, 2004); Christian Smith with Patricia Snell, *Souls in Transition: The Religious and Spiritual Lives of Emerging Adults* (New York: Oxford University Press, 2009); Jeffrey Jensen Arnett and Jennifer Lynn Tanner, *Emerging Adults in America: Coming of Age in the 21st Century (Decade of Behavior)* (Washington, DC: American Psychological Association Press, 2005).

8. This is a fictionalized detail. I have taken some literary license to make theoretical points, in this case about the Pygmalion effect and leadership.

9. Blake E. Ashforth and Deepa Vaidyanath, "Work Organizations as Secular Religions," *Journal of Management Inquiry* 11, no. 4 (2002): 367.

10. Smith, *Courage and Calling*; Douglas T. Hall and Dawn E. Chandler, "Psychological Success: When the Career Is a Calling," *Journal of Organizational Behavior* 26, no. 2 (2005): 155–76.

11. Sharan B. Merriam, Rosemary S. Caffarella, Lisa M. Baumgartner, *Learning in Adulthood: A Comprehensive Guide* (San Francisco, CA: John Wiley/Jossey-Bass, 2007).

12. Patricia A. Reuter-Lorenz and Paul B. Baltes, eds., *Lifespan Development and the Brain: The Perspective of Biocultural Co-Constructivism* (New York: Cambridge University Press, 2006).

13. Mark J. DeHaven, B. Hunter Irby, Wilder Laura, W. Walton James, and Berry Jarett, "Health Programs in Faith-Based Organizations: Are They Effective?," *American Journal of Public Health* 94, no. 6 (2004): 1030; Valerie L. Myers, *An Interdisciplinary Analysis of Faith-Based Human Services: Analyzing Latent Organizational, Social and Psychological Processes* (PhD diss., University of Michigan, 2003).

14. Uri Bronfenbrenner, "Human Development, Bioecological Theory Of," in *International Encyclopedia of the Social and Behavioral Sciences*, ed. N. J. Smelser and P. B Battles, 6963–70 (Washington, D.C.: American Psychological Association, 2001).

15. Ibid.

16. Richard Sennett, *The Craftsman* (New Haven, CT: Yale University Press, 2008).

17. Robert N. Bellah, Richard Madsen, William M. Sullivan, Ann Swidler, and Steven M. Tipton, *Habits of the Heart: Individualism and Commitment in American Life: Updated Edition with a New Introduction* (Berkeley: University of California Press, 1996).

18. N. Brady and D. Hart, "An Exploration into the Developmental Psychology of Ethical Theory with Implications for Business Practice and Pedagogy," *Journal of Business Ethics* 76 (2007): 397–412.

19. Lawrence Kohlberg, *The Psychology of Moral Development: The Nature and Validity of Moral Stages, Essays on Moral Development,* vol. 2 (San Francisco: Harper & Row, 1984).

20. Arnett, "Emerging Adulthood"; Carolyn McNamara-Barry and Larry J. Nelson, "The Role of Religion in the Transition to Adulthood for Young Emerging Adults," *Journal of Youth and Adolescence* 34, no. 3 (2005): 245–55; Christian Smith, with Patricia Snell, *Souls in Transition.*

21. Smith, *Souls in Transition.*

22. Melissa Bopp and Benjamin Webb, "Health Promotion in Megachurches: An Untapped Resource with Megareach?" *Health Promotion Practice* 13, no. 5 (2012): 679–686.

23. Jeff Levin and Jay F. Hein, "A Faith-Based Prescription for the Surgeon General: Challenges and Recommendations," *Journal of Religion and Health* 51, no. 1 (2012): 57.

24. Ron Zemke, Claire Raines, and Bob Filipczak, *Generations at Work: Managing the Clash of Veterans, Boomers, Xers, and Nexters in Your Workplace* (New York: American Management Association, 2000).

25. Lori A. Fox, "The Role of the Church in Career Guidance and Development: A Review of the Literature 1960–Early 2000s," *Journal of Career Development* 29, no. 3 (2003): 167–82.

26. Brady and Hart, "An Exploration into the Developmental Psychology of Ethical Theory."

27. Lake Lambert III, *Spirituality Inc.: Religion in the American Workplace* (New York: New York University Press, 2009), 116; Daniel T. Rodgers, *The Work Ethic in Industrial America, 1850–1920* (Chicago: University of Chicago Press, 1978).

28. Brady and Hart, "An Exploration into the Developmental Psychology of Ethical Theory."

29. Lambert, Spirituality Inc., 101.

30. Ibid., 116.

31. For Yale's Center for Faith and Culture, see http://www.yale.edu/faith/esw/esw.htm; the Tyson Center for Faith and Spirituality in the Workplace, see http://tfsw.uark.edu/; Princeton's Faith and Work Initiative, see http://www.princeton.edu/faithandwork/; and Coram Deo, see http://webuser.bus.umich.edu/organizations/coramdeo/.

32. Myers, *An Interdisciplinary Analysis of Faith-Based Human Services.*

33. James O. Porchaska, Carlo C. DiClemente, and John C. Norcross, "In Search of How People Change: Applications to Addictive Behaviors," *The American Psychologist* 47, no. 9 (1992): 1102–14.

34. Lawrence W. Green and Marshall W. Kreuter, *Health Promotion Planning: An Educational and Ecological Approach* (Mountain View, CA: Mayfield, 1999).

35. Myers, *An Interdisciplinary Analysis of Faith-Based Human Services.*
36. DeHaven et al., B. Hunter Irby, Wilder Laura, W. Walton James, and Berry Jarett, "Health Programs in Faith-Based Organizations"; Melissa Bopp and Elizabeth A. Fallon, "Individual and Institutional Influences on Faith-Based Health and Wellness Programming," *Health Education Research* 26, no. 6 (2011): 1107–19; Maureen R. Benjamins, Christopher G. Ellison, Neal M. Krause, and John P. Marcum, "Religion and Preventive Service Use: Do Congregational Support and Religious Beliefs Explain the Relationship between Attendance and Utilization?" *Journal of Behavioral Medicine,* Special Issue *Spirituality in Behavioral Medicine Research* 34, no. 6 (2011): 462–76; Amber M. Gum, Mary Ann Watson, Bernard A. Smith, Richard Briscoe, Johnetta Goldsmith, and Britney Henley, "Collaborative Design of a Church-Based, Multidimensional Senior Wellness Program by Older Adults, Church Leaders, and Researchers," *Journal of Religion, Spirituality and Aging* 24, no. 3 (2012): 213–34.
37. C. S. Skinner, R. K. Sykes, B. S. Monseos, D. S. Andriole, C. L. Arfken, and E. B. Fisher, "Learn, Share and Live: Breast Cancer Education for Older, Urban Minority Women," *Health Education and Behavior* 25, no. 1 (1998): 60–78; Diane M. Becker, Joel Gittelsohn, Dyann Matson Koffman, Taryn F. Moy, and Lisa R. Yanek, "Project Joy: Faith Based Cardiovascular Health Promotion for African American Women," *Public Health Reports* 116, no. 1 (2001): S68; Stillman et al., 1993; Voorhees et al., 1996.
38. Roscoe C. Brown, "The National Negro Health Week Movement," *The Journal of Negro Education* 6, no. 3 (1937): 553–64; R. C. Engs, *Clean Living Movements: American Cycles of Health Reform* (Westport, CT: Praeger, 2000).
39. Howard E. Gardner, Mihaly Csikszentmihalyi, and William Damon, *Good Work: When Excellence and Ethics Meet* (New York: Basic Books, 2001).
40. John Calvin, "Institutes of the Christian Religion," in *Callings: Twenty Centuries of Christian Wisdom on Vocation,* ed. William C. Placher, 232–38 (Grand Rapids, MI: Eerdsman, 2005).
41. Jane Kise and David Stark, *Working with Purpose: Finding a Corporate Calling for You and Your Business* (Minneapolis, MN: Ausberg Fortress, 2004).

Epilogue

Calling is sacred meaning imputed to ordinary activities in ways that result in "good work." The sacred meaning of calling and instructions about how to live it were once defined and reinforced by traditional institutions, communities, and national culture. Absent those influences, what is sacred has increasingly been defined by work organizations and a capitalistic culture that, in making profits, winning, bigness and the individual sacred, have diminished but not erased the essence of calling—duty to excellent role performance, character strengths, adaptive coping, and, yes, fitting work that are cultivated in community. One need not be religious to recognize that this shift serves neither individuals, organizations, nor society.

That said, I have shown that there has been no revolutionary shift in the meaning of calling, at best an evolutionary shift has occurred and it has been diluted. Still, calling is a robust idea, the original meaning of which has persisted, despite the lack of institutional supports, as is evident in practitioner perspectives, personal narratives, and individual quests for sacred meaning through self-directed searches and involvement in workplace ministries. Whether or not these tools are effective, we don't know. Much research is needed to understand the ways in which a calling ethic is cultivated and enacted. Toward that end, I've proposed a theory; it is not revolutionary or evolutionary, it is revelatory. It reveals historic insights about how institutions and communities educated people to live their callings and can once again.

I hope that the insights and research presented throughout this book will be a catalyst for new conversations about calling in traditional institutions, various communities, and ultimately the culture more broadly. To promote education, I've also created a suite of teaching cases about Joseph to facilitate conversations about calling in community—in undergraduate and graduate school classrooms, within professional groups and associations, in executive and leadership development programs, community centers, faith at work groups, and so forth.[1] The case study includes information from Christianity, Islam, and Judaism, thereby making it relevant to a broad constituency.

I have successfully used the "Not Your Average Joe" (which is available through GlobaLens.com) case to teach graduate courses in management at the University of Michigan to students from various disciplines (e.g., MBAs, engineering, Information Technology, Hospital Administration, Health Sciences and Social Work). In that setting, we do not discuss religion, but issues that are germane to any organization such as leadership, ethics, innovation, diversity, team work, and the secular elements of calling (duty, disposition, destiny, and cosmologies). The content has resonated with atheists, Hindus, and people who consider themselves spiritual but not religious, as well as religious adherents who are surprised by its theoretical relevance to modern life. It is useful for a "spiritual but not religious" dialogue. The content may also be customized, as I have done with student and professional groups, to explicitly emphasize connections between faith, work, and calling. Or it can be adapted to facilitate cross-cultural and interfaith dialogues that promote understanding. Given the historically important role that narratives, stories, songs, axioms, rituals and poems have played in cultivating calling, I hope that this case and book will be the impetus for creating many new conversations that reconstitute and reinforce the concept in practice and help others live their calling.

NOTE

1. Valerie Myers "Calling and Talent Development: Not Your Average Working Joe." Published by GlobaLens.com, Business Case #1-429-200. Copyright © 2011 by Valerie L. Myers.

   The suite of business cases and teaching notes are available for purchase through GlobaLens.com.

   To learn more, please visit www.conversationsaboutcalling.com

Bibliography

Abbott, Jennifer, and Mark Achbar, dir. *The Corporation*. New York: Zeitgeist Films, 2003.

Abu-Raiya, Hisham, Kenneth Pargament, and Annette Mahoney. "Examining Coping Methods with Stressful Interpersonal Events Experienced by Muslims Living in the United States Following the 9/11 Attacks." *Psychology of Religion and Spirituality* 3, no. 1 (2011): 1–14.

Aburdene, John, and Patricia Naisbitt. *Megatrends 2000: Ten New Directions for the 1990s*. New York: Avon Books, 1990.

Albertson, Quist. *The Gods of Business: The Intersection of Faith in the Marketplace*. Los Angeles, CA: Trinity University Alumni Press, 2007.

Alvesson, Mats, and Jörgen Sandberg. "Has Management Studies Lost Its Way? Ideas for More Imaginative and Innovative Research." *Journal of Management Studies* (2012): doi: 10.1111/j.1467-6486.2012.01070.x.

Alvesson, Mats, and Kaj Skoldberg. "(Post-)Positivism, Social Constructionism, Critical Realism: Three Reference Points in the Philosophy of Science." In *Reflexive Methodology: New Vistas for Qualitative Research*, 2nd ed., ed. Mats Alvesson and Kaj Skoldberg. Thousand Oaks, CA: Sage, 2009.

Anderson, Peter J. J., Ruth Blatt, Marlys K. Christianson, Adam M. Grant, Eric J. Neuman, Scott Sonenshein, and Kathleen M. Sutcliffe. "Understanding Mechanisms in Organizational Research: Reflections from a Collective Journey." *Journal of Management Inquiry* 15, no. 2 (2006): 102.

Anderson, Philip, and Michael L. Tushman. "Technological Discontinuities and Dominant Designs: A Cyclical Model of Technological Change." *Administrative Science Quarterly* 35, no. 4 (1990): 604–33.

Arnett, Jeffrey J. "Emerging Adulthood: A Theory of Development from the Late Teens through the Twenties." *American Psychologist* 55, no. 5 (2000): 469–80.

Ashforth, Blake E., and Deepa Vaidyanath. "Work Organizations as Secular Religions." *Journal of Management Inquiry* 11, no. 4 (2002): 359.

Baker, A. E., ed. *A Christian Basis for the Post-War World: A Commentary on the Ten Peace Points*. Preface by the Bishop of Carlisle. New York: Morehouse-Gorham, 1942.

Baltes, Paul B., and Patricia A. Reuter-Lorenz, eds. *Lifespan Development and the Brain: The Perspective of Biocultural Co-Constructivism*. New York: Cambridge University Press, 2006.

Banks, R., D. Poehler, and R. Russell. "Spirit and Human-Spiritual Interactions as a Factor in Health and in Health Education." *Journal of Health Education* 15 (1984): 16–19.

Barboza, Steven, ed. *The African American Book of Values: Classic Moral Stories.* New York: Doubleday Dell, 1998.

Barley, Stephen R., and Gideon Kunda. "Design and Devotion: Surges of Rational and Normative Ideologies of Control in Managerial Discourse." *Administrative Science Quarterly* 37, no. 3 (1992): 363–99.

Baumeister, R. F. *Work, Work, Work, Work: Meanings of Life.* New York: The Guilford Press, 1991.

Baumgartner, Sharan B., Rosemary S. Merriam, and Lisa M. Caffarella. *Learning in Adulthood: A Comprehensive Guide.* San Francisco, CA: John Wiley/Jossey-Bass, 2007.

Baxter, Richard. "Directions about Our Labor and Callings." In *Callings: Twenty Centuries of Christian Wisdom on Vocation,* edited by William Placher, 278–85. Grand Rapids, MI: Erdsman, 2005.

Beil, Gail. "Wiley College's Great Debaters" (February 2008), http://www.humanitiestexas.org/news/articles/wiley-colleges-great-debaters.

Bellah, Robert N., Richard Madsen, William M. Sullivan, Ann Swidler, and Steven M. Tipton. *Habits of the Heart: Individualism and Commitment in American Life: Updated Edition with a New Introduction.* Berkeley: University of California Press, 1996.

Benjamins, Maureen R., Christopher G. Ellison, Neal M. Krause, and John P. Marcum. "Religion and Preventive Service Use: Do Congregational Support and Religious Beliefs Explain the Relationship between Attendance and Utilization?" *Journal of Behavioral Medicine,* Special Issue *Spirituality in Behavioral Medicine Research* 34, no. 6 (2011): 462–76.

Berg, Justin M., Adam M. Grant, and Victoria Johnson. "When Callings Are Calling: Crafting Work and Leisure in Pursuit of Unanswered Occupational Callings." *Organization Science* 21, no. 5 (2010): 973–94.

Bloch, Deborah P., and Lee J. Richmond. "Complexity, Chaos, and Nonlinear Dynamics: A New Perspective on Career Development Theory." *The Career Development Quarterly* 53, no. 3 (2005): 194–207.

Bopp, Melissa, and Elizabeth A. Fallon. "Individual and Institutional Influences on Faith-Based Health and Wellness Programming." *Health Education Research* 26, no. 6 (2011): 1107–19.

Bopp, Melissa, and Benjamin Webb. "Health Promotion in Megachurches: An Untapped Resource with Megareach?" *Health Promotion Practice* 13, no. 5 (2012): 679–86.

Bourdieu, Pierre. *Distinction: A Social Critique of the Judgement of Taste.* London: Routledge, 1984.

Brady, N., and D. Hart. "An Exploration into the Developmental Psychology of Ethical Theory with Implications for Business Practice and Pedagogy." *Journal of Business Ethics* 76 (2007): 397–412.

Brennfleck, Kevin, and Kay Marie Brennfleck. *Live Your Calling: A Practical Guide to Finding and Fulfilling Your Mission in Life.* San Francisco, CA: Jossey Bass, 2005.

Bronfenbrenner, Uri. "Human Development, Bioecological Theory Of." In *International Encyclopedia of the Social and Behavioral Sciences,* edited by N. J. Smelser and P. B Battles, 6963–70. Washongton, D.C.: American Psychological Association, 2001.

Bronson, Po. "What Should I Do with My Life, Now?" *FastCompany* (2009), http://www.fastcompany.com/1130055/what-should-i-do-my-life-now.

Brown, Roscoe C. "The National Negro Health Week Movement." *The Journal of Negro Education* 6, no. 3 (1937): 553–64.

Bunderson, J. Stuart, and Jeffrey A. Thompson. "The Call of the Wild: Zookeepers, Callings, and the Dual Edges of Deeply Meaningful Work." *Administrative Science Quarterly* 54, no. 32 (2009): 32–57.

Bunyan, John. *The Pilgrim's Progress*. New York: Signet, 1964.

Cain, Susan. *Quiet: The Power of Introverts in a World That Can't Stop Talking*. New York: Crown-Random House, 2012.

Calhoun, Lawrence G., and Richard G. Tedeschi. "The Foundations of Posttraumatic Growth: An Expanded Framework." In *Handbook of Posttraumatic Growth: Research and Practice*, edited by Lawrence G. Calhoun and Richard G. Tedeschi, 3–23. New York: Psychology Press, Routledge Taylor Francis Group, 2009.

Calhoun, Lawrence G., and Richard G. Tedeschi, eds. *Handbook of Posttraumatic Growth: Research and Practice*. Mahwah, NJ: Lawrence Erlbaum, 2006.

Calvin, John. "Institutes of the Christian Religion." In *Callings: Twenty Centuries of Christian Wisdom on Vocation*, edited by William C. Placher, 232–38. Grand Rapids, MI: Erdsman, 2005.

Campbell, Colin. "Do Todays Sociologists Really Appreciate Weber's Essay *The Protestant Ethic and the Spirit of Capitalism*?" *The Sociological Review* 54 (2006): 207.

Cardador, M. Teresa, Erik Dane, and Michael G. Pratt. "Linking Calling Orientations to Organizational Attachment via Organizational Instrumentality." *Journal of Vocational Behavior* 79, no. 2 (2011): 367–78.

Carnegie, Dale. *How to Win Friends and Influence People*. New York: Simon and Schuster, 1936.

Case, Thomas. *Two Sermons Lately Preached Ii*. London, 1642.

Chatters, L. M. "Religion and Health: Public Health and Practice." *Annual Review of Public Health* 21 (2000): 335–67.

Chatters, L. M., J. S. Levin, and R. J. Taylor. "Antecedents and Dimensions of Religious Involvement among Older Black Adults." *Journal of Gerontology* 47, no. 6 (1992): S269–S278.

Chopra, Deepak. *The Seven Spiritual Laws of Success: A Practical Guide to the Fulfillment of Your Dreams*. San Rafael, CA: New World Library, 1994.

Ciulla, Joanne B. *The Working Life: The Promise and Betrayal of Modern Work*. New York: Times Books, 2000.

Clark, Glenn. *The Man Who Talks with Flowers: The Life Story of Dr. George Washington Carver*. Austin, MN: Macalester Park Publishing Company, 1939.

Cohen, Albert K. "A General Theory of Subcultures [1955]." In *Subcultures Reader*, edited by Ken Gelder and Sarah Thornton, 44–54. New York: Routledge, 1997.

Collins, Travis. *Directionally Challenged: How to Find and Follow God's Course for Your Life*. Birmingham, AL: New Hope Publishers, 2007.

Conklin, T. "Work Worth Doing: A Phenomenological Study of the Experience of Discovering and Following One's Calling." *Journal of Management Inquiry* 21, no. 3 (2012): 298.

Conlin, Michelle. "Religion in the Workplace: The Growing Presence of Spirituality in Corporate America." *Business Week,* November 1, 1999.

Crawford, Krysten. "Lay Surrenders to Authorities: Ex-Enron Ceo Turns Himself in after Indictment, Pleads Not Guilty in Massive Accounting Fraud." *CNN/Money,* July 12, 2004, http://money.cnn.com/2004/07/08/news/newsmakers/lay/.

Crawford, Matthew B. *Shop Class as Soulcraft: An Inquiry into the Value of Work.* New York: Penguin Press, 2009.

Damon, W. "The Moral Development of Children." *Scientific American* (August 1999): 76.

Davidson, J. D., and D. P. Caddell. "Religion and the Meaning of Work." *Journal of Scientific Study of Religion* 33, no. 2 (1994): 135–47.

Davies, J. Llewelyn. *The Christian Calling.* London: Macmillan, 1875.

Davis, Gerald F. "Mechanisms and the Theory of Organizations." *Journal of Management Inquiry* 15, no. 2 (2006): 114–18.

DeHaven, Mark J., B. Hunter Irby, Wilder Laura, W. Walton James, and Berry Jarett. "Health Programs in Faith-Based Organizations: Are They Effective?" *American Journal of Public Health* 94, no. 6 (2004): 1030.

Deming, W. Edwards. *Quality Productivity and Competitive Position.* Cambridge, MA: Massachusetts Institute of Technology Press, 1982.

The Devil's Oak: Or, His Ramble in a Tempestuous Night Where He Happen'd to Discourse with Men of Several Callings of His Own Colour and Complexion. To a Very Pleasant New Tune. London: printed for C. Bates, at the Sun and Bible in Pye-corner, 1685.

Dik, B. J., and R. D. Duffy. "Calling and Vocation at Work: Definitions and Prospects for Research and Practice." *The Counseling Psychologist* 37, no. 3 (2009): 424–50.

Dik, Bryan J., and Ryan D. Duffy. *Make Your Job a Calling: How the Psychology of Vocation Can Change Your Life at Work.* West Conshohocken, PA: Templeton Press, 2012.

Dik, Bryan J., and Michael F. Steger. "Randomized Trial of a Calling-Infused Career Workshop Incorporating Counselor Self-Disclosure." *Journal of Vocational Behavior* 73, no. 2 (2008): 203–11.

DiMaggio, P. J., and W. W. Powell. "The Iron Cage Revisited: Institutional Isomorphism and Collective Rationality in Organizational Fields." In *The New Institutionalism in Organizational Analysis,* edited by W. W. Powell and P. J. DiMaggio, 63–82. Chicago: University of Chicago Press, 1991.

Dobrow, S. "Dynamics of Calling: A Longitudinal Study of Musicians." *Journal of Organizational Behavior* (2012). doi: 10.1002/job.1808.

Dobrow, S. "Extreme Subjective Career Success: A New Integrated View of Having a Calling." Paper presentation at the Academy of Management Annual Conference, August 2004.

Dobrow, S. R., and J. Tosti-Kharas. "Calling: The Development of a Scale Measure." *Personnel Psychology* 64, no. 4 (2011): 1001–49.

Duffy, R. D. "Spirituality, Religion and Work Values." *Journal of Psychology and Theology* 38, no. 1 (2010): 52–61.

Duffy, Ryan D., and William E. Sedlacek. "The Presence of and Search for a Calling: Connections to Career Development." *Journal of Vocational Behavior* 70, no. 3 (2007): 590–601.

Ehrenreich, Barbara. *Fear of Falling: The Inner Life of the Middle Class.* New York: Harper Perennial, 1990.

Engs, R. C. *Clean Living Movements: American Cycles of Health Reform.* Westport, CT: Praeger, 2000.

Fornaciari, Charles J., and Kathy Lund Dean. "Making the Quantum Leap: Lessons from Physics on Studying Spirituality and Religion in Organizations." *Journal of Organizational Change Management* 14, no. 4 (2001): 335–51.

Fox, Lori A. "The Role of the Church in Career Guidance and Development: A Review of the Literature 1960–Early 2000s." *Journal of Career Development* 29, no. 3 (2003): 167–82.

Frankel, David, dir. *The Devil Wears Prada.* Beverly Hills, CA: 20th Century Fox, 2006.

Freidson, E. *Doctoring Together: A Study of Professional Social Control.* New York: Elsevier, 1975.

Fuller, Robert W. *Somebodies and Nobodies: Overcoming the Abuse of Rank.* Gabriola Island, British Columbia, Canada: New Society Publishers, 2004.

Furey, Robert J. *Called by Name: Discovering Your Unique Purpose in Life.* New York: Crossroad, 1996.

Gardner, Howard E., Mihaly Csikszentmihalyi, and William Damon. *Good Work: When Excellence and Ethics Meet.* New York: Basic Books, 2001.

Gersick, Connie J. G., and J. Richard Hackman. "Habitual Routines in Task-Performing Groups." *Organizational Behavior and Human Decision Processes* 47, no. 1 (1990): 65–97.

Gladden, Washington. *Working People and Their Employers.* Boston: Lockwood, Brooks, 1876.

Glynn, Mary Ann. "Evangelical Domesticity and Martha Stewart Living Magazine, 1990–2002." In *Interdisciplinary Committee on Organization Studies,* edited by University of Michigan. Ann Arbor: University of Michigan, 2003.

Golden-Biddle, Karen, Karen Locke, and Trish Reay. "Using Knowledge in Management Studies: An Investigation of How We Cite Prior Work." *Journal of Management Inquiry* 15, no. 3 (2006): 237–54.

Green, Lawrence W., and Marshall W. Kreuter. *Health Promotion Planning: An Educational and Ecological Approach.* Mountain View, CA: Mayfield, 1999.

Gum, Amber M., Mary Ann Watson, Bernard A. Smith, Richard Briscoe, Johnetta Goldsmith, and Britney Henley. "Collaborative Design of a Church-Based, Multidimensional Senior Wellness Program by Older Adults, Church Leaders, and Researchers." *Journal of Religion, Spirituality and Aging* 24, no. 3 (2012): 213–34.

Hackman, J. Richard, and Greg R. Oldham. "Motivation through the Design of Work: Test of a Theory." *Organizational Behavior and Human Performance* 16, no. 2 (1976): 250–79.

Hagmaier, Tamara, and Andrea E. Abele. "The Multidimensionality of Calling: Conceptualization, Measurement and a Bicultural Perspective." *Journal of Vocational Behavior* 81, no. 1 (2012): 39–51.

Hall, Douglas T., and Dawn E. Chandler. "Psychological Success: When the Career Is a Calling." *Journal of Organizational Behavior* 26, no. 2 (2005): 155–76.

Hall, Richard H. "Professionalization and Bureaucratization." *American Sociological Review* 33, no. 1 (1968): 92–104.

Hardy, Lee. *The Fabric of This World: Inquiries into Calling, Career Choice, and the Design of Human Work*. Grand Rapids, MI: Eerdsman, 1990.

Harzer, Claudia, and Willibald Ruch. "When the Job Is a Calling: The Role of Applying One's Signature Strengths at Work." *The Journal of Positive Psychology* 7, no. 5 (2012): 362–71.

Hawks, S. "Spiritual Health: Definition and Theory." *Wellness Perspectives* 10 (1994): 3–13.

Hegewisch, Ariane, Claudia Williams, and Anlan Zhang. "The Gender Wage Gap: 2011." Institute for Women's Policy Research (2012), http://www.iwpr.org/publications/pubs/the-gender-wage-gap-2011.

Hernandez, Esperanza F., Ben K. Beitin, and Pamela F. Foley. "Hearing the Call: A Phenomenological Study of Religion in Career Choice." *Journal of Career Development* 38, no. 1 (2011): 62–88.

Hevesi, Dennis. "Willa Ward, Gospel Singer, Dies at 91." *New York Times,* August 12, 2012.

Hirschi, Andreas. "Callings in Career: A Typological Approach to Essential and Optional Components." *Journal of Vocational Behavior* 79, no. 1 (2011): 60–73.

Holland, J. L. *Making Vocational Choices: A Theory of Careers*. Englewood Cliffs, NJ: Prentice-Hall, 1973.

Holland, J. L. *Professional Manual for the Self-Directed Search*. Palo Alto, CA: Consulting Psychologist Press, 1970.

Holland, John L. *The Self-Directed Search*. Palo Alto, CA: Consulting Psychologist Press, 1970.

Howe, Jeff. *Crowdsourcing: Why the Power of the Crowd Is Driving the Future of Business*. New York: Three Rivers Press, 2008.

Hunter, I., B. J. Dik, and J. H. Banning. "College Students' Perceptions of Calling in Work and Life: A Qualitative Analysis." *Journal of Vocational Behavior* 76, no. 2 (2010): 178–86.

Inge-Barry, Leoneda. "Career Lessons from the Biblical Joseph." *Michigan Today* 32, no. 2 (2000).

Johnson, B. R., R. B. Tompkins, and D. Webb. *Objective Hope—Assessing the Effectiveness of Faith-Based Organizations: A Review of the Literature*. Baylor Institute for Studies of Religion, 2002.

Jones, Laurie Beth. *Jesus, CEO: Using Ancient Wisdom for Visionary Leadership*. New York: Hyperion, 1996.

Kalberg, S. "Should the 'Dynamic Autonomy' of Ideas Matter to Sociologists? Max Weber on the Origin of Other-Worldly Salvation Religions and the Constitution of Groups in American Society Today." *Journal of Classic Sociology* 1 no. 3 (2001): 291–327.

King, James E. "(Dis)Missing the Obvious: Will Mainstream Management Research Ever Take Religion Seriously?" *Journal of Management Inquiry* 17 (2008): 214.

Kise, Jane, and David Stark. *Working with Purpose: Finding a Corporate Calling for You and Your Business*. Minneappolis, MN: Ausberg Fortress, 2004.

Kise, Jane A. G., David Stark, and Sandra Krebs Hirsh. *Lifekeys: Discover Who You Are*. Minneapolis, MN: Betheny House, 2005.

Koehn, Nancy. "The History of Black Friday." *Marketplace Commentary* (2011), http://www.marketplace.org/topics/life/commentary/history-black-friday.

Kohlberg, Lawrence. *The Psychology of Moral Development: The Nature and Validity of Moral Stages.* Essays on Moral Development, vol. 2. San Francisco: Harper & Row, 1984.

Kosmin, Barry A., and Ariela Keysar, with Ryan Cragun and Juhem Navarro-Rivera. "American Nones: The Profile the No Religion Population 2008." Report published from the American Religious Identification Survey 2008 (2009), http://commons.trincoll.edu/aris/publications/american-nones-the-profile-of-the-no-religion-population/.

Kosmin, Barry A., Egon Mayer, and Ariela Keysar. "American Religious Identification Survey." (2001). http://commons.trincoll.edu/aris/surveys/aris-2001/.

Kovan, Jessica T., and John M. Dirkx. "'Being Called Awake': The Role of Transformative Learning in the Lives of Environmental Activists." *Adult Education Quarterly* 53, no. 2 (2003): 99–118.

Kreider, Tim. "The 'Busy' Trap." *New York Times*, June 30, 2012.

Krumrei, Elizabeth J., Annette Mahoney, and Kenneth I. Pargament. "Divorce and the Divine: The Role of Spirituality in Adjustment to Divorce." *Journal of Marriage and Family* 71, no. 2 (2009): 373–83.

Lambert, Lake, III. *Spirituality Inc.: Religion in the American Workplace.* New York: New York University Press, 2009.

Laudan, Larry. *Progress and Its Problems: Toward a Theory of Scientific Growth.* Berkeley: University of California Press, 1977.

Lazarus, Richard S., and Susan Folkman. *Stress, Appraisal, and Coping.* New York: Springer, 1984.

Lebow, Victor. "Price Competition 1955." *Journal of Retailing*, Spring (1955). http://ablemesh.co.uk/PDFs/journal-of-retailing1955.pdf.

Lehmann, Hartmut, and Guenther Roth, eds. *Weber's Protestant Ethic: Origins, Evidence, Contexts.* Cambridge: Cambridge University Press, 1987.

Levin, Jeff, and Jay F. Hein. "A Faith-Based Prescription for the Surgeon General: Challenges and Recommendations." *Journal of Religion and Health* 51, no. 1 (2012): 57.

Levine, Lawrence W. *Black Culture and Black Consciousness: Afro-American Folk Thought from Slavery to Freedom.* New York: Oxford University Press, 1977.

Levoy, Gregg Michael. *Callings: Finding and Following an Authentic Life.* New York: Three Rivers Press, 1997.

Lewis, C. S. *Surprised by Joy: The Shape of My Early Life.* Orlando, FL: Harcourt, Brace, Jovanovich, 1955.

Lincoln, C. Eric, and Lawrence H. Mamiya. *The Black Church in the African American Experience.* Durham, NC: Duke University Press, 1990.

Lips-Wiersma, M. "The Influence of Spiritual 'Meaning Making' on Career Behavior." *Journal of Management Development* 21 (2002): 497–520.

Lomax, A. *Afro-American Spirituals, Work Songs, and Ballads* [Sound Recording 1933–1939]. Cambridge, MA: Rounder Records, 1998.

Markham, Gervase, Simon Harward, William Lawson, and George Sawbridge. *A Way to Get Wealth: Containing Six Principal Vocations, or Callings, in Which Every Good Husband or House-Wife May Lawfully Imploy Themselves.* London: Printed by E. H. for George Sawbridge, 1676.

McGee, J.J., and A.L. Delbecq. "Vocation as a Critical Factor in Spirituality for Executive Leadership in Business." In *Business, Religion and Spirituality: A New*

Synthesis, edited by Oliver F. Williams, 94–110. Notre Dame, IN: University of Notre Dame Press, 2003.

McLaughlin, Ross. "Tracking Down Stewart Parnell, Owner of the Peanut Corporation of America." *11 Alive News,* Mar 25, 2010. http://www.11alive.com/news/local/story.aspx?storyid = 142129.

McNamara-Barry, Carolyn, and Larry J. Nelson. "The Role of Religion in the Transition to Adulthood for Young Emerging Adults." *Journal of Youth and Adolescence* 34, no. 3 (2005): 245–55.

Meyerson, D. E. *Tempered Radicals: How People Use Difference to Inspire Change at Work.* Cambridge, MA: Harvard Business School Press, 2001.

Miller, David W. "The Faith at Work Movement." *Theology Today* 60, no. 3 (2003): 301.

Miller, David W. *God at Work: The History and Promise of the Faith at Work Movement.* New York: Oxford University Press, 2007.

Mizzoni, J. "Perspectives on Work in American Culture." *Journal of Interdisciplinary Studies* 16 nos. 1/2 (2004): 97–110.

Myers, Valerie L. "Calling and Talent Development: Not Your Average Working Joe Case #1-429-200." GlobaLens Business Case. *GlobaLens.com* (2011).

Myers, V. L. "Cultivating Calling: A Faith-Based Approach to Work Orientation and Spirituality at Work." Paper presented at the Symposium at the Society of Industrial Organizational Psychologists Annual Conference, Dallas, Texas, May 2006.

Myers, Valerie L. *An Interdisciplinary Analysis of Faith-Based Human Services: Analyzing Latent Organizational, Social and Psychological Processes.* PhD dissertation. University of Michigan, 2003.

Myers, Valerie L. "An Ontology of Calling: Examining Mechanisms and the Transcendent Possibilities of Work Orientation Theory." In *Critical Management Studies Conference Proceedings.* Convened by Scott Taylor, Emma Bell, and Roy Jacques. Manchester, UK: Manchester Business School, 2007.

Myers, V. L. "Planning and Evaluating Faith-Based Interventions: Closing the Theory-Practice Divide." In *Independent Sector Conference Spring Research Forum: The Role of Faith-based Organizations in the Social Welfare System.* Competition hosted by the Rockefeller Institute, Washington, D.C., February 2003.

Myers, Valerie L. "What Did Weber Say? A Comprehensive Materialization of His Implicit Theory of Calling." In *Academy of Management Annual Conference—Management, Spirituality and Religion Division.* Organized by Debu Mukerji. Chicago, IL: Academy of Management, 2009.

Neafsey, John. *A Sacred Voice Is Calling: Personal Vocation and Social Conscience.* Maryknoll, NY: Orbis Books, 2006.

Norman, Warren T. "Toward an Adequate Taxonomy of Personality Attributes: Replicated Factor Structure in Peer Nomination Personality Ratings." *Journal of Abnormal Psychology* 66 (1963): 574–83.

Novak, Michael. *Business as a Calling: Work and the Examined Life.* New York: Free Press, 1996.

Oates, Kerris, M. Elizabeth Lewis Hall, and Tamara Anderson. "Calling and Conflict: A Qualitative Exploration of Interrole Conflict and the Sanctification of Work in Christian Mothers in Academia." *Journal of Psychology and Theology* 33, no. 3 (2005): 210–23.

Overton, Willis F., and Michelle D. Ennis. "Relationism, Ontology, and Other Concerns." *Human Development* 49, no. 3 (2006): 180–83.

Page, Scott E. *The Difference: How the Power of Diversity Creates Better Groups, Firms, Schools, and Societies.* Princeton, NJ: Princeton University Press, 2007.

Palmer, P. J. *Let Your Life Speak: Listening to the Voice of Vocation.* San Francisco: Jossey-Bass, 2000.

Panichas, George E. "Introduction." *Journal of Business Ethics* 10, no. 8 (1991): 559–60.

Pargament, Kenneth I. *The Psychology of Religion and Coping: Theory, Research, Practice.* New York: Guilford Press, 1997.

Pargament, Kenneth I., Kavita M. Desai, and Kelly M. McConnell. "Spirituality: A Pathway to Posttraumatic Growth or Decline?" In *Handbook of Posttraumatic Growth: Research and Practice,* edited by Lawrence G. Calhoun and Richard G. Tedeschi, 121–37. Mahwah, NJ: Lawrence Erlbaum Associates, 2006.

Pargament, Kenneth I., Gina M. Magyar, Ethan Benore, and Annette Mahoney. "Sacrilege: A Study of Sacred Loss and Desecration and Their Implications for Health and Well-Being in a Community Sample." *Journal for the Scientific Study of Religion* 44, no. 1 (2005): 59–78.

Pargament, Kenneth I., and Annette Mahoney. "Sacred Matters: Sanctification as a Vital Topic for the Psychology of Religion." *The International Journal for the Psychology of Religion* 15, no. 3 (2005): 179–98.

Parsons, F. *Choosing a Vocation.* Boston: Houghton Mifflin, 1909.

Perkins, William. "A Treatise of the Vocations." In *Callings: Twenty Centuries of Christian Wisdom on Vocation,* edited by William Placher, 262–73. Grand Rapids, MI: Erdsman, 2005.

Peterson, Christopher, Nansook Park, Nicholas Hall, and Martin E. Seligman. "Zest and Work." *Journal of Organizational Behavior* 30, no. 2 (2009): 161–72.

Peterson, Christopher, and Martin E. P. Seligman. *Character Strengths and Virtues: A Handbook and Classification.* New York: Oxford University Press, 2004.

Placher, William C., ed. *Callings: Twenty Centuries of Christian Wisdom on Vocation.* Grand Rapids, MI: Erdsman, 2005.

Pope, Liston. *Millhands and Preachers: A Study of Gastonia.* New Haven, CT: Yale University Press, 1942.

Porchaska, James O., Carlo C. DiClemente, and John C. Norcross. "In Search of How People Change: Applications to Addictive Behaviors." *The American Psychologist* 47, no. 9 (1992): 1102–14.

Pratt, M. G., and B. E. Ashforth. "Fostering Meaningfulness in Working and at Work." In *Positive Organizational Scholarship: Foundations of a New Discipline,* edited by J. E. Dutton, K. S. Cameron, and R. E. Quinn, 309–27. San Francisco: Berrett-Koehler, 2003.

Ramo, Joshua Cooper. *The Age of the Unthinkable: Whey the New World Disorder Constantly Surprises Us and What We Can Do About It.* New York: Little, Brown and Company, 2009.

Richards, Lysander Salmon. *Vocophy: The New Profession—A System Enabling a Person to Name the Calling or Vocation One Is Best Suited to Follow.* East Marshfield, MA: Pratt Brothers, Steam Job Printers, 1881.

Rodgers, Daniel T. *The Work Ethic in Industrial America, 1850–1920.* Chicago: University of Chicago Press, 1978.

Rokeach, Milton. *Understanding Human Values: Individual and Societal.* New York: Free Press, 1979.

Rosso, B. D., K. H. Dekas, and A. Wrzesniewski. "On the Meaning of Work: A Theoretical Integration and Review." *Research in Organizational Behavior* 30 (2010).

Ruef, M. "Social Ontology and the Dynamics of Organizational Forms: Creating Market Actors in the Healthcare Field, 1966–1994." *Social Forces* 77, no. 4 (1999): 1403–33.

Sandberg, J., and M. Alvesson. " Routes to Research Questions: Beyond Gap-Spotting." *Organization* 18 (2011): 22–44.

Sayers, Dorothy L. "Vocation in Work." In *A Christian Basis for the Post-War World: A Commentary on the Ten Peace Points,* edited by A. E. Baker, 89–105. New York: Morehouse-Gorham, 1942.

Sayers, Dorothy L. "Why Work?" In *Creed or Chaos? And Other Essays in Popular Theology,* 63–84. Manchester: Sophia Institute Press, 1948/1999.

Schmit, Julie. "Peanut Boss Refuses to Testify at Salmonella Hearing." *USA Today* (2009), http://usatoday30.usatoday.com/news/washington/2009-02-11-house-salmonella_N.htm#.

Schorr, Philip. "Public Service as a Calling: An Exploration of a Concept." *International Journal of Public Administration* 10, no. 5 (1987): 465–93.

Schorr, Philip. "Public Service as a Calling: An Exploration of a Concept. Part II." *International Journal of Public Administration* 13, no. 5 (1990): 649–88.

Schwehn, Mark R., and Dorothy C. Bass, eds. *Can I Control What I Shall Do and Become? Leading Lives That Matter: What We Should Do and Who We Should Be.* Grand Rapids, MI: W. B. Eerdmans, 2006.

Scott, W. Richard. *Institutions and Organizations.* Foundations for Organizational Science. Thousand Oaks, CA: Sage, 1995.

Sennett, Richard. *The Craftsman.* New Haven, CT: Yale University Press, 2008.

Shapiro, Richard J., and David A. Leider. *Whistle While You Work: Heeding Your Life's Calling.* Williston, VT: Berrett-Koehler Publishers, 2001.

Shephard, Thomas. *Certain Select Cases Resolved, Specially, Tending to the Right Ordering of the Heart That We May Comfortably Walk with God in Our Generall and Particular Callings.* London: Printed for John Rothwel, 1655.

Shils, A., and H. A. Finch. *Max Weber on the Methodology of the Social Sciences.* Glencoe, IL: Free Press, 1949.

Shulman, Shmuel, Benni Feldman, Sidney J. Blatt, Omri Cohen, and Amalya Mahler. "Emerging Adulthood: Age-Related Tasks and Underlying Self Processes." *Journal of Adolescent Research* 20, no. 5 (2005): 577–603.

Smith, Christian, with Patricia Snell. *Souls in Transition: The Religious and Spiritual Lives of Emerging Adults.* New York: Oxford University Press, 2009.

Smith, Gordon T. *Courage and Calling: Embracing Your God-Given Potential.* Downers Grove, IL: InterVarsity Press, 2011.

Spielberg, Steven, dir. *Schindler's List.* Hollywood, CA: Universal Studios, 1993.

Steele, Richard. *The Religious Tradesman; or, Plain and Serious Hints of Advice for the Tradesman's Prudent and Pious Conduct . . . of Religion; of Leaving Our Callings.* Charlestown [MA]: Printed by Samuel Etheridge, and sold by him at the Washington head bookstore, 1804.

Steele, Richard. *The Trades-Man's Calling. Being a Discourse Concerning the Nature, Necessity, Choice, & C. Of a Calling in General: And Directions for the Right.* London, 1684.

Steger, Michael F., N. K. Pickering, B. J. Dik, and J. Y. Shin. "Calling in Work." *Journal of Career Assessment* 18, no. 1 (2010): 82–96.

Stevens, Paul R. *The Other Six Days: Vocation, Work, and Ministry in Biblical Perspective.* Grand Rapids, MI: Wm. B. Eerdmans Publishing Company, 2000.

Stowe, S. M. "Seeing Themselves at Work: Physicians and the Case Narrative in the Mid-Nineteenth-Century American South." *American Historical Review* 101, no. 1 (1996): 41–79.

Strong, Edward K. *Vocational Interests of Men and Women.* Stanford, CA: Stanford University Press, 1943.

Suddath, Claire. "Top 10 Ceo Scandals: Kenneth Lay, Enron." *Time Magazine,* August 10, 2010.

Super, D. E. "A Life-Span, Life-Space Approach to Career Development." *Journal of Vocational Behavior* 16, no. 3 (1980): 282–98.

Super, D. E., J. O. Crites, R. C. Hummel, H. P. Moser, P. Overstreet, and C. F. Warnath. *Vocational Development: A Framework for Research.* New York: Teachers College Press, 1957.

Sutton, Robert I., and Barry M. Staw. "What Theory Is Not." *Administrative Science Quarterly* 40, no. 3 (1995): 371–84.

Sweetman, Paul. "Twenty-First Century Dis-Ease? Habitual Reflexivity or the Reflexive Habitus." *The Sociological Review* 51, no. 4 (2003): 528–49.

Taylor, Frederick Winslow. *The Principles of Scientific Management.* New York: Harper & Brothers, 1911.

Terkel, Studs. *Working: People Talk About What They Do All Day and How They Feel About What They Do.* New York: The New Press, 1972.

Terry, Lynne. "2 Oregonians Help Lead Fight for Prosecution of Former Peanut Corp. Chief Stewart Parnell over Salmonella Outbreak." *The Oregonian* (2011), http://www.oregonlive.com/health/index.ssf/2011/02/two_oregonians_helping_lead_fi.html.

Treadgold, R. "Transcendent Vocations: Their Relationship to Stress, Depression, and Clarity of Self-Concept." *Journal of Humanistic Psychology* 39, no. 1 (1999): 81–105.

True Blew the Plowman . . . Character of Several Callings Which He Could Not Freely Fancy, When He Found Their Grand Deceit. [London]: Printed for P. Brooksby, 1685.

A True Character of Sundry Trades and Callings . . . Licensed According to Order. New Ditty of Innocent Mirth. London: Printed for P[hilip]. Brooksby, at the Golden-Ball in Pye-corner, 1670.

Volf, Miroslav. *Work in the Spirit: Toward a Theology of Work.* Eugene, OR: Wipf & Stock Publishers, 2001.

Walters, Barbara. *Audition: A Memoir.* New York: Alfred A. Knopf, 2008.

Walters, Barbara. *The View.* Disney–ABC Television Group, 2011.

Ward-Royster, Willa, and Toni Rose. *How I Got Over: Clara Ward and the World-Famous Ward Singers.* Philadelphia: Temple University Press, 1997.

Warren, Robert. *Industry and Diligence in Our Callings Earnestly Recommended in a Sermon Preached . . . March 17, 1736–7. At the Parish-Church of St. Bride, . . . London.*

By Robert Warren, D.D. . . . . Published at the Unanimous Request of the Trustees. London: printed for W. Meadows, 1737.

Washington, Denzel, dir. *The Great Debaters.* Los Angeles, CA: Genius Products, 2007.

Weber, Klaus. "From Nuts and Bolts to Toolkits: Theorizing with Mechanisms." *Journal of Management Inquiry* 15, no. 2 (2006): 119.

Weber, Max. *The Protestant Ethic and the Spirit of Capitalism.* London: Routledge, 1904/1992.

Weber, Max, and Edward Shils. *Max Weber on the Methodology of the Social Sciences.* Glencoe, IL: Free Press, 1949.

Weick, Karl E. "The Collapse of Sensemaking in Organizations: The Mann Gulch Disaster." *Administrative Science Quarterly* 38, no. 4 (1993): 628–52.

Weiss, J. W., M. F. Skelley, J. C. Haughey, and D. T. Hall. "Callings, New Careers and Spirituality: A Reflective Perspective for Organizational Leaders and Professionals." *Research in Ethical Issues in Organizations* 5 (2004): 175–201.

Wilson, Thomas. *A Sermon Preached in August the 13. 1610. In Canterbury to the Corporation of Black-Smiths . . . By Thomas Wilson Preacher, Sermon Preached before the Corporation of Black-Smiths.* London: Printed [by N. Okes] for Simon Waterson, dwelling in Pauls Church-yard at the signe of the Crowne, 1610.

Work, John Wesley. *Folk Song of the American Negro.* Nashville, TN: Tennessee Press of Fisk University, 1915.

Wrzesniewski, A., K. Dekas, and B. Rosso. "Calling." In *The Encyclopedia of Positive Psychology,* edited by S. J. Lopez and A. Beauchamp, 115–18. Chichester, UK: Blackwell Publishing, 2009.

Wrzesniewski, Amy, and Jane E. Dutton. "Crafting a Job: Revisioning Employees as Active Crafters of Their Work." *The Academy of Management Review* 26, no. 2 (2001): 179–201.

Wrzesniewski, Amy, Clark McCauley, Paul Rozin, and Barry Schwartz. "Jobs, Careers, and Callings: People's Relations to Their Work." *Journal of Research in Personality* 31, no. 1 (1997): 21–33.

Wrzesniewski, Amy, and Jennifer Tosti, eds. "Career as a Calling." In *Encyclopedia of Career Development.* Thousand Oaks, CA: Sage, 2006.

Wuthnow, Robert. *The Crisis in the Churches: Spiritual Malaise, Fiscal Woe.* New York: Oxford University Press, 1997.

Zemke, Ron, Claire Raines, and Bob Filipczak. *Generations at Work: Managing the Clash of Veterans, Boomers, Xers, and Nexters in Your Workplace.* New York: American Management Association, 2000.

Zimbardo, Philip. *The Lucifer Effect: Understanding How Good People Turn Evil.* New York: Random House, 2008.

Index

Printed in the United States
by Baker & Taylor Publisher Services